Palgrave Macmillan Studies in Banking and Financial Institutions

Series Editor
Jonathan Williams, University of Surrey, Guildford, UK

The Palgrave Macmillan Studies in Banking and Financial Institutions series is international in orientation and includes studies of banking systems in particular countries or regions as well as contemporary themes such as Islamic Banking, Financial Exclusion, Mergers and Acquisitions, Risk Management, and IT in Banking. The books focus on research and practice and include up to date and innovative studies that cover issues which impact banking systems globally.

Enzo Scannella • Jonathan Williams
Editors

Trends, Issues, and Challenges in Banking and Finance

Financial and Non-Financial Risks, Corporate Governance, and Regulation

palgrave
macmillan

Editors
Enzo Scannella
University of Palermo
Palermo, Italy

Jonathan Williams
University of Surrey
Guildford, UK

ISSN 2523-336X ISSN 2523-3378 (electronic)
Palgrave Macmillan Studies in Banking and Financial Institutions
ISBN 978-3-031-96065-9 ISBN 978-3-031-96066-6 (eBook)
https://doi.org/10.1007/978-3-031-96066-6

This Palgrave Macmillan imprint is published by the registered company Springer Nature Switzerland AG
The registered company address is: Gewerbestrasse 11, 6330 Cham, Switzerland

Acknowledgements

The book provides the latest scholarly researches in the field of banking and finance and brings together a selection of papers presented at the "Annual Conference 2024" of the European Association of University Teachers of Banking and Finance (Wolpertinger), organized by the University of Palermo, Italy, August 28–31, 2024.

We would like to thank all the participants of the conference for presenting and discussing their research papers, the authors of the chapters for debating and sharing their research results, the reviewers for their fruitful comments and suggestions, the publisher for having accepted this editorial project in the book series "Palgrave Macmillan Studies in Banking and Financial Institutions." A special thanks to Tula Weis, executive editor and head of economics and finance at Palgrave Macmillan, for her kind assistance and guidance during the editorial process.

Finally, we would like to thank the institutional partners of the conference—Bank of Italy, the Italian Association of University Teachers of Banking and Finance (Adeimf), the Municipality of Palermo—and the sponsors of the conference for their financial support: Sicilbanca, Fondazione Sicana, KPMG, BCC Banca Don Rizzo, Fidimed, SEDA Experts, and the Italian Association of Financial Consultants (Anasf).

Contents

Notes on Contributors

Omar Al-Bataineh is an assistant professor in banking and financial services with the Department of Business Administration, the Hashemite University. He gained a PhD at Kent Business School, University of Kent under the supervision of Professor Timothy King and Dr Abdullah Iqbal. His research interests include corporate governance, corporate financial decisions, and corporate social responsibility, specializing in social networks, social capital, and board attributes.

Federico Beltrame is an associate professor in corporate finance in the Department of Economics and Statistics, University of Udine, where he teaches corporate finance. He graduated in economics at the University of Udine, where he also received his PhD in business science. His main research interests are related to SMEs' cost of capital, banks' capital structure, and mutual guarantee credit institutions.

Giorgio Stefano Bertinetti is a full professor of corporate finance at the Venice School of Management—Ca' Foscari University, where he served as director of the Department of Economics and Business Management. He currently teaches the following courses: "Financial Policies and M&A Strategies," "Corporate Risk Management," and "International Financial Management." He conducts research at Ca' Foscari University of Venice and collaborates with various master's programs in Italy and abroad. As a founding partner of Akos S.r.l., he works as a consultant for several companies and institutions, mainly in the areas of financial analysis and planning, business valuation, and M&A transactions. He has served and continues to serve as a board member, auditor, and statutory auditor in various companies and banks.

Marco Boso is a chartered public accountant based in Venice, Italy. He graduated in accounting and finance at the University of Venice "Ca' Foscari" in 2023, with a strong focus on subjects such as corporate finance, valuation, and financial accounting. His field of work allowed him to develop expertise in financial reporting, tax planning, and business advisory services. His main research interests include the study of interactions between accounting standards, mainly IAS/IFRS, and their possibility to convey useful information to investors.

Violeta Bringas Fernández based in Santander, Spain, is a researcher in economic and business sciences. Currently, she is pursuing a PhD at the University of Cantabria, focusing on climate risks in the banking sector, supported by a prestigious pre-doctoral contract from the Spanish Ministry of Universities. Violeta's professional journey includes an impactful internship at the Santander Financial Institute (SANFI). Her research has been showcased at international conferences, and she has published highlighting her expertise in B-Corp certification and climate risk analysis. In addition to her research, Violeta teaches Financial Management and Sustainable Development Goals. Her academic credentials include an MBA and a bachelor's degree in business administration and management from the University of Cantabria, where she graduated with honors. Fluent in English and proficient in French, Violeta has enriched her international perspective through academic stays in France and Poland. Her dedication to community service is evident through her volunteer work with the Red Cross and the Erasmus Student Network (ESN).

María Cantero Saiz is an associate professor in banking and finance at the University of Cantabria (Spain) and researcher at Santander Financial Institute (SANFI), teaching in undergraduate and postgraduate programs. Her research interests focus on banking, monetary policy, sovereign risk, climate risks, corporate finance, and sustainable finance. She has published many articles in prestigious scientific journals, such as *Research in International Business and Finance*; *Journal of International Money and Finance*; *International Review of Economics and Finance*; *Finance Research Letters*; *Journal of Macroeconomics*; *Journal of Regulatory Economics*; *Journal of*

Asian Economics; *Journal of Money, Credit and Banking*; or *BRQ Business Research Quarterly*, among others. She has also collaborated in several books, presented numerous papers at national and international conferences, and received several awards for her research, such as "Doctoral Theses Santander Financial Institute Award (2016)." She has taken part in numerous national and international research projects. She was visiting researcher at Norwich Business School (University of East Anglia, United Kingdom; 2013–2014), Berlin School of Economics and Law (2017), and University of Palermo (Italy; 2022–2023; 2024–2025). Since 2015, she has been in charge of the University of Cantabria Classroom Debate to promote communicative skills among students.

Andrea Cerri is an academic fellow at SDA Bocconi and deputy coordinator of the European FS Tech Hub at ICE SDA Bocconi. He teaches finance lab at Università Bocconi, as well as courses in international financial markets and venture capital at IES Abroad, Milan. His research focuses on corporate finance and financial intermediation, with publications in international journals and books published by Palgrave Macmillan and Bocconi University Press (BUP). He holds a degree in management and a PhD in management from Università Cattolica in Milan.

Giusy Chesini is an Associate Professor in Banking and Finance at the Department of Management of the University of Verona. She teaches Economics of Financial Intermediaries and Financial Markets with a focus on portfolio selection and investment topics. She graduated in Economics from the University of Verona and received a PhD in the Economics of Financial Markets from the University of Bergamo. Recent research topics include the role of banks in the green transition, the sovereign green bonds, and the evolution of the activity of the European Central Bank (ECB).

Radosław Ciukaj, PhD, is an assistant professor at the Institute of Finance of Cracow University of Economics. Previously, he worked for a company providing investment fund management services. His research interest centers around credit risk, including NPL resolution methods in the EU countries, and international finance.

Licia Ferranna holds a PhD in economics from Ca' Foscari University of Venice. She is a researcher at the Italian National Institute of Statistics where she contributes to quarterly national accounts and quarterly sector accounts. She has expertise in econometrics and data analysis, and she has collaborated on various academic research projects.

Myriam García-Olalla is professor of finance and accounting at the University of Cantabria, Spain. She holds a PhD in economics and business from the University of Oviedo (Spain) and she has been professor at the University of Oviedo and visiting researcher at the universities of Berkley (United States) and Bangor (United Kingdom). She has carried out several positions at her university and UCEIF Foundation. Her main research interests are banking, corporate governance, and corporate finance. She has published scientific books and articles in relevant international economics and finance journals, and she is a member of scientific associations and editorial boards.

Gloria Gardenal graduated with honors in economics and finance from Ca' Foscari University of Venice, and she obtained a PhD in business from the same university and completed a visiting period at UCL, London (UK). She is currently an associate professor at the Venice School of Management—Ca' Foscari University, where she teaches "Corporate finance," "Financing High Growth Firms," and "Financial Reporting." Her research focuses on corporate risk management, investment decisions both at individual and corporate levels, financial advisory, and trust. She is also serving as a board member in a cooperative bank.

Gimede Gigante is a director of ICE—Innovation and Corporate Entrepreneurship—at SDA Bocconi and director of the European FS Tech Hub of Milan. He is a tenured faculty member in financial intermediaries economics at the Department of Finance, Bocconi University, where he also serves as a director of the international management—China MiM program. He teaches principles of international finance, financial systems, investment banking, and international finance at Bocconi University and corporate finance at the Bocconi China Master in International Management, a double degree program with Fudan University. Previously, he held postdoctoral research positions at the Salomon Center for the Study of Financial Institutions (Stern-NYU) and Columbia Business School. His research focuses on banking, fintech, and financial intermediation, with publications in leading journals and books by Palgrave Macmillan, Routledge, and Bocconi University Press (BUP). Since 2020, he has been an advisory council member at Harvard Business Review, and since 2021, a Board Member of Assofintech. He holds a degree in business administration from Bocconi University, a PhD in banking and finance, and completed the International Teaching Programme at SDA Bocconi.

Beatrice Gobbo holds a double MSc degree in international management from Bocconi University in Milan and Fudan University in Shanghai. She currently works at UBS as a structured lending specialist for MEA, CEE, and TIGA, specializing in margin lending and cash flow-backed lending.

Karim Henide is a liquid alternatives portfolio manager with experience managing a sustainable fixed income UCITS fund. He holds a master's degree from the London School of Economics and is completing his PhD in finance at Northumbria Business School. Karim's research has been cited by the Banca d'Italia, IMF, and ESMA, among others.

Abdullah Iqbal is a senior lecturer in accounting and finance and chair of the Kent Business School Research Ethics Advisory Group at Kent Business School, University of Kent. He had worked as a visiting professor at National University of Sciences and Technology (NUST) Business School and Lahore University of Management Sciences, Pakistan. Abdullah received his master's in Finance and PhD in Accounting and Finance degrees from the University of Manchester, UK. He is also a Fellow of the Higher Education Academy, UK. He has published in well-respected international journals, including the *British Journal of Management, Journal of Business Ethics* and *Journal of Banking and Finance.*

Christos Kallandranis is an assistant professor in the Department of Accounting and Finance at the University of West Attica and external research associate at the Bank of Greece. He earned his PhD in Financial Economics from the University of Patras, Greece, specializing in Credit Markets and Business Investment Decisions. His research interests lie within the framework of real economic decisions under capital market imperfections. In addition, Christos is involved in several thematic areas, such as climate finance, trust in institutions, non-traditional markets, economic growth, and government spending. Throughout his career, Christos has published numerous articles in peer-reviewed journals such *as Journal of Economic Behavior and Organizations, Risk Analysis, Journal of Business Research, Finance Research Letters* and presented his work at national and international conferences.

Krzysztof Kil, PhD, is an assistant professor at the Institute of Finance of Cracow University of Economics and a lecturer at the Jagiellonian University in Cracow. He is the author of publications on risk management in banking, financial stability and efficiency, and consumer protection in the financial market. He is a member of the Presidium of Qualification Standards in Banking of the Polish Banking Association.

Timothy King is a full professor of finance and director of the Finance and Financial Accounting research group (FRG) at the School of Accounting and Finance, University of Vaasa. His ongoing research focuses on the theme of climate and corporate social responsibility, with a strong focus on the banking sector. He is an Editor-in-Chief of the *Multinational Finance Journal* and an associate editor for several other leading journals. He has also organized various international conference sessions and conferences including the 2023 Wolpertinger conference (the annual meeting of the European Association of Teachers of Banking and Finance) hosted at the University of Vaasa. He is a highly experienced academic and former research center director who has published in numerous leading academic journals including 4/4* ranked CABS journals such as the *Journal of Corporate Finance* and the *British Journal of Management*.

Ewa Miklaszewska is a professor of finance and the chair of the Department of Banking and Global Financial System at the Institute of Finance of Cracow University of Economics. She is also a lecturer at the Jagiellonian University in Cracow and a member of the managing committee of The European Association of University Teachers in Banking and Finance—the Wolpertinger Group. She is the author of several publications on bank stability, efficiency, and financial and social performance.

Maurizio Polato, PhD, is a full professor of banking and finance at Udine University, Italy. His research fields mainly relate to the securities and exchange industry and bank performance. He is the author of various publications on the topic, which address issues related to the industry's structure, performance, and value measurement for securities trading and regulation.

Begoña Torre Olmo is an associate professor in banking and finance and director of Santander Financial Institute (SANFI), a research center at the University of Cantabria. Her research interests include banking and corporate finance, topics in which she has published numerous articles in prestigious scientific journals and books. She has supervised several doctoral theses and participated in international conferences. She has served as the dean of the Business and Economics School of the University of Cantabria. She is a member of the board of directors of public and private companies as an independent vocal.

Eleuterio Vallelado is a professor of financial markets, financial intermediaries, and corporate finance at the University of Valladolid. He has been involved in over thirty distinct research projects, with many led by him. His research has been extensively published in prestigious journals that specialize in corporate finance, banking, and behavioral finance. Recently, he resumed his position as chair of financial economics and accounting after serving 4 years as a seconded national expert in DG FISMA, specifically in the Euro Area Financial System Unit (Unit E1). Furthermore, he has served as vice chairman for strategic planning at the University of Valladolid and functioned as a consultant for various financial institutions in the United States and EU, including San Paolo Bank, Chase Manhattan, and Banco Hispano Americano. He is also a former Fulbright Scholar who participated in a postgraduate program.

Ioannis Vlassas is a PhD candidate at the University of West Attica in the Department of Accounting and Finance. He has also managed to gain a full scholarship as a distinct young researcher. He holds a BSc and MSc in Business Administration and Economics from Athens University of Economics and Business. His research focuses on how different firm characteristics affect access to bank finance and how credit rationing impacts firm's real decisions, with a special emphasis on small- and medium-sized enterprises (SMEs). Ioannis' work has already been published or is under review in highly ranked journals and has participated in national and international conferences.

Jonathan Williams is a professor of banking and finance in the discipline of finance and accounting, Surrey Business School, University of Surrey. He is the series editor of the Palgrave Macmillan Studies on Banking and Financial Institutions and co-editor of *Digital Transformation and the Economics of Banking: Economic, Institutional, and Social Dimensions* (2024) and *Disruptive Technology in Banking and Finance: An International Perspective on FinTech* (2021). He is the chair of the European Association of University Teachers of Banking and Finance (Wolpertinger). His early research examined the efficiency and productivity of banks and policy-related issues, such as competition and privatization. More recently, he has published on banking union and negative interest rate policy. Currently, he is conducting research on executive compensation and corporate governance in banking as well as fintech and macroprudential policy.

Gianni Zorzi is an adjunct professor of corporate finance in the Department of Economics and Statistics, University of Udine, where he teaches corporate and international finance. He holds a PhD in finance from the University of Trieste and his main areas of expertise are corporate finance, financial markets, and credit ratings. His main fields of interest are credit risk and credit rating activities, risk management, and fintech.

Introduction

Enzo Scannella and Jonathan Williams

The banking and financial industry is undergoing a radical shift, driven by new regulatory frameworks, changing business models, increasing competitive pressures at national and international level, the emergence and rapid growth of new disruptive technologies, the growing importance of non-financial risks, and mounting awareness of stakeholders, regulators, and supervisors of the importance of sustainable finance.

Risks play a pivotal role in the economics and management of financial institutions. New risks emerge and evolve over time, such as climate risks and risks associated with the spread of diseases, and financial institutions face challenges to detect, monitor, manage, and mitigate them effectively, in addition to assessing their potential consequences. In a wider perspective of analysis, the emerging risks are strictly interrelated with traditional risks (credit, liquidity, and market risks), demonstrating that the implementation of a holistic approach is strategically important. Regulators at national and international levels require financial intermediaries to develop and implement adequate risk management strategies for both financial and nonfinancial risks, with intention to increase both the soundness of financial system and the level of financial stability.

E. Scannella (✉)
Department of Economics, Business and Statistics, University of Palermo, Palermo, Italy
e-mail: enzo.scannella@unipa.it

J. Williams
Department of Finance and Accounting, Surrey Business School,
University of Surrey, Guildford, UK
e-mail: jon.williams@surrey.ac.uk

Digital innovation has a significant impact on the finance industry and has become increasingly crucial to enhance competitiveness, productivity, and sustainability. The COVID-19 pandemic also created more demand for digitalized financial services and has significantly increased the importance of digitalization. In addition, the emergence of new operators, variously specialized across the whole range of financial intermediation activities (financing, investing, payments, insurance), has significantly widened the boundary of the financial sector.

Environmental problems are priorities in political agendas nowadays and the financial sector plays a key role in fostering the change toward sustainability and actively stimulating innovation, sustainable consumption, and production. Banks and other financial institutions can promote and finance the ecological transition, creating conditions for sustainable economic development. From this point of view, the changes are not only managerial but also organizational, operational, technological, and regulatory.

Corporate governance mechanisms and the efficiency and effectiveness of financial markets are crucial factors that significantly impact the value creation process in the financial intermediation value chain.

The evolution of the banking and financial system poses challenges for financial institutions and regulators, and, at the same time, it offers new opportunities to banking and finance scholars to conduct theoretical and empirical research to investigate in-depth the implications of such evolution and the emergence of new financial paradigms and scenarios.

This book collects papers analyzing several trends, issues, and challenges in the banking and finance industry, with particular reference to financial and non-financial risks, corporate governance, and financial regulation. In particular, the book chapters cover topics related to the soundness and performance of financial institutions, efficiency of financial markets, resilience of the financial sector to exposure to financial and non-financial risks, governance of financial institutions, and performance in a longitudinal way and across European countries.

Chapter 1 analyzes the transmission of the COVID-19 shock to the returns of real estate companies through their asset base. The authors account for the relationship between the spread of the virus and REITs' performances in Europe while considering the role played by localization and the diversification of properties in real estate portfolios. The chapter shows that COVID-19 had heterogeneous impacts depending on property types. Moreover, risks associated with COVID-19 may be captured by synthetic indexes that represent the degree of vulnerability of economic activities carried out in real estate sectors.

Chapter 2 reviews the extant scholarly research on climate risk in banking and its effects on financial stability. The chapter provides a framework to facilitate a comprehensive understanding of the significance of climate risks for sustainable finance and economic stability. The authors analyze the risks that banking institutions face, how financial stability is affected, and the regulations and policies implemented. Despite the recent and growing interest in research related to climate risk and its implications for the financial sector, the literature is in a formative stage. The authors conclude that the literature on climate risk in the financial sector can play a pivotal role in enhancing understanding of the most effective supervisory approaches and disclosures.

Chapter 3 investigates the effects of credit rationing for small- and medium-sized enterprises (SMEs) on employment development from 2014 to 2022 by employing a comprehensive survey microdata set compiled by the European Central Bank. The findings suggest that SMEs may recruit fewer staff when they fail to obtain the amount of credit they desire. The authors propose the adoption of a more holistic approach that considers both supply and demand dynamics in formulating counter-employment initiatives. This can help SMEs reduce their dependence on bank lending by enhancing access to alternative capital sources.

Chapter 4 examines the relationship between managerial social capital (MSC), based on a structural definition of social capital (SC), and firm risk in the United Kingdom. Using data on listed firms from 2006 to 2017, the authors find that MSC is associated with lower firm risk. Although MSC closely embodies a structural social capital definition, the authors expand the analyses to consider firms' corporate social responsibility (CSR) as an alternative measure of firm social capital which is more aligned with the cognitive SC dimension. The chapter shows that CSR is associated with an increase in firm risk.

Chapter 5 provides an estimation of the cumulative average abnormal returns for 2,644 announcements of turnover in CEO and Chair positions at 915 nonfinancial European companies between 2002 and 2021. The authors provide evidence that markets respond vigorously to news of changes in CEO compared to changes in the Chair which are smaller and mostly insignificant. The chapter represents a starting point to disentangle the question of how to explain market reactions to changes in top management. Further research should explore the functioning of corporate boards which affects decision-making, including the turnover of top management.

Chapter 6 compares the value relevance of the transition to accounting standard IFRS 9 from its predecessor IAS 39 for a sample of 139 European banks. The analysis shows that accounting items defined according to each accounting standard are value relevant in terms of the effects on the stock price. Further results show that the impact on the stock price of changes in equity resulting from the transition to accounting standards is ambiguous, whereas the effect of changes in loans and advances to customers is meaningful. The transition to IFRS 9 is more value relevant to countries which are identified as equity strong.

Chapter 7 provides an analysis of the benefit of market timing in the European mergers and acquisitions (M&A) market, with particular reference to the short- and long-run returns for bidding companies that decided to time the market, and others that chose not to exploit their stock overvaluation. Results show that companies timing the market and using their overvalued equity as a payment method generate higher returns compared to those companies that do not. The empirical analysis provides evidence of the perks associated with market timing in M&A.

Chapter 8 explores the implications of bank-affiliated dealers directing their best trades to bank-affiliated mutual funds, resulting from Basel III leverage ratio requirements, which are of concern to risks of anticompetitive behavior, long-term consumer welfare, sound market functioning, and systemic stability. The chapter sets out some hypotheses on the motivation for such behaviors, offering propositions relating to how the adverse effects of preferential trading practices may be mitigated.

Chapter 9 takes as its motivation the sudden collapses of US and European banks early in 2023. The chapter provides a forensic analysis of the causes of the troubles and, by analyzing a sample of 75 EU banks and 89 US banks from 2005 to 2024, it identifies important differences in regulations and profitability between the United States and Europe. The chapter includes an empirical analysis of factors affecting the probability of default for the two samples of banks and discusses the implications of the results.

Chapter 10 analyzes the effectiveness of the post-GFC restructuring programs, particularly those aiming to reduce NPL portfolios and incentivizing banks to extend loans in general and corporate loans in particular. The empirical analysis covers the period from 2014 to 2022. The evidence shows that the methods of restructuring low-quality loan portfolios and the intensity of measures used were an important determinant not only for the change in the quality of the loan portfolio, but also in extending bank lending to the economy, particularly the corporate loans. The chapter endorses a positive role for public involvement in reducing bank fragility and resolving obstacles to the efficient allocation of credit.

To conclude, this book offers new and fresh perspectives of analysis on emerging risks (climate, pandemic) and their effects on bank performance and sustainability, alongside cross-country analyses on financial regulation and accounting frameworks and their impacts on bank lending, financial stability, and bank performance. Other contributions analyze corporate governance dynamics, the efficiency of financial markets, and M&A activity mostly with reference to European countries. The book chapters raise crucial issues and challenges for bank managers, financial regulators, and stakeholders of the financial industry. The way they act and interact will significantly affect the value creation process, business models, and the stability and sustainability of the banking industry. For these reasons, the audience of this book is not limited to banking and finance scholars, but also includes policymakers, students, and financial practitioners, who wish to explore how financial institutions are facing incredibly significant challenges under turbulent economic, financial, and environmental conditions.

CHAPTER 1

Impact of COVID-19 on European Real Estate Investment Trusts

The Role of Property Type, Localization, and Diversification

Licia Ferranna, Giorgio Stefano Bertinetti, and Gloria Gardenal

1.1 Introduction

The real estate sector has been one of the most affected by the COVID-19 pandemic and one of the last to recover (Wen and Arbogast 2021; Canton et al. 2021). The implementation of lockdowns and social-distancing

The views and opinions expressed are solely those of the author and do not necessarily reflect those of the Italian National Institute of Statistics – Istat.

L. Ferranna
Researcher at Istat – Italian National Institute of Statistics, Rome, Italy
e-mail: licia.ferranna@istat.it

E. Scannella and J. Williams (eds.), *Trends, Issues, and Challenges in Banking and Finance*, Palgrave Macmillan Studies in Banking and Financial Institutions,
https://doi.org/10.1007/978-3-031-96066-6_1

policies has undermined tenants' rental payment capacities (Akinsomi 2021), resulting in a reduction in cash flow for those real estate companies that derive most of their revenue from renting properties. High uncertainty about rental income and increased risk-aversion behavior resulted in higher risk premia and declining property values (Duca et al. 2020). In the commercial real estate sector, the effects of confinement measures have been heterogeneous across property types (Balemi et al. 2021). For example, buildings hosting hotels have been directly hit by rental reductions due to the decrease in both international tourist arrivals and business travels. Similarly, real estates with retail activities have suffered the restrictive policies because they needed to provide in-person services. In many offices instead employees were able to offer the required services by teleworking from home. Therefore, office buildings have remained vacant, and the effective experience of remote working has cast some doubts on the future of office space demand. However, manufacturing activities have continued their production with fewer problems, and storage and logistics spaces have been busy all over the pandemic period.

In the paper, we endeavor to assess how much the shock of COVID-19 has been transmitted to the returns of real estate companies through their asset base, considering that the intensity of the sanitary emergency has been heterogeneous across European territory—with the number of positive cases that have varied from region to region—and heterogeneous across sectors and real estate types—with some economic activities and professions more vulnerable than others. We evaluate the significance of synthetic measures of firms' pandemic-related risk by means of indices that measure the degree of sectoral vulnerability to the diffusion of the virus. For this, we followed Sanchez et al. (2020), Dingel and Neiman (2020), and Avdiu and Nayyar (2020) who suggested to divide jobs into three categories: those that are essential, those that can be done from home, and those that require face-to-face interactions to be performed. For each economic sector (following the Ateco 2007 sector classification), the authors associate a

---

G. S. Bertinetti
Full Professor of Corporate Finance at the Venice School of Management, Ca' Foscari University, Venice, Italy
e-mail: bertinet@unive.it

G. Gardenal (✉)
Associate Professor of Corporate Finance, Venice School of Management, Ca' Foscari University, Venice, Italy
e-mail: ggardenal@unive.it

percentage that indicates the share of workers that satisfy the criterion. By linking each property type to its most likely economic sector, it is possible to derive measures of essentiality, tele workability and face-to-face interactivity for each property type. Stock returns of real estate companies may also be influenced by the economic specialization of the surrounding region (Coulson et al. 2020; Bai and Zhu 2018). Among the others, Coulson et al. (2013) show that housing prices are significantly driven by certain locally concentrated industries. The same may apply to commercial properties. Therefore, we rely on the concept of economic base[1] (Hoyt 1954; North 1955; Tiebout 1956) to understand whether the occupational composition of the regional economy, in which Real Estate Investment Trusts (REITs) own properties, is important for the performance of real estate companies. Finally, we test whether environmental, social, and governance ("ESG") scores may have mitigated the COVID-19 shock (Broadstock et al. 2021; Demers et al. 2021; Engelhardt et al. 2021).

Since the beginning of the pandemic, many studies have tried to disentangle market reactions to the spread of coronavirus disease by looking at firm-level returns. For example, Ding et al. (2021) try to determine the relationship between corporate characteristics and the performance of stock returns to COVID-19 cases; Ramelli and Wagner (2020) exploit the exogenous shock due to the pandemic outbreak to identify the drivers of firm value; He et al. (2022) analyze Chinese firms' exposure to COVID-19 and they observe that a lower COVID exposure is associated with higher cash holding. Other studies instead focus on index-level returns: Gormsen and Koijen (2020) use the S&P 500 for the United States, the Euro Stoxx 50 for European Union, and the Nikkei 225 for Japan; Doko Tchatoka et al. (2022) examine Morgan Stanley Capital International (MSCI) market index data, while Szczygielski et al. (2022) analyze the reaction of industrial groupings. In the real estate sector, several studies evaluating the effects of COVID-19 concentrated on the housing market (Zhao et al. 2020; Layser et al. 2020; Gupta et al. 2022) even at the regional level (Del Giudice et al. 2020; Allen-Coghlan and McQuinn 2021; Duca et al. 2021; Zhang et al. 2023). D'Lima et al. (2022) were the first to document the effect of the

[1] According to the theory of the economic base (Hoyt 1954; North 1955; Tiebout 1956), in a regional economic system it is possible to distinguish between: (1) "basic" activities, which are addressed to an external demand, and (2) "nonbasic" activities, which are locally provided services that strictly depend on their growth on the level of basic activities. The first group identifies the sectoral specialization of the area and basic activities are also determinant for the occupational growth of the nonbasic activities via sectoral interdependencies.

disease spread on US residential property transactions, highlighting a significant decrease in sales and a modest decrease in prices in densely populated locations. Liu and Su (2021) found that the diffusion of teleworking has shifted the US demand for houses away from dense neighborhoods. Turning to commercial properties, most of the studies look at index-level returns (Gherghina et al. 2021 for Romania, Chong and Phillips 2022 with the estimation of the impact of COVID-19 on REITs' index returns in the absence of fiscal and monetary policies). For example, Van Dijk et al. (2020) analyze the performance of Real Capital Analytics (RCA) Commercial Property Price Indexes for eight major US metro markets; Gholipour et al. (2021) consider the effect of market participants' perceived uncertainty on both REITs and commercial property price index for the United States. Among those looking at real estate sub-sectoral indexes, Akinsomi (2021) found that the top three REIT sector losers in the United States are lodging/resort, retail, and office; Hoesli and Malle (2021) for the European Union conclude that retail and hospitality properties (and to a lesser extent office buildings) have been affected the most by COVID-19, while the residential and industrial sectors have been less affected by the crisis. Ling et al. (2020) are the first to evaluate the effect of the pandemic on stock returns in the real estate market through the firm's underlying assets. The authors relate US REITs' abnormal returns to a weighted average of daily growth rates of COVID-19 cases in the counties in which the REITs own properties. By distinguishing between commercial real estate sectors, they show that hospitality and retail trade are those that have had the poorest performance. Similarly, Xie and Milcheva (2020) studied the Hong Kong case by considering the proximity of real estates to infections in the early stage of the pandemic. The results show that REITs with properties within two miles from a COVID-19 case have a 0.02% lower return the day after the disclosure of the case. Milcheva (2022) analyzed the variation in the risk–return relationship before and after the outbreak of COVID-19 in the United States, Singapore, Hong Kong, and Japan. She found that the spread of the disease is associated with an increase in risk and a decrease in returns, which makes the risk–return relationship negative, especially in the United States. The most affected sectors are retail and accommodation in the United States and offices in Asian countries. Cai and Xu (2022) distinguished the consequences of COVID-19 from that of recessions, finding that the latter had negatively affected office and residential REITs' returns while the former had a positive influence on industrial REITs' returns. Finally, other studies have evaluated firm-level exposure to pandemic even by relying on different measures. For example, Allan et al. (2021) evaluate the impact of the COVID-19 pandemic on commercial property rent dynamics in the Asia-Pacific region, finding that rents had a decline of approximately 15% during the first 6 months of 2020. The most severe drops are associated with real estates located in areas with more COVID-19 cases.

To this literature, we made several original contributions. First, while most of the studies look at the United States or Far East context, we focus on the European context for which evidence is scarce and confined to index-level returns. Second, we construct specific measures of real estate companies' vulnerability to evaluate the risk associated with COVID-19 diffusion. On this issue, Wang and Zhou (2021) limited their analysis to the impact of face-to-face interactions. Finally, we evaluate the importance of the regional economic base for real estate firms' performance and the importance of ESG scores. The remainder of the paper is structured as follows: Sect. 1.2 describes the empirical methodology followed and the data that have been used, Sect. 1.3 analyzes the empirical results, and Sect. 1.4 concludes the paper.

1.2 Empirical Methodology and Data Description

The empirical analysis evaluates the consequences of the diffusion of COVID-19 on the returns of the real estate sector. To achieve the aim, we consider the performance of 60 REITs, which (a) are among the constituents of the S&P Developed REIT Index and (b) have their headquarters in one of the European countries,[2] in the period between March 2020 and December 2021.

To evaluate the impact of COVID-19 exposure on firm-level stock returns, we adopt an event study methodology (Fama et al. 1969) according to which the effect of an event on stock prices is measured by the difference between the expected and the actual return, which is called abnormal return. As expected returns are not observed; they need to be estimated. In the empirical analysis, the expected return model that is implemented is the market model according to which the return on stock i at time t ($R_{i,t}$) is determined by the return on the market at time t (M_t). The relationship is supposed to be linear, as in Eq. 1.1:

$$R_{i,t} = \alpha_i + \beta_i M_t + \varepsilon_{i,t} \tag{1.1}$$

[2] Europe is intended as the geographic region; therefore, REITs based in the United Kingdom are included in the analysis.

which is estimated for a reference period, preceding the event to be evaluated, to obtain the estimated relationship for normal returns. In our case the reference period lasts from January 3, 2019 to December 31, 2019, and the reference market is represented by the STOXX Europe 600 Index. Data on stock prices are obtained from the Bloomberg database, and daily returns are calculated as log differences of day-to-day last prices. Subsequently, expected returns are computed for the period of interest by using the previously estimated parameters $\hat{\alpha}_i$ and $\hat{\beta}_i$, as in Eq. 1.2:

$$ER_{i,t+k} = \hat{\alpha}_i + \hat{\beta}_i M_{t+k} \tag{1.2}$$

Finally, abnormal returns for the period $t+k$ are derived as the difference between actual stock returns ($R_{i,t+k}$) and normal returns that have been predicted in the previous step ($ER_{i,t+k}$), as in Eq. 1.3:

$$AR_{i,t+k} = R_{i,t+k} - ER_{i,t+k} \tag{1.3}$$

Estimated daily abnormal returns are the dependent variable in the second step of the empirical analysis, where we evaluate the significance of a set of explicative variables through linear regressions estimated using the OLS methodology. The period examined extends from March 2, 2020 to December 31, 2021; therefore, our sample includes data for 60 equity REITs examined for 480 (working) days, for a total of 28,740 observations. We proceed starting from a baseline regression and gradually including more independent variables.

In the baseline regression we investigate the effect of regional COVID-19 daily growth rates on the REITs' returns of the day after. The growth rate of confirmed COVID-19 cases is computed at the Nomenclature of Territorial Units for Statistics (NUTS) 3 level,[3] by relying on the data collected by Naqvi (2021)[4] for the publicly accessible COVID-19 European regional tracker. To assign, for each point in time, unique values of REITs' vulnerability to COVID-19, we compute a measure of REITs' exposure to COVID-19 which is a geographically weighted average of the growth rates obtained by multiplying the NUTS 3 growth rates of COVID-19

[3] The NUTS classification is a hierarchical system for dividing up the economic territory of the EU and the United Kingdom. NUTS 3 regions correspond to the lower tier.

[4] Data on daily COVID-19 cases at the subnational level for European countries are available at https://github.com/asjadnaqvi/COVID19-European-Regional-Tracker

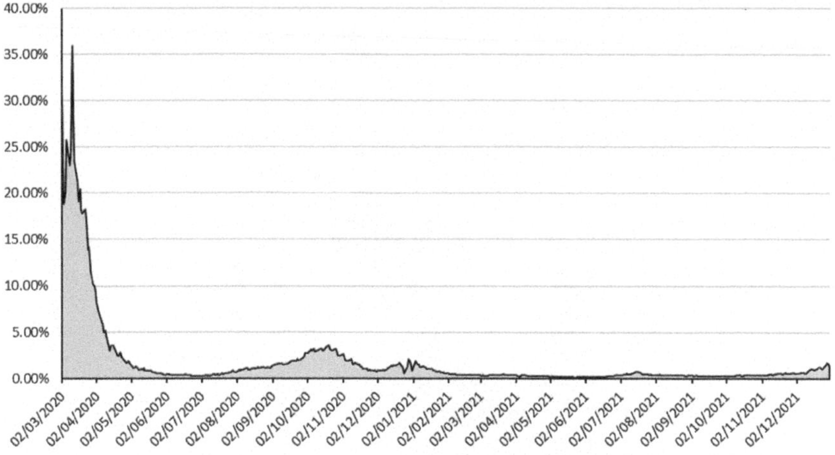

Fig. 1.1 GeoCovid evolution March 2020–December 2021

with the percentages of portfolio allocated in each NUTS 3 (*GeoCovid*). Figure 1.1 reports the evolution of geographically weighted growth rate of COVID-19 for the period March 2020–December 2021.

Data about companies' real estate portfolios are manually collected using information available in the annual reports. In particular, we compiled the list of real estate properties, reporting geographical location and type of property. The percentage of property portfolio located in each NUTS 3 is computed in terms of sizes (sqm) of real estate present in each NUTS 3 at the end of 2019. The total number of properties belonging to the sixty REITs considered in the analysis is 5,252.[5] Figure 1.2 represents the geographic extent of the analysis.

Data on the geographic localization of the real estate properties are collected at the NUTS 3 level. In the map, NUTS 3 regions with real estate belonging to the portfolios of the REITs considered in the analysis are colored in gray. Most of the properties are in Western Europe. In particular, the countries involved in the analysis are Austria, Belgium, Czech Republic, Denmark, France, Germany, Ireland, Italy, Luxembourg, the Netherlands, Norway, Poland, Portugal, Romania, Slovakia, Spain, Sweden, and the

[5] One REIT (LAND LN equity) does not report the full list of real estate belonging to its portfolio; in this case we considered only the top ten real estates.

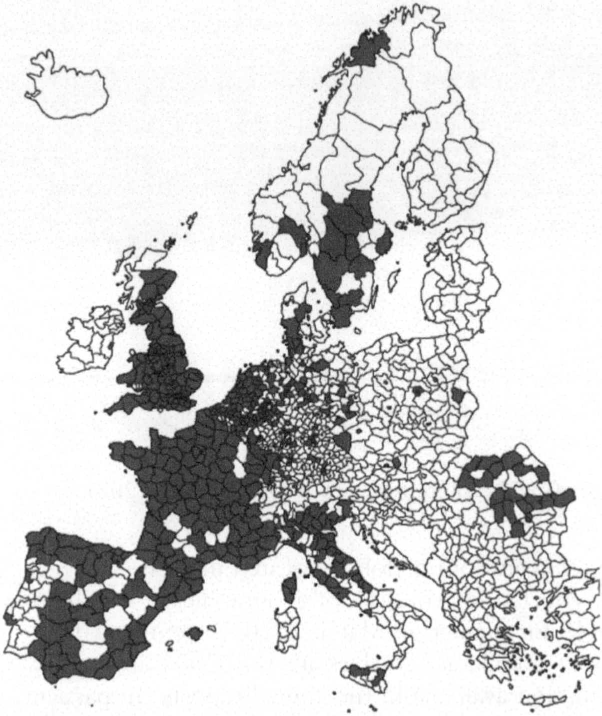

Fig. 1.2 Geographical location of real estate properties

UK. In the baseline regression we use *GeoCovid* reported on day $t-1$ as a predictor for REITs' stock returns on day t, in order to test the hypothesis that news related to the diffusion of COVID-19 in the NUTS 3 in which REITs own properties has an effect on abnormal returns.

Subsequently, we investigate the role played by property types in determining the gap between actual and expected returns. The baseline regression is then enriched to account for diverse reactions across property types, that we derive from companies' annual reports. As discussed in the Sect. 1.1, REITs focused on different property types that experienced substantial variations in returns both before and after the onset of the pandemic. Figure 1.3 reports the distribution of property types across companies' portfolios.

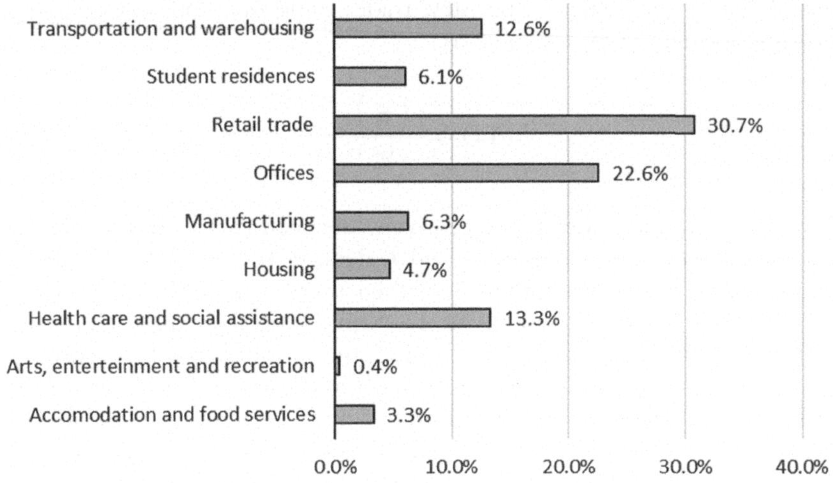

Fig. 1.3 Composition of property portfolios by type of activity

Retail trade represents the most diffused type of property (30.7% of the total number of observations) followed by offices (22.6%). The least represented sectoral activities are those related to the arts, entertainment, and recreation (0.4%), as well as the accommodation and food services (3.3%). Types of properties are classified into nine categories: manufacturing, transportation and warehousing, offices, student residences, housing, retail trade, healthcare and social assistance, accommodation and food services, and arts entertainment and recreation. The significance of property type in explaining abnormal returns is tested in a second regression, where we include dummies for each category.

In the empirical analysis we also assess the relevance of the economic structure of the region in which the REITs own real estate properties. In order to identify which economic sectors represent the economic base of the NUTS 2 region surrounding the NUTS 3 in which REITs own real estate properties, we use the criterion of the location quotient, according to which a sector is considered as "basic" activity if the number of jobs (relative to the total number of jobs in the region) in that sector is higher than the corresponding national average. For each possible "basic" sector considered in the analysis (industry, trade, transport, and services), the location quotient (LQ_{sj}) is equal to

$$LQ_{sj} = \frac{\left(\frac{E_{sj}}{E_j}\right)}{\left(\frac{E_{sn}}{E_n}\right)} \tag{1.4}$$

where j, s, and n define, respectively, the sector, the region (NUTS 2), and the nation under analysis, and E denotes the number of employees. If the ratio is greater than one, then there is a surplus of production, and the sector represents an economic base for exports. For the economic activities identified as "basic," the number of jobs exceeding the national average indicates the strength of the sector. In the empirical analysis we calculate the sectoral composition of the employment surplus of the regions (NUTS 2) in which REITs own real estate properties and then we compute for each REIT weighted averages based on the percentages of portfolio allocated in each NUTS 2. We evaluate the significance of the economic base in explaining abnormal returns in the third version of the model.

Finally, to investigate property-type specific effects of GeoCovid, we augment the model with variables that result from the interaction between GeoCovid and the property-type dummies. The resulting interaction variables allow us to determine the different impacts of GeoCovid depending on the types of real estate properties in the REITs' portfolios. For example, for the category *Accommodation and food services*, the estimated coefficient associated with the corresponding interaction variable expresses the difference in the impact of GeoCovid between the hospitality and the nonhospitality type of property.

We repeat the steps of the analysis using three indexes of COVID vulnerability in place of property type. The indexes refer to the degree of essentiality of the jobs, the possibility of teleworking, and the necessity of face-to-face interactions to perform the activity. The first measure, developed by Sanchez et al. (2020), indicates the percentages of jobs considered essential in each economic sector of the NACE 1 classification[6] (*Ess*). For some categories, such as Public Administration, Human Health and Social Work Activities, and Water Supply, 100% of the jobs are supposed to be essential; on the other hand, other sectors have been considered as

[6] Sanchez et al. (2020), table 2, p. 2.

nonessential at all. The latter comprise, for example, Arts, Entertainment, and Recreation, Accommodation, and Food Service Activities. We reconduct Sanchez et al. (2020) percentages to sectoral activities associated with the property types considered in the empirical analysis. Once we determine the rate of essential jobs for each type of property, we compute for each REIT the proportion of essential jobs performed in the portfolio's real estate properties. The second measure of COVID-related risk exposure concerns the possibility of teleworking (*Tel*). Dingel and Neiman (2020) quantify the fraction of employees that are in teleworkable occupations for each economic sector in the NAICS two-digit classification.[7] There is significant variation across occupations. For example, office workers are largely able to work from home while transport, construction, and production workers cannot. As before, we adapt the information to sectoral activities associated with the property types considered in the empirical analysis and we compute for each REIT the proportion of teleworkable jobs performed in the portfolio's real estate properties. The same procedure is adopted for the third measure, which is related to the necessity of face-to-face interactions with other workers or with customers to best perform the job. To determine an index of interactions intensity applied to the NAICS two-digit economic sectors, Avdiu and Nayyar (2020)[8] considered the necessity of (a) establishing and maintaining personal relations, (b) assisting and caring for the others, (c) working directly with the public, and (d) selling or influencing purchases. Although the measure of interaction intensity (*FtoF*) may seem similar to that of teleworkability, for some sectors the two indicators differ. For example, many jobs in manufacturing require physical presence in the workplace but do not require much face-to-face interaction. On the contrary, teaching is likely to be carried out electronically, but it requires a strong component of interaction between teacher and student, and this may have influenced the performance of student residences.

As control variables, we use quarterly accounting data, obtained from the Bloomberg database. In particular, we consider determinants of daily stock returns reported in previous studies (e.g., Ling et al. 2020; Milcheva 2022). *Leverage* refers to financial leverage, and it is calculated as average total assets divided by average total common equity; *Tobin's Q* is the ratio of the market value of a firm to the replacement cost of the firm's assets.

[7] Dingel and Neiman (2020), table 3, p. 8.

[8] Avdiu and Nayyar (2020), figure 1, appendix A.

The numerator is the sum of market cap, total liabilities, preferred equity, and minority interest; the denominator is total assets. *Assets* indicate the size of the REIT and are the total of all short- and long-term assets as reported on the balance sheet; *Cash* is the sum of cash and cash equivalents divided by lagged total assets; *LagRet* are REITs' returns in the last quarter of 2019. We also include two Herfindahl–Hirschman kind of indexes to account for firms' degree of concentration related either to the type of property (*SecHHI*) or to the geography (*NutsHHI*). Finally, we use as control variables three indicators of economic prosperity at the national level as industrial production (*IndProd*), unemployment (*Unempl*), and exports (*Exp*) and Bloomberg ESG (*Environmental—BESGENV, Governance—BESGGOV, Social—BESGSOC*) scores.

1.3 Empirical Results

The results of the baseline regression are reported in the first column of Table 1.1, where we investigate the effect of regional COVID-19 daily growth rates (*GeoCovid*) on abnormal returns on the following day.

The findings are in line with expectations: the estimated coefficient for *GeoCovid* is negative and highly significant: returns react negatively to the spread of the virus in regions where REITs own real estates. In the second column of Table 1.1, we investigate the reaction of REITs' returns to different property types in the period of COVID-19 diffusion. Three categories present a significantly negative sign, while another four have experienced positive returns in the pandemic period. The former group includes real estates dedicated to arts, entertainment, and recreation activities, retail trade, and offices; the latter comprises buildings with healthcare and social assistance functions, or real estates used for manufacturing, transportation, and warehousing. Finally, housing has maintained positive returns, although poorly significant. Column (3) of Table 1.1 presents the estimation results of the regression in which we introduce the three indexes of COVID vulnerability, essentiality (*Ess*), teleworkability (*Tel*) and interaction intensity (*FtoF*) in place of property type. The results indicate that, during the sanitary emergency, the ownership of real estates in which highly teleworkable activities were conducted revealed to be harmful to stock returns. The same applies to those activities which need face-to-face interaction to be performed. While the former category may be associated with office work, the latter well represents retail trade. As noted with the previous estimates, offices and shops

Table 1.1 Column 1: Baseline results—abnormal returns and geographically weighted COVID-19 growth. Column 2: Extended regression 1a—abnormal returns and property types. Standard errors clustered at firm level. Column 3: Extended regression 1b—abnormal returns and vulnerability

Variables	*(1) Abnormal returns*	*(2) Abnormal returns*	*(3) Abnormal returns*
GeoCovid	-1.831***	-1.838***	-1.837***
	(0.337)	(0.339)	(0.338)
Accommodation and food services		-0.020	
		(0.019)	
Arts, entertainment, and recreation activities		-0.042*	
		(0.021)	
Healthcare and social assistance		0.024*	
		(0.014)	
Retail trade		-0.033**	
		(0.013)	
Manufacturing		0.069***	
		(0.020)	
Transportation and warehousing		0.078***	
		(0.017)	
Offices		-0.034**	
		(0.015)	
Student residences		0.001	
		(0.0138)	
Housing		0.033*	
		(0.019)	
Tel			-0.180*
			(0.028)
Ess			0.053***
			(0.015)
FtoF			-0.129***
			(0.025)
Constant	-0.024***	-0.019	0.084***
	(0.009)	(0.014)	(0.024)
Observations	28,740	28,740	28,740
R^2	0.042	0.043	0.043

***, **, and * indicate statistical significance at the 1%, 5%, and 10% levels, respectively.

have suffered during the pandemic period. However, less teleworkable and in need of face-to-face interactions activities have performed better during COVID-19 spread. This is the case with manufacturing activities and warehousing. Finally, real estate where essential jobs were performed experienced significantly positive returns. Healthcare and social assistance belong to this class of activities.

The influence of different local economic structures in determining REITs' performances, as well as the impact of their financial characteristics, is investigated in Table 1.2.

The first column reports the estimation results when the property type dummies are included in the analysis; in the second column the binary variables are substituted with vulnerability indicators. In both cases, the coefficient of the main variable of interest, *GeoCovid*, is significant and maintains the expected negative sign. For what concerns the economic base, REITs surrounded by regions with commercial specialization, were favored during the pandemic period. The reason behind this result may be that regions highly specialized in commerce tend to be more residential than regions with, for example, an industrial specialization, where the retail trade may have been replaced by e-commerce, favoring warehouses. Control variables related to the economic dimension are industrial production, unemployment, and exports. The former and the latter have significant coefficients, both positive. The other covariates, *Tobin's Q*, *Leverage*, *Asset*, *LagRet*, *Cash*, *NutsHHI*, and *SecHHI*, are all not significant except for the sum of cash and cash equivalents divided by lagged total assets. In the second version of the analysis, when vulnerability indexes substitute property types, also the two Herfindahl–Hirschman indexes are slightly significant.

Subsequently, we determine property-type specific effect of *GeoCovid* by augmenting the previous models with interaction variables resulting from *GeoCovid* multiplied by property type dummies (Table 1.3, Column 1) or vulnerability indicators (Table 1.3, Column 2).

The estimated coefficients indicate the difference in the impact of *GeoCovid* between the category of interest and the other categories. Reading Column 1 of Table 1.3, the specific impact of COVID-19 on retail trade is negative, while *GeoCovid* has been beneficial for the healthcare sector and the transportation and warehousing activities, maybe due to the significant increase in e-commerce experienced in the pandemic period. Looking at the second version of the model, with vulnerability indexes instead of property types, it turns out that the more teleworkable and highly interactive the activities are, the more they have been damaged by the spread of the virus.

Finally, we restrict our sample to those REITs with Bloomberg ESG (Environmental—BESGENV, Governance—BESGGOV, Social—BESGSOC) scores and we evaluate their impact in determining abnormal returns during the pandemic period. Table 1.4 presents the results. REITs with higher scores in social activities have been rewarded during the pandemic period.

Table 1.2 Abnormal returns and geographically weighted COVID-19 growth. Economic structure and financial controls included. Column 1: Dummies for property types included. Column 2: Vulnerability indexes included. Standard errors clustered at firm level

Variables	*(1)* *Abnormal returns*	*(2)* *Abnormal returns*
GeoCovid	−1.309***	−1.293***
	(0.382)	(0.379)
EB_industry	0.014	0.008
	(0.043)	(0.035)
EB_trade	0.223**	0.195**
	(0.108)	(0.086)
EB_transport	0.067	0.049
	(0.059)	(0.049)
EB_services	0.007	0.008
	(0.046)	(0.044)
IndProd	0.005***	0.005***
	(0.002)	(0.002)
Unempl	−0.003	−0.001
	(0.004)	(0.003)
Exp	0.002***	0.002***
	(0.001)	(0.001)
Tobin's Q	−0.041	−0.098
	(0.063)	(0.064)
Leverage	−0.014	−0.002
	(0.016)	(0.014)
Asset	0.002	0.001
	(0.001)	(0.001)
Cash	0.674**	0.680***
	(0.274)	(0.255)
NutsHHI	0.025	0.054*
	(0.039)	(0.028)
SecHHI	0.050	0.052*
	(0.040)	(0.027)
LagRet	0.001	0.001
	(0.001)	(0.001)
Constant	−0.667***	−0.470***
	(0.182)	(0.162)
Property types' dummies	Yes	No
Vulnerability indicators	No	Yes
Observations	28,740	28,740
R-squared	0.043	0.043

***, **, and * indicate statistical significance at the 1%, 5%, and 10% levels, respectively.

Table 1.3 Abnormal returns and geographically weighted COVID-19 growth. Interaction variables, economic structure, and financial controls included. Column 1: Dummies for property types included. Column 2: Vulnerability indexes included. Standard errors clustered at firm level

Variables	(1) *Abnormal returns*	(2) *Abnormal returns*
GeoCovid	−1.089*	−0.714
	(0.592)	(0.702)
Accommodation*GeoCovid	0.018	
	(0.016)	
Entertainment*GeoCovid	−0.028	
	(0.019)	
Healthcare*GeoCovid	0.025***	
	(0.009)	
Retail*GeoCovid	−0.015*	
	(0.008)	
Manufacturing*GeoCovid	0.010	
	(0.007)	
Transportation*GeoCovid	0.018***	
	(0.006)	
Offices*GeoCovid	−0.007	
	(0.007)	
Student*GeoCovid	−0.005	
	(0.010)	
Housing*GeoCovid	0.003	
	(0.006)	
Tel*GeoCovid		−0.033***
		(0.011)
Ess*GeoCovid		0.037***
		(0.009)
FtoF*GeoCovid		−0.0257***
		(0.009)
Constant	−0.657***	−0.450***
	(0.182)	(0.151)
Property types' dummies	Yes	No
Vulnerability indicators	No	Yes
Control variables	Yes	Yes
Observations	28,740	28,740
R-squared	0.045	0.045

***, **, and * indicate statistical significance at the 1%, 5%, and 10% levels, respectively.

Table 1.4 Abnormal returns and geographically weighted COVID-19 growth. The role of ESG scores. Economic structure and financial controls included. Dummies for property types included

Variables	*Abnormal returns*
GeoCovid	−2.106**
	(0.769)
BESGENV	−0.003
	(0.021)
BESGGOV	−0.011
	(0.014)
BESGSOC	0.033***
	(0.010)
Constant	−1.117***
	(0.364)
Observations	13,412
R^2	0.006

***, **, and * indicate statistical significance at the 1%, 5%, and 10% levels, respectively.

1.4 Conclusions

The paper investigates the transmission of COVID-19 shock to the returns of real estate companies through their asset base. Results show that day-after returns are negatively related to the spread of the virus in regions where REITs own properties. The effect of COVID-19 shock has been heterogeneous across property types with some economic activities and professions more vulnerable than others: real estates dedicated to arts, entertainment, and recreation activities, retail trade, and offices have suffered the most in the pandemic period. However, properties comprising buildings with healthcare and social assistance functions, or real estates used for manufacturing, transportation, and warehousing, have reacted positively to the sanitary emergency. Moreover, lower stock returns are associated with the ownership of real estates in which highly teleworkable or interactive activities were conducted. The type of economic base of the region where REITs own properties contributed to determine variations in returns: regions highly specialized in commerce were favored during the pandemic. Finally, REITs with higher scores in social activities were rewarded during the pandemic period.

References

Akinsomi, O. (2021). How resilient are REITs to a pandemic? The COVID-19 effect. *Journal of Property Investment & Finance, 39*(1). 19–24. https://doi.org/10.1108/JPIF-06-2020-0065

Allan, R., Liusman, E., Lu, T., & Tsang, D. (2021). The COVID-19 pandemic and commercial property rent dynamics. *Journal of Risk and Financial Management, 14*(8), 360.

Allen-Coghlan, M. and McQuinn, K.M. (2021). The potential impact of Covid-19 on the Irish housing sector, *International Journal of Housing Markets and Analysis, 14*(4), 636–651. https://doi.org/10.1108/IJHMA-05-2020-0065

Avdiu, B., & Nayyar, G. (2020). When face-to-face interactions become an occupational hazard: Jobs in the time of COVID-19. *Economic Letters*, (197), 1–4.

Bai, Q., & Zhu, L. (2018). The effects of industry specific and local economic factors on credit default swap spreads: Evidence from REITs. *Journal of Financial Services Research, 54*(3), 293–321.

Balemi, N., Füss, R., & Weigand, A. (2021). COVID-19 's impact on real estate markets: review and outlook. *Financial Markets and Portfolio Management, 35*(4), 495–513.

Broadstock, D. C., Chan, K., Cheng, L. T., & Wang, X. (2021). The role of ESG performance during times of financial crisis: Evidence from COVID-19 in China. *Finance Research Letters, 38*, 101716.

Cai, Y., & Xu, K. (2022). Net impact of COVID-19 on REIT returns. *Journal of Risk and Financial Management, 15*(8), 359.

Canton, E., Colasanti, F., Durán, J., Garrone, M., Hobza, A., Simons, W., & Vandeplas, A. (2021). *The sectoral impact of the COVID-19 crisis. An unprecedented and atypical crisis* (No. 069). Directorate General Economic and Financial Affairs (DG ECFIN), European Commission.

Chong, J., & Phillips, G. M. (2022). COVID-19 losses to the real estate market: An equity analysis. *Finance Research Letters, 45*, 102131.

Coulson, N. E., Liu, C. H., & Villupuram, S. V. (2013). Urban economic base as a catalyst for movements in real estate prices. *Regional Science and Urban Economics, 43*(6), 1023–1040.

Coulson, N. E., McCoy, S. J., & McDonough, I. K. (2020). Economic diversification and the resiliency hypothesis: Evidence from the impact of natural disasters on regional housing values. *Regional Science and Urban Economics, 85*, 103581.

Del Giudice, V., De Paola, P., & Del Giudice, F. P. (2020). COVID-19 Infects Real Estate Markets: Short and Mid-Run Effects on Housing Prices in Campania Region (Italy). *Social Sciences, 9*(7), 114. https://doi.org/10.3390/socsci9070114

Demers, E., Hendrikse, J., Joos, P., & Lev, B. (2021). ESG did not immunize stocks during the COVID-19 crisis, but investments in intangible assets did. *Journal of Business Finance & Accounting, 48*(3–4), 433–462.

Ding, W., Levine, R., Lin, C., & Xie, W. (2021). Corporate immunity to the COVID-19 pandemic. *Journal of Financial Economics, 141*(2), 802–830.

Dingel, J. I., & Neiman, B. (2020). How many jobs can be done at home? *Journal of Public Economics*, 189, 104235.

D'Lima, W., Lopez, L. A., & Pradhan, A. (2022). COVID-19 and housing market effects: Evidence from US shutdown orders. *Real Estate Economics*, *50*(2), 303–339.

Doko Tchatoka, F., Puellbeck, J., & Masson, V. (2022). Stock returns in the time of COVID-19 pandemic. *Applied Economics*, *54*(9), 1071–1092.

Duca, J. V., Ling, D. C. (2020). The other (commercial) real estate boom and bust: The effects of risk premia and regulatory capital arbitrage. *Journal of Banking & Finance*, *112*. https://doi.org/10.1016/j.jbankfin.2018.03.006

Duca, J. V., Hoesli, M., & Montezuma, J. (2021). The resilience and realignment of house prices in the era of Covid-19. *Journal of European Real Estate Research*, 14(3), 421–431.

Engelhardt, N., Ekkenga, J., & Posch, P. (2021). ESG ratings and stock performance during the COVID-19 crisis. *Sustainability*, *13*(13), 7133.

Fama, E. F., Fisher, L., Jensen, M. C., & Roll, R. (1969). The adjustment of stock prices to new information. *International Economic Review*, *10*(1), 1–21.

Gherghina, Ş. C., Armeanu, D. Ş., & Joldeş, C. C. (2021). COVID-19 pandemic and Romanian stock market volatility: A GARCH approach. *Journal of Risk and Financial Management*, *14*(8), 341.

Gholipour, H. F., Tajaddini, R., Farzanegan, M. R., & Yam, S. (2021). Responses of REITs index and commercial property prices to economic uncertainties: A VAR analysis. *Research in International Business and Finance*, *58*, 101457.

Gormsen, N. J., & Koijen, R. S. (2020). Coronavirus: Impact on stock prices and growth expectations. *The Review of Asset Pricing Studies*, *10*(4), 574–597.

Gupta, A., Mittal, V., Peeters, J., & Van Nieuwerburgh, S. (2022). Flattening the curve: Pandemic-induced revaluation of urban real estate. *Journal of Financial Economics*, *146*(2), 594–636.

He, Z., Suardi, S., Wang, K., & Zhao, Y. (2022). Firms' COVID-19 pandemic exposure and corporate cash policy: Evidence from China. *Economic Modelling*, *116*, 105999.

Hoesli, M., & Malle, R. (2021). Commercial real estate prices and COVID-19. *Journal of European Real Estate Research*, *15*(2), 295–306.

Hoyt, H. (1954). Homer Hoyt on development of economic base concept. *Land Economics*, 30(2), 182–186.

Layser, M. D., De Barbieri, E. W., Greenlee, A. J., Kaye, T. A., & Saito, B. G. (2020). Mitigating housing instability during a pandemic. *Oregon Law Review*, *99*, 445.

Ling, D. C., Wang, C., & Zhou, T. (2020). A first look at the impact of COVID-19 on commercial real estate prices: Asset-level evidence. *The Review of Asset Pricing Studies*, *10*(4), 669–704.

Liu, S., & Su, Y. (2021). The impact of the COVID-19 pandemic on the demand for density: Evidence from the US housing market. *Economics Letters*, *207*, 110010.

Milcheva, S. (2022). Volatility and the cross-section of real estate equity returns during Covid-19. *The Journal of Real Estate Finance and Economics*, *65*(2), 293–320.

Naqvi, A. (2021). COVID-19 European regional tracker. *Scientific Data*, *8*(1), 1–14.

North, D. C. (1955). Location theory and regional economic growth. *Journal of Political Economy*, *63*(3), 243–258.

Ramelli, S., & Wagner, A. F. (2020). Feverish stock price reactions to COVID-19. *The Review of Corporate Finance Studies*, *9*(3), 622–655.

Sanchez, D. G., Parra, N. G., Özden, Ç., & Rijkers, B. (2020). Which Jobs are Most Vulnerable to COVID-19? What an Analysis of the European Union Reveals. *World Bank Research and Policy Briefs No. 148384*, 1–7.

Szczygielski, J. J., Charteris, A., Bwanya, P. R., & Brzeszczyński, J. (2022). The impact and role of COVID-19 uncertainty: A global industry analysis. *International Review of Financial Analysis*, *80*, 101837.

Tiebout, C. M. (1956). A pure theory of local expenditures. *Journal of Political Economy*, *64*(5), 416–424.

Van Dijk, D., Kinsella Thompson, A., & Geltner, D. (2020). Recent drops in market liquidity may foreshadow major drops in US commercial real estate markets. *MIT Center for Real Estate Research Paper*, (2). Available at SSRN: https://ssrn.com/abstract=3604606 or http://dx.doi.org/10.2139/ssrn.3604606

Wang, C. & Zhou (2021). T. Trade-offs between Asset Location and Proximity to Home: Evidence from REIT Property Selloffs. *The Journal of Real Estate Finance and Economics*, *63*, 82–121. https://doi.org/10.1007/s11146-020-09770-9

Wen and Arbogast. (2021). *How COVID-19 has impacted stock performance by industry*. On the Economy Blog, Federal Reserve Bank of St. Louis, March 21. https://www.stlouisfed.org/on-the-economy/

Xie, L., & Milcheva, S. (2020). *Proximity to COVID-19 cases and REIT equity returns*. Working Paper, University College London.

Zhang, L., Leonard, T., & Bitzan, J. (2023). Impacts of the COVID-19 pandemic on house prices: Heterogeneous impacts over time and across the house price distribution. *Journal of Real Estate Research*, *45*(1), 1–22.

Zhao, Y., Zakharova, D. V., & Zettelmeyer, J. (2020). US Housing Market during COVID-19: Aggregate and Distributional Evidence. *IMF Working Papers*, *2020*(212), 1–47. Available at SSRN: https://ssrn.com/abstract=3744679

CHAPTER 2

Climate Risks in Banking

State of the Art and Future Research Directions

Violeta Bringas Fernández, Begoña Torre Olmo, and María Cantero Saiz

2.1 Introduction

The perception of climate change has undergone a significant shift in recent years, transitioning from a primarily environmental concern to a matter of pressing relevance to humanity, businesses, and national and global economic interests. Indeed, the phenomenon of climate risk has gradually evolved into an unprecedented threat with the potential to cause significant damage to human assets, posing a threat to the ecological environment, human health, and economic development (Heutel et al. 2021; Rising et al. 2022). For instance, between 1999 and 2019, the number of extreme weather events worldwide exceeded 10,000, resulting in over 475,000 fatalities and direct economic losses amounting to approximately

V. Bringas Fernández (✉) • B. Torre Olmo • M. Cantero Saiz
Santander Financial Institute (SANFI), Universidad de Cantabria – Fundación UCEIF, Santander, Spain
e-mail: Bringasv@unican.es

E. Scannella and J. Williams (eds.), *Trends, Issues, and Challenges in Banking and Finance*, Palgrave Macmillan Studies in Banking and Financial Institutions,
https://doi.org/10.1007/978-3-031-96066-6_2

US $2.56 trillion (Eckstein et al. 2021). Furthermore, in 2020, natural disasters were responsible for damages amounting to US $210 billion (MunichRe). These instabilities have the potential to spread to the financial sector and climate change is increasingly recognized as a new source of risk affecting global economic development and financial stability (Rezai et al. 2018; Kahn et al. 2021). Furthermore, there has been a marked increase in the frequency of banking crises, with a 26%–248% rise in occurrences attributable to climate change (Lamperti et al. 2019). Indeed, climate change and environmental factors pose a substantial concern for the banking sector due to their unpredictable and non-diversifiable characteristics (Battiston 2021; Rudebusch 2021), creating potential risks and opportunities for the financial sector.

From a financial and international perspective, climate change has been identified as one of the major international challenges of recent years (Numan et al. 2023). In 2020, the Federal Reserve indicated that climate change can aggravate economic and financial vulnerability. The World Economic Forum's Global Risk Report, published in 2022, identified extreme weather events as among the top three most severe risks in the next decade. In the long run, this risk could potentially create greater challenges than the 2008–2009 global financial crisis (Chiavuzzo 2018). Indeed, Central Banks have warned of the potentially destabilizing effects of climate risks (Bank of England 2017; De Nederlandsche Bank 2017) and the European Central Bank's Financial Stability Review specified that these risks could negatively impact the balance sheets of financial institutions, particularly if markets mispriced these risks (Giuzio et al. 2024).

The financial sector and its assets are highly exposed to climate risks and the numerous regulations and policies adopted to try to mitigate them. However, this sector also plays a pivotal role in implementing global initiatives (e.g., the Paris Agreement or COP26) aimed at reducing greenhouse gas (GHG) emissions, financing low-carbon transitions, and reallocating essential resources (Lang et al. 2023; Spinaci 2021). In this regard, the financial sector's function in directing investment flows from high-emission activities to low-carbon or sustainable ones, as well as the development of innovative financial instruments such as green loans, bonds, investment funds, and sustainable indices, can be considered a significant contribution to the broader transformation toward a more sustainable economy (Amargant Arnau and del Arroyo González 2022).

In this chapter, we undertake a review of the extant scholarly research focusing on climate risk in banking and its effects on financial stability.

It is observed that the strands of literature focusing on climate risks and their effects on banking institutions are increasingly growing, although still in their initial stage. The present study aims to provide suitable guidelines to facilitate a comprehensive understanding of the significance of climate risks for sustainable finance and economic stability. The present study contributes to the literature by shedding light on the evolution of this research topic in an attempt to foster the academic debate on this relevant topic.

The remainder of this chapter is structured as follows: Sect. 2.2 provides an overview of climate risks and financial stability, focusing on typologies of climate risks, sustainability regulations, and the overall impact of climate change on the financial stability of the banking industry; Sect. 2.3 describes the state of the art of climate risk research in the banking industry; Sect. 2.4 analyzes the methodologies for assessing climate risks; Sect. 2.5 suggests an avenue for future research; finally, Sect. 2.6 concludes the chapter.

2.2 Climate Risks and Financial Stability

2.2.1 Typologies of Climate Risks

Climate risk has the potential to compromise the financial stability of banking institutions (Shabir et al. 2024; Le et al. 2023). It is therefore essential for banks to incorporate climate risk considerations into their risk frameworks (Caby et al. 2022). In 2015, the governor of the Bank of England asserted that climate change poses three distinct types of climate-related risk to the banking sector: climate physical risks, climate transition risks, and climate liability risks.

Physical risks are derived from extreme weather events and consistent changes in climate patterns, including floods, hurricanes, and heatwaves (Chalabi-Jabado and Ziane 2024). Such events result in significant disruptions to operations, pose a threat to the profitability of banks, and increase compliance costs (Lee and Alam, 2024). The impact of climate change on physical assets and the production capacity of firms can escalate the credit risk of banking institutions, precipitate financial losses within the insurance sector, and compromise the financial stability of governments (Battiston et al. 2021). Physical risk can be categorized into two distinct types: acute and chronic (as we can see in Table 2.1). The former encompasses all extreme natural phenomena that result in immediate

Table 2.1 Classification of physical risks (adapted from the European Commission Taxonomy Delegated Act of April 2021 [C(2021) 2800/3 Annex 1, Appendix A])

Temperature	*Wind*	*Water*	*Solid mas*
Chronic			
Changing temperature (air, freshwater, marine water)	Changing wind patterns	Changing precipitation patterns and types (rain, hail, snow/ice)	Coastal erosion
Heat stress		Precipitation or hydrological variability	Soil degradation
Temperature variability		Ocean acidification	Soil erosion
Permafrost thawing		Saline intrusion	Solifluction
Acute			
Heat wave	Cyclones, hurricanes, typhoons	Sea level rise Water stress Drought	Avalanche
Cold wave/frost	Storm (including blizzards, dust storms, and sandstorms)	Heavy precipitation (rain, hail, snow/ice)	Landslide
Wildfire	Tornado	Flood (coastal, fluvial, pluvial, ground water) Glacial lake outburst	Subsidence

destruction, such as heatwaves or hurricanes (Chabot and Bertrand 2023). These events have the capacity to induce temporary or permanent interruptions to business operations, exerting a detrimental effect on companies' production assets and their partners within supply and distribution chains (Pankratz and Schiller 2023). In contrast, chronic risks refer to events that occur over time but have a more prolonged and significant impact on the financial stability of institutions (Bank for International Settlements [BIS] 2021).

Transition risks are associated with the repercussions of alterations in regulations, business models, technologies, and consumer preferences that are intended to be in accordance with the transition to a low-carbon economy (Ojea-Ferreiro et al. 2024). Moreover, the transition to a low-carbon economy has the potential to precipitate unanticipated adjustments to asset prices (both positive and negative) and changes in defaults for entire asset classes, giving rise to financial shocks for asset managers, institutional investors, and bank portfolios (Battiston et al. 2021). Transition risks can arise from a variety of factors, including climate regulations and policies, such as the Paris Agreement. Technological change is another potential cause, as new policies may lead to the substitution of energy sources from existing technologies toward greener and more sustainable sources or technologies that enable energy storage, which is costly. Furthermore, market sentiment can play a significant role, as shifts in investor and consumer preferences toward sustainable economic propositions can have a substantial impact on asset valuations.

Finally, liability risks emerge from the escalating compensation provided to individuals and enterprises adversely affected by physical and transitional climate-related risks (Bayangos et al. 2021; Wu et al. 2023).

A number of particularities are associated with climate risks. Firstly, they will occur over a long period of time, although their effects are uncertain as they are unprecedented and it is not possible to establish when, where, how often, or how severe they will be. Secondly, physical and transition risks are interrelated—the higher the transition risks, the lower the future physical risks. The initiation of robust and expeditious measures to mitigate climate change will elevate transition risks, concomitantly reducing the frequency and severity of natural disasters, thereby lowering physical risks (Monasterolo 2020; González and Nuñez 2021). Thirdly, the impacts of climate change vary across geographical regions and economic sectors. However, the sectors requiring prompt attention are coastlines, water resources, terrestrial ecosystems, and human health (García-León and Ciscar 2022). Despite the progress that has already been made, such as the European Union's Taxonomy Regulation and the European Banking Authority's environmental, social, and governance (ESG) risk disclosure standards, there is a need for common definitions in order to facilitate the correct assessment of climate risks and global standards for their disclosure (NGFS 2020).

Climate risks have been demonstrated to be linked to financial risks through macro- and microeconomic transmission channels. These channels illustrate how climate risk factors exert a direct and indirect influence on institutions, their assets, and the economies in which they operate. In essence, these channels can be regarded as the medium through which climate change manifests as a source of financial risk (NGFS 2019). The distinction between micro and macro channels is made to facilitate a more nuanced analysis of how financial risks impact banks, particularly with regard to the differentiation between microeconomic effects on banks' counterparties and their exposures to financial assets, as well as indirect macroeconomic effects (BIS 2021).

The microeconomic transmission channels are defined as the mechanisms that are employed to measure the effects that climate risks may have on the borrowers or financial assets of institutions. These risks affect banks' financial risks, for example, through their operations and their ability to fund themselves. Thus, in the event of deterioration of physical capital due to natural disasters, firms will require liquidity to make new investments, which translates into higher leverage and reduced revenues as their productive capacity is reduced, impacting the banks that finance them. Furthermore, microeconomic transmission channels also reflect indirect effects on banks' specific financial assets such as bonds or equities.

Macroeconomic transmission channels have been defined as the mechanisms through which climate risk factors affect the macroeconomy. These channels refer to the negative effect that physical and transition risks have on economic growth or labor productivity, with the effects on banks having an impact on the economic environment in which they operate. Furthermore, the effects of climate change on macroeconomic variables such as interest rates, inflation, or exchange rates are also captured (BIS 2021).

2.2.2 *Impact on Financial Stability*

The repercussions of climate change on financial stability present substantial challenges to central banks and financial regulators (Campiglio and Dafermos 2018). Indeed, climate change engenders a series of financial fluctuations, thereby triggering systemic financial risk and threatening the safety and stability of the financial sector (Liu et al. 2024). Specifically, climate change may affect the stability of the financial system through the previously explained physical and transitional risks.

Dafermos et al. (2018) posit that climate change is likely to have adverse effects on the liquidity of firms and negatively impact credit expansion and financial stability. Roncoroni et al. (2021) conducted a study on the impact of climate transition risks and market conditions on financial stability. They estimated the direct and indirect consequences of a disorderly transition to a low-carbon economy on a financial system comprising banks and investment funds. Their findings demonstrated that financial contagion effects have the potential to compromise financial stability in scenarios where there is a disorderly transition, particularly when accompanied by weak market conditions. Concurrently, Ojea-Ferreiro et al. (2024) assess the potential influence of climate transition risk, as reflected in its effect on asset prices, on financial stability. Their results demonstrate that banking institutions anticipate a more significant systemic impact in the event of a disorderly transition, with the magnitude of this impact exhibiting considerable variation based on the specific financial firm's type and geographical location. In their study, Chabot and Bertrand (2023) sought to estimate the impact of national climate conditions and extreme events on financial stability, measured at the individual financial institution and system levels. The results of the study demonstrated that transition and physical risks exert a highly significant negative influence on financial stability at both the institution and financial system levels. By focusing on physical risks, Liu et al. (2024) investigated the correlation among these risks and financial stability. The findings demonstrated that climate risk negatively impacts financial stability, and this adverse impact will vary among different levels of economic and financial development across countries.

These studies revealed that climate risk has a detrimental impact on financial stability as the economic impact caused by climate risk may change the value of financial assets held by enterprises and sovereign entities (Battiston et al. 2021). The impact may also adversely affect the liquidity (Lang et al. 2023; Lee et al. 2022), leverage (Jiang et al. 2025; Zhang et al. 2025), solvency (Gramlich et al. 2023), and stock volatility (Kruttli et al. 2019) of the financial institutions resulting in financial risk. Also, the interconnection within the financial sector will further impact financial risk. In fact, physical and transition risks are interrelated and constitute a major source of systemic risk when they cause losses to financial intermediaries, disruptions in the functioning of financial markets, and sudden increases in the volatility of large asset classes, with spillover effects on the real economy (Monasterolo et al. 2017; Brunetti et al. 2021; Curcio et al. 2023).

2.2.3 *Sustainable Finance Regulations*

Previous studies urge regulators to mandatorily require the assessment and disclosure of corporate climate risks to allow banks to adjust their prudential capital requirements. Consequently, the evaluation of the repercussions of climate change risks on financial entities and on the financial system's stability is currently a primary concern on the agendas of central banks, regulatory authorities, and investors (Campiglio and Dafermos 2018). Indeed, research findings indicate that a country's macro-prudential policies can effectively contribute to maintaining financial stability in the face of climate-related financial risks. Moreover, it has been evidenced that a comprehensive national governance system can serve as a mitigating factor against the detrimental consequences of climate risk on financial stability (Liu et al. 2024).

In September 2015, the United Nations adopted 17 Sustainable Development Goals (SDGs). Numerous goals address environmental concerns, including SDGs 13 (Climate action) and 15 (Life on land), thus underscoring the significance of climate in achieving global sustainability. In order to achieve them, it is essential to involve the financial sector to promote responsible investment and to drive innovative financial products. Furthermore, 65% of banks have already launched products, services, or commercial initiatives aligned with the UN SDGs. Another relevant international treaty is the Paris Agreement, whose second article aims to ensure that financial flows are consistent with a pathway toward low GHG emissions and climate-resilient development. This agreement represents the third significant international legal instrument to address climate change, following the United Nations Framework Convention on Climate Change and the Kyoto Protocol. Indeed, in the period following the ratification of the Paris Agreement, the nexus between climate risk and financial stability has emerged as a pivotal issue in policy discourse (Carney 2015).

The Financial Stability Board (FSB) was assigned the responsibility of clarifying the short- and long-term risks to financial stability and considering measures to mitigate them. For instance, in 2017, the FSB established the Task Force on Climate-related Financial Disclosures (TCFD). The primary objective of the initiative was to formulate a series of voluntary and consistent recommendations concerning the information that companies should provide to investors, lenders, and insurance providers regarding their climate-related financial risks. The 2021 status report demonstrates a growing trend in climate-related financial reporting, with a total of 2,600 organizations having adopted the TCFD framework. These include 1,069 financial institutions responsible for US $194 trillion in assets. Furthermore, the Network for Greening the Financial System (NGFS) was established in 2017 as an international body composed of central banks and financial supervisory authorities. The central objective of the NGFS is to promote the development of environmental and climate risk management within the financial sector, while also mobilizing mainstream financial resources to support the transition toward a sustainable economy. In 2019, the NGFS promulgated the utilization of climate stress tests for the evaluation of the financial stability implications of climate risks (NGFS 2019), and in 2020, it provided a set of climate scenarios intended to guide investors in the assessment of climate-related financial risks (NGFS 2020). In order to ascertain whether a financial institution is committed to promoting green investment and aligning its practices with sustainability principles, the United Nations launched the United Nations' Environment Program Finance Initiative (UNEP FI). This initiative comprises a group of banks that are recognized for being green banks.

The European Central Bank (ECB) initiated its regulatory efforts concerning climate risk in 2020, subsequent to the identification of climate-related risks as a pivotal risk driver in the Systemic Risk Map (SRM) for the euro area banking system. To this end, the ECB promulgated a guide (Guide on climate-related and environmental risks) outlining its expectations for supervised institutions to identify, acknowledge, and address climate-related and environmental risks as drivers of existing risk categories when developing and implementing business strategies, governance frameworks, and risk management models. In 2022, the ECB established the first climate risk tests with the objective of raising awareness of climate risk among supervisory institutions and facilitating the identification of banks' vulnerabilities to, and resilience against, the materialization of climate-related risks (ECB 2022).

Other financial polices addressing climate risks, while fostering climate change mitigation are: (a) green Basel-type capital requirements, (b) green public guarantees to credit, and (c) carbon-risk adjustment in credit ratings. The Green Basel II policy scheme is a regulatory framework that facilitates the exclusion of loans to green firms from banks' capital requirements regulation. This regulatory intervention has the effect of relaxing the credit constraints experienced by green firms, thereby enhancing their relative performance (Lamperti et al. 2021; Oehmke and Opp 2023). In the context of green public guarantees, the government assumes responsibility for providing a guarantee on the total amount of credit in the event that a green firm applies for a loan. Consequently, government-backed green loans are exposed to the same default risk as sovereign bonds. This, in turn, results in green firms being placed at the top of banks' credit rankings (Buchetti et al. 2025). Finally, the concept of carbon-risk adjustment in credit ratings involves the disclosure of information pertaining to the carbon footprint of businesses and their exposure to climate-related events (Safiullah et al. 2021; Breitenstein et al. 2022).

2.3 Current State of Research

Climate change represents one of the most significant challenges facing the world's economies in the coming decades. In response to this challenge, a substantial body of literature has been developed by academics and regulators to investigate the risks and consequences of climate change on the banking system.

Climate change is a recognized risk factor in financial markets, with the potential to trigger significant fluctuations in the value of assets. Indeed, the matter of the pricing of climate risk by financial markets has been the focus of an expanding body of literature concerning asset pricing. Demetriades and Politsidis (2025) discovered that loans extended to fossil fuel enterprises incur a cost that is a minimum of 7% higher than for other types of enterprise. The findings of Ge et al. (2024) indicate that financial institutions apply higher interest rates to borrowers who are considered to be more exposed to climate risk. Degryse et al. (2022) conducted a study to ascertain whether and how environmental consciousness is reflected in the pricing of bank credit. The findings suggested that green banks do indeed offer more favorable loan terms to environmentally conscious firms. Similarly, Ehlers et al. (2022) demonstrated that financial institutions impose a risk premium on borrowing firms with higher carbon intensities since the Paris Agreement. However, they also revealed that although green banks may be lending less to high carbon emitters than other banks, they do not appear to be charging a higher carbon premium. Nguyen et al. (2023) concentrate on residential mortgage markets and demonstrate that lenders impose higher interest rates on mortgages relating to properties exposed to a greater risk of sea level rise. In their work, Javadi and Masum (2021) demonstrated that firms in areas with greater exposure to climate change exhibit significantly elevated spreads on their bank loans. This finding suggests that financial institutions perceive climate change as a significant risk factor. In this line of research, various studies propose the pricing of climate risk in bond markets (Badía et al. 2024; Painter 2020), equity markets (Ilhan et al. 2021), and the real estate market (Garbarino et al. 2024; Baldauf et al. 2020).

As highlighted in other studies, investor demands for compensation for exposure to climate risks are increasing. This is due to a deeper understanding of the financial risks associated with global warming and associated policies. It is therefore likely that investors will direct capital toward investments that offer environmental benefits while simultaneously mitigating climate-related financial risks (Krueger et al. 2020; Bolton and Kacperczyk 2021). In addition, Alessi et al. (2023) demonstrated that investors in the European equity market generally exhibit a propensity to accept lower returns, under conditions of ceteris paribus, and to hold assets that are greener and more transparent. Azmi et al. (2021) demonstrated that environmentally friendly initiatives have the most significant impact on bank value. Reghezza et al. (2022) showed that after the Paris Agreement European firms reallocated credit away from polluting firms, and Mésonnier (2019) established that in France, there was a reduction in credit provision to fossil-based sectors by banks. In addition, Mueller and Sfrappini (2022) showed that EU banks are lending more to companies that could benefit from environmental regulation, and Gambacorta et al. (2023) revealed that banks which provide higher levels of environmental disclosure tend to lend more to low-polluting firms and less to brown firms. In this regard, it is evident that climate risk exerts a substantial influence on the reputation of banking institutions. Indeed, the TCFD has determined that climate change poses significant reputational risks for banks, particularly with regard to stakeholders' perceptions of their capacity to contribute effectively to the transition toward a low-carbon economy. As stated by Choi et al. (2022), financial institutions with elevated reputational risks associated with environmental concerns frequently experience a decline in deposits from countries that are particularly vulnerable to the consequences of severe climate change.

In contrast to previous studies, a report by the ECB and the European Systemic Risk Board (ECB/ESRB 2023) demonstrates that banking institutions persist in extending credit to high-emitting sectors to a disproportionate extent, with these sectors receiving 75% more in lending than their share in economic activity. In fact, the results of the first climate stress test for European systemically important banks showed that most banks do not incorporate climate risk in their credit risk models, only 20% consider climate risk in their lending decisions, and about two thirds of their income from nonfinancial companies comes from heavily polluting industries (ECB 2022). Elderson (2022) stated that over 50% of the revenue generated by banks from nonfinancial corporate customers is derived from industries characterized by significant GHG emissions. Demetriades and Politsidis (2025) discovered that loan amounts to fossil fuel firms are approximately 22% larger, suggesting substantial financing of brown activities. Giannetti et al. (2024) demonstrate that financial institutions which make comprehensive environmental disclosures tend to extend more loans to so-called "brown borrowers" and provide less credit to firms operating within the green sector. In addition, Elliot and Löfgren (2022) found that while banking institutions have been implementing an increasing number of climate change actions since the introduction of the Paris Agreement, there is a lack of explicit commitments regarding their financing of fossil fuels. These findings suggest the existence of greenwashing as banks perceived as environmentally responsible may be more attractive to investors and customers, which may lead to increased profits and market share (Galleta et al. 2024; Yip and Bocken 2018).

Physical loss of assets and the increase in extreme weather events will cause damage to infrastructure, housing, and other physical assets (Giglio et al. 2021). In fact, following a physical risk event, customers may encounter difficulties in meeting their loan obligations, as these events may result in substantial loss or harm to their capital, leading to an increase in nonperforming loans. Similarly, Dafermos et al. (2018) posits that climate change destroys corporate capital, reduces corporate profitability, worsens corporate liquidity, and leads to higher default rates. This would, in turn, have a detrimental effect on the capacity and ability to repay loans, potentially leading to missed repayment deadlines (Faiella and Natoli 2018). It is evident that when the ability of borrower firms to repay loans is diminished by climate losses, there is an increase in banks' credit risk and a decline in loan quality.

Climate change is associated with events that possess the potential to destabilize capital markets and lead to grave detrimental consequences for financial markets and institutions. Consequently, climate change is deemed to pose considerable systemic risks to all financial markets (Nieto 2019). In fact, Curcio et al. (2023) demonstrated that particular extreme events have the capacity to amplify financial systemic risk. Nevertheless, as Birindelli et al. (2024) demonstrated, financial institutions that exhibit a heightened level of engagement with the issue of climate change are more likely to decrease their contribution to systemic risk, underscoring the significance of implementing effective climate policies.

2.4 Methodologies for Assessing Climate Risks

The economic and financial repercussions of climate change have the potential to occasion considerable present and future losses for banking institutions, so they are becoming increasingly concerned about measuring and understanding the exposure of their assets to climate risks. Furthermore, it is important to assess and price in advance the potential financial risks and opportunities associated with climate change, in order to provide investors with the necessary information and ensure the proper functioning of the market. Nevertheless, a significant challenge in this domain is the absence of standardized information concerning the climate-related characteristics of firms and financial products, as well as the complexity in identifying low-carbon and high-carbon assets.

In principle, it is plausible to adapt some conventional risk measures to assess climate-related financial risk. Indeed, the traditional Value at Risk (VaR) framework is utilized by numerous academic articles to assess the consequences of climate change on the balance sheets of financial institutions (Dietz et al. 2016; Curcio et al. 2023; Wu et al. 2024). Another methodology employed in the evaluation of climate risks is the analysis of scenarios. The NGFS designed a set of hypothetical scenarios to provide a common and up-to-date reference point for understanding how climate change (i.e., physical risk) and trends in climate policy and technology (i.e., transition risk) could evolve in the future (NGFS 2019). These scenarios are widely used to assess climate risks (Holden et al. 2024; Ge et al. 2024; Darracq et al. 2024). Nevertheless, these are not the sole scenarios employed for this purpose, as other supervisory authorities (i.e., the Bank of Canada; Bank of England 2021) also consider and establish different possible scenarios (Acharya et al. 2023). In order to assess climate-related financial risks and impacts, Battiston et al. (2019) developed a new methodology denoted CLIMAFIN that combined climate scenarios with financial risk metrics and methods in a transparent methodological framework.

A further conventional risk measure that has been adapted for the assessment of climate-related risk are stress tests, which represent a specific subset of scenario analysis (BIS 2021). These tests constitute quantitative assessments of the resilience of individual banks and the financial system to severe, though plausible, adverse economic scenarios (Acharya et al. 2023). A considerable number of regulators and central banks have conducted climate stress tests and scenario analysis, frequently utilizing the aforementioned NGFS scenarios. Indeed, in 2022 the ECB conducted a climate stress test which was divided into three distinct modules. The first module entailed the administration of a qualitative questionnaire, with the objective of providing a uniform and standardized assessment of banks' climate risk stress-testing capabilities. The second module incorporated two climate risk metrics, providing insights into the sensitivity of banks' income to transition risk and their exposure to carbon emission-intensive industries as of the reference date. The third module entailed a bottom-up stress test component, wherein banks were tasked with providing projections for a number of different scenarios and risk areas (ECB 2022). A significant body of research has been dedicated to the development of methodologies for climate stress testing, with these methodologies being applied to a variety of scenarios in order to assess climate risks (Battiston et al. 2017; Jan Reinder et al. 2023; Faiella et al. 2022).

The measurement of transition risk in relation to financial institutions is largely based on the level of GHG emissions associated with bank lending (Chabot and Bertrand 2023). Alternative approaches measure climate risks based on the Palmer Drought Severity Index (PDSI) (Javadi and Masum 2021; Huynh et al. 2020).

2.5 Future Research Directions

The issue of climate risk in the banking sector is a relatively recent area of research, and there is a need for further exploration of this topic within the academic literature. It is evident that considerable advancement has been made in recent years; nevertheless, there are significant knowledge gaps that necessitate further analysis.

The interconnected nature of physical and transition risks has significant implications for systemic risk, given their capacity to precipitate financial intermediary losses, market dysfunction, and pronounced fluctuations in the volatility of major asset classes, resulting in deleterious spillover consequences for the real economy (Monasterolo et al. 2017; Curcio et al. 2023). From a micro-level perspective, there is an absence of systematic theoretical explanations and empirical evidence to demonstrate how changes in climate state in the short term impact the level of systemic risk. In addition, recent research has focused on the potential impact of climate transition risk on financial stability, leading to an increase in systemic risk by the development of new methodologies and frameworks (Stolbova et al. 2018; Jung et al. 2023). Nevertheless, the analysis of physical risk is not as extensively explored. The integration of physical risk into extant methodologies, or the development of novel ones, would represent a significant contribution to the existing body of literature.

To date, there has been a dearth of research into whether bank environmental disclosure practices truly reflect the bank's actual behavior in combating climate change and acting as a socially and environmentally responsible lending institution (Giannetti et al. 2024). Indeed, despite efforts to enhance the comparability and transparency of sustainable financing instruments, there remains a paucity of transparent and consistent sustainability disclosures. This poses a significant challenge for customers and stakeholders when evaluating a bank's actual environmental impact. Moreover, the regulatory frameworks and oversight mechanisms that have been implemented within the banking sector have yet to demonstrate an adequate degree of robustness, which is essential for the effective monitoring and prevention of greenwashing practices.

Another area in this field that requires further exploration is the effectiveness of green financial instruments in mitigation climate risk as identifying which instruments are better at offsetting possible losses due to climate risk is essential (Wu et al. 2024). Banks offer different credit products to firms to support their efforts to incorporate sustainability into their strategies and projects. It is the case that green bonds are among the most recognized instruments for financing green projects, and they are the focus of the majority of research in this field (Zhou et al. 2025; Mertzanis et al. 2025; Wang et al. 2024). However, banking institutions offer a variety of products and services that are specifically designed to promote sustainability. These include green loans, green venture capital, and green grants. It is an area that requires further research in order to analyze the impact on bank profitability, investor reaction, and the policies associated with them.

Another significant gap in the research is the interrelationship between digital transformation and green finance. Indeed, there is a need for further investigation to be made into the manner in which digital transformation affects the development of green financial products and the existing range of such products across a variety of different economic and cultural backgrounds (Mertzanis et al. 2025). Additionally, there is a lack of research on the relationship between green financial policies and firms' technological and investment decisions (Wang and Zhao 2022; Tong et al. 2022; Xiong and Dai 2023).

Climate risks could negatively impact banks through credit risk, market risk, liquidity risk, operational risk, and reputational risk. A greater volume of research is available on credit and market risk; therefore, it would be beneficial to develop a more comprehensive understanding of the impact of climate change on bank liquidity and operational risks.

2.6 Conclusions

In recent years, there has been a growing need to manage the social and economic impacts of climate change. Coupled with the climate risks (physical and transitional) faced by financial institutions, the increasing regulation of the financial sector, in terms of sustainability (stress tests, taxonomy, etc.) and the changing behavior of individuals demanding increasingly greener investments, has led to a boom in academic research into banking climate risk.

In this chapter, we undertake a review of the extant literature focusing on climate risks in the banking industry, with a particular focus on their inter-relationships, and their impact on financial stability. Moreover, we identify gaps in the extant literature and propose avenues for future research.

In the field of banking practices, the issue of climate risk has emerged as a prominent and rapidly evolving subject in the academic literature. Climate change represents a significant concern and a substantial challenge for the banking sector, as it currently impacts all aspects of human life and is present in all countries. The financial stability of the banking sector and its assets is also impacted, and it is highly exposed to climate risks and the regulations and agreements adopted to mitigate them, such as the Paris Agreement (2015) or the climate stress tests to which financial institutions are exposed. Furthermore, financial institutions with heightened exposure to climate risks exhibit deteriorated balance sheets, attributable to the exacerbation of conventional risks, encompassing credit, market, liquidity, operational, reputational, and legal hazards (González and Núñez 2021). This heightened risk environment is expected to lead to increased challenges and costs in accessing financial resources, as investors are likely to demand higher returns in response to these risks (Azmi et al. 2021). Additionally, clients may be hesitant to deposit their funds into institutions whose reputations are compromised (Paulet et al. 2015). Conversely, the banking sector plays a pivotal role in the global effort to combat climate change, given its capacity to channel investment flows toward environmentally beneficial activities, mobilize resources, and create financial instruments that promote sustainability (Spinaci 2021).

A potentially significant avenue for future research would be the analysis of how changes in climate state in the short term affect the level of systemic risk, and the development of new methodologies regarding physical risks. In the context of this field, further exploration is required with respect to the efficacy of green financial instruments in mitigating climate risk. It is important to identify which instruments are more effective in offsetting potential losses due to climate risk, with a particular focus on less well-known products such as green loans and grants. Further research is required to ascertain the impact of climate change on liquidity, operational risk, and reputational risk, with the latter including the issue of greenwashing.

It is concluded that the literature focusing on climate risk in the financial sector, particularly with regard to banking and their interrelationships, can play a pivotal role in enhancing comprehension of the most effective supervisory approaches and disclosures. This is imperative to achieve a balance between sustainability, climate protection, banking interests and profits, as well as sound and transparent corporate governance and environmental and social sustainability in the banking sector.

References

Acharya, V. V., Berner, R., Engle, R., Jung, H., Stroebel, J., Zeng, X., & Zhao, Y. (2023). Climate stress testing. *Annual Review of Financial Economics, 15*, 291–326. https://doi.org/10.1146/annurev-financial-110921-101555

Alessi, L., Ossola, E., & Panzica, R. (2023). When do investors go green? Evidence from a time-varying asset-pricing model. *International Review of Financial Analysis, 90*, 102898. https://doi.org/10.1016/j.irfa.2023.102898

Amargant Arnau, R., & del Arroyo González, F. G. (2022). El efecto del cambio climático y la transición energética sobre el sector financiero y la reacción al desafío por parte de la UE. *Papeles de Energía, Funcas* (16), 65–115.

Azmi, W., Hassan, M. K., Houston, R., & Karim, M. S. (2021). ESG activities and banking performance: International evidence from emerging economies. *Journal of International Financial Markets, Institutions and Money, 70*, 101277. https://doi.org/10.1016/j.intfin.2020.101277

Badía, G., Cortez, M. C., & Silva, F. (2024). Do investors benefit from investing in stocks of green bond issuers? *Economic Letters, 242*, 111859. https://doi.org/10.1016/j.econlet.2024.111859

Baldauf, M., Garlappi, L., & Yannelis, C. (2020). Does climate change affect real estate prices? Only if you believe in it. *Review of Financial Studies, 33*(3), 1256–1295. https://doi.org/10.1093/rfs/hhz073

Bank for International Settlements (BIS). (2021). *Climate related risk drivers and their transmission channels*. ISBN 978-92-9259-472-5. https://www.bis.org/bcbs/publ/d517.pdf

Bank of England. (2017). *The Bank of England's response to climate change*. Bank of England, Quarterly Bulletin. https://www.bankofengland.co.uk/-/media/boe/files/quarterly-bulletin/2017/the-banks-response-to-climate-change.pdf

Battiston, S., Dafermos, Y., & Monasterolo, I. (2021). Climate risks and financial stability. *Journal of financial stability*, *54*, 100867. https://doi.org/10.1016/j.jfs.2021.100867

Battiston, S., Mandel, A., & Monasterolo, I. (2019). CLIMAFIN Handbook: Pricing Forward-Looking Climate Risks Under Uncertainty. https://dx.doi.org/10.2139/ssrn.3476586

Battiston, S., Mandel, A., Monasterolo, I. Schütze, F., & Visentin, G. (2017). A climate stress-test of the financial system. *Nature Clim Change*, *7*, 283–288. https://doi.org/10.1038/nclimate3255

Bayangos, V. B., Cachuela, R. A., & Del Prado, F. L. (2021). Impact of extreme weather episodes on the Philippine banking sector—Evidence using branch-level supervisory data. *Latin American Journal of Central Banking*, *2*(1), 100023. https://doi.org/10.1016/j.latcb.2021.100023

Birindelli, G., Chiappini, H., & Jalal, R. (2024). Greenwashing, bank financial performance and the moderating role of gender diversity. *Research in International Business and Finance*, *69*, 102235. https://doi.org/10.1016/j.ribaf.2024.102235

Bolton, P., & Kacperczyk, M. (2021). Do investors care about carbon risk? *Journal of Financial Economics*, *142*(2), 517–549. https://doi.org/10.1016/j.jfineco.2021.05.008

Breitenstein, M., Ciummo, S., & Walch, F. (2022). *Disclosure of climate change risk in credit ratings*. Occasional Paper Series No 303, European Central Bank. https://www.ecb.europa.eu/pub/pdf/scpops/ecb.op303~eaa6fe6583.en.pdf

Brunetti, C., Dennis, B., Gates, D., Hancock, D., Ignell, D., Kiser, E., Kotta, G., Kovner, A., Rosen, R., & Tabor, N. (2021). Climate change and financial stability. *FEDS Notes*, No 2021-03-19-3. https://dx.doi.org/10.17016/2380-7172.2893

Buchetti, B., Lin, L., Miquel-Flores, I., Perdichizzi, S., & Reghezza, A. (2025). *Loan guarantee and portfolio greening: Evidence from European credit registers*. Working Paper Series No 2916, Europe. https://www.ecb.europa.eu/pub/pdf/scpwps/ecb.wp2916~f95e083a6e.en.pdf

Caby, J., Ziane, Y., & Lamarque, E. (2022). The impact of climate change management on banks profitability. *Journal of Business Research*, *142*, 412–422. https://doi.org/10.1016/j.jbusres.2021.12.078

Campiglio, E., & Dafermos, Y. (2018). Climate change challenges for central banks and financial regulators. *Nature Climate Change*, *8*(6), 462–468. http://dx.doi.org/10.1038/s41558-018-0175-0

Carney, M. (2015). *Breaking the Tragedy of the Horizon—climate change and financial stability*. Lloyd's of London, 29, 220–230. https://www.bankofengland.co.uk/-/media/boe/files/speech/2015/breaking-the-tragedy-of-the-horizon-climate-change-and-financial-stability.pdf

Chabot, M., & Bertrand, J. L. (2023). Climate risks and financial stability: Evidence from the European financial system. *Journal of Financial Stability*, *69*, 101190. https://doi.org/10.1016/j.jfs.2023.101190

Chalabi-Jabado, F., & Ziane, Y. (2024). Climate risks, financial performance and lending growth: Evidence from the banking industry. *Technological Forecasting and Social Change, 209*, 123757. https://doi.org/10.1016/j.techfore.2024.123757

Chiavuzzo, F. (2018). *Climate change impacts on finance: Managing one of the biggest threats to the global economy* [Master's thesis]. Italy: Ca'Foscari University of Venice. https://unitesi.unive.it/retrieve/82ed30fd-a945-4e38-8f03-12360a827b61/842852-1214001.pdf

Choi, D., Gam, Y., & Shin, H. (2022). Environmental reputation and bank liquidity: Evidence from climate transition. *Journal of Business Finance & Accounting, 50*(6–7), 1274–1304. https://doi.org/10.1111/jbfa.12669

Curcio, D., Igor, G., & Davide, V. (2023). Climate change and financial systemic risk: Evidence from US banks and insurers. *Journal of Financial Stability, 66*, 101132. https://doi.org/10.1016/j.jfs.2023.101132

Dafermos, Y., Nikolaidi, M., & Galanis, G. (2018). Climate change, financial stability and monetary policy. *Ecological Economics, 152*, 219–234. https://doi.org/10.1016/j.ecolecon.2018.05.011

Darracq Pariès, M., Dées, S., De Gaye, A., Parisi, L., & Sun, Y. (2024). *NGFS climate scenarios for the euro area—role of fiscal and monetary policy conduct—opening up the macroeconomic toolbox and its sensitivity to policy settings.* European Central Bank. https://doi.org/10.2866/872021

Degryse, H., Goncharenko, R., Theunisz, C., & Vadasz, T. (2022). When green meets green. *Journal of Corporate Finance, 78*, 102355. https://doi.org/10.1016/j.jcorpfin.2023.102355

Demetriades, E., & Politsidis, P. N. (2025). Bank lending to fossil fuel firms. *Journal of Financial Stability, 76*, 101349. https://doi.org/10.1016/j.jfs.2024.101349

De Nederlandsche Bank. (2017). *Climate risk and the financial sector: Sharing of good practices.* The Sustainable Finance Platform. https://www.dnb.nl/media/zvunexjb/climate-risk-and-the-financial-sector-sharing-of-good-practices-_tcm46-389956.pdf

Dietz, S., Bowen, A., Dixon, C., & Gradwell, P. (2016). "Climate value at risk" of global financial assets. *Nature Climate Change, 6*(7), 676–679. http://dx.doi.org/10.1038/nclimate2972

Eckstein, D., Künzel, V., & Schäfer, L. (2021). *The Global Climate Risk Index 2021.* Germanwatch. https://bvearmb.do/handle/123456789/1306

Ehlers, T., Packer, F., & de Greiff, K. (2022). The pricing of carbon risk in syndicated loans: Which risks are priced and why? *Journal of Banking and Finance, 136*, 106180. https://doi.org/10.1016/j.jbankfin.2021.106180

Elderson, F. (2022, July 8). *Climate Risk Stress Test. Final Results.* European Central Bank. https://www.bankingsupervision.europa.eu/ecb/pub/pdf/annex/ssm.pr220708_annex2.en.pdf?

Elliott, J., & Löfgren, Å. (2022). If money talks, what is the banking industry saying about climate change? *Climate Policy, 22*(6), 743–753. https://doi.org/10.1080/14693062.2022.2036090

European Central Bank & European Systemic Risk Board (2023). *Towards macroprudential frameworks for managing climate risk.* https://www.esrb.europa.eu/pub/pdf/reports/esrb.report202312~d7881028b8.en.pdf

European Central Bank. (2022). *2022 climate risk stress test.* European Central Bank. https://doi.org/10.2866/97350

European Commission. (2021, April). *Taxonomy Delegated Act of April 2021 (C(2021) 2800/3 ANNEX 1, Appendix A).* https://ec.europa.eu/finance/docs/level-2-measures/taxonomy-regulation-delegated-act-2021-2800-annex-1_en.pdf

Faiella, I., Lavecchia, L., Michelangeli, V., & Mistretta, A. (2022). A climate stress test on the financial vulnerability of Italian households and firms. *Journal of Policy Modeling, 44*(2), 396–417. https://doi.org/10.1016/j.jpolmod.2021.11.001

Faiella, I., & Natoli, F. (2018). *Natural catastrophes and bank lending: the case of flood risk in Italy.* Bank of Italy Occasional Paper No. 457. https://dx.doi.org/10.2139/ssrn.3429210

Galleta, S., Mazzù, S., Naciti, V., & Paltrinieri, A. (2024). A PRISMA systematic review of greenwashing in the banking industry: A call for action. *Research in International Business and Finance, 69*, 102262. https://doi.org/10.1016/j.ribaf.2024.102262

Gambacorta, L., Polizzi, S., Reghezza, A., & Scannella, E. (2023). *Do banks practice what they preach? Brown lending and environmental disclosure in the euro area.* (ECB Working Paper No. 2872). European Central Bank. https://www.ecb.europa.eu/pub/pdf/scpwps/ecb.wp2872~b91ebffb71.en.pdf

Garbarino, N., Guin, B., & Lee, J. (2024). The effect of subsidized flood insurance on real estate markets. *Journal of Risk and Insurance, 91*(44), 991–1024. https://doi.org/10.1111/jori.12491

García-León, D., & Ciscar, J. C. (2022). *Impacts and risks of climate change in Spain: A brief panoramic overview.* Papeles de Energía No. 16, Funcas. https://www.funcas.es/articulos/impactos-y-riesgos-del-cambio-climatico-en-espana-una-breve-panoramica/

Ge, W., Qu, Z., Wu, Z., & Yu, L. (2024). Abnormal temperatures, climate risk disclosures and bank loan pricing: International Evidence. *British Journal of Management, 36*, 726–744. https://doi.org/10.1111/1467-8551.12867

Giannetti, M., Jasova, M., Loumioti, M., & Mendicino, C. (2024). *"Glossy Green" Banks: The Disconnect Between Environmental Disclosures and Lending Activities.* Swedish House of Finance Research Paper No. 23–07, European Corporate Governance Institute—Finance Working Paper No. 919/2023. https://dx.doi.org/10.2139/ssrn.4424081

Giglio, S., Kelly, B., & Stroebel, J. (2021). Climate finance. *Annual Review of Financial Economics, 13*, 15–36. https://doi.org/10.1146/annurev-financial-102620-103311

Giuzio, M., Krusec, D., Levels, A., Melo, A. S., Mikkonen, K., & Radulova, P. (2024). *Climate change and financial stability.* Financial Stability Review of the European Central Bank. https://www.ecb.europa.eu/press/financial-stability-publications/fsr/special/html/ecb.fsrart201905_1~47cf778cc1.en.html

González, C. I., & Núñez, S. (2021). *Markets, financial institutions and central banks in the face of climate change: Challenges and opportunities.* Documentos Ocasionales Banco de España, 2126. https://www.bde.es/f/webbde/SES/Secciones/Publicaciones/PublicacionesSeriadas/DocumentosOcasionales/21/Files/do2126e.pdf

Gramlich, D., Walker, T., Zhao, Y., & Bitar, M. (2023). After the storm: Natural Disasters and Bank Solvency. *International Journal of Central Banking, 19*(2).

Heutel, G., Miller, N. H., & Molitor, D. (2021). Adaptation and the mortality effects of temperature across U.S. Climate Regions. *The Review of Economics and Statistics, 103*(4), 740–753. https://doi.org/10.1162/rest_a_00936

Holden, L., King., J., Richards, H., Siegert, C., & Krebel, L. (2024). *Measuring climate—related financial risks using scenario analysis.* Bank of England Quarterly Bulletin 2024. https://dx.doi.org/10.2139/ssrn.4947406

Huynh, T. D., Nguyen, T. H., & Truong, C. (2020). Climate risk: The price of drought. *Journal of Corporate Finance, 65,* 101750. https://doi.org/10.1016/j.jcorpfin.2020.101750

Ilhan, E., Sautner, Z., & Vilkov, G. (2021). Carbon tail risk. *The Review of Financial Studies, 34*(3), 777–799. https://dx.doi.org/10.2139/ssrn.3204420

Jan Reinder, H., Schoenmaker, D., & Van Dijk, M. (2023). A finance approach to climate stress testing. *Journal of International Money and Finance, 131,* 102797. https://doi.org/10.1016/j.jimonfin.2022.102797

Javadi, S., & Masum, A. A. (2021). The impact of climate change on the cost of bank loans. *Journal of Corporate Finance, 69,* 102019. https://doi.org/10.1016/j.jcorpfin.2021.102019

Jiang, C., Li, Y., Zhang, X., & Zhao, Y. (2025). Climate risk and corporate debt decision. *Journal of International Money and Finance, 151,* 103261. https://doi.org/10.1016/j.jimonfin.2024.103261

Jung, H., Engle, R. F., & Berner, R. (2023). *CRISK: Measuring the climate risk exposure of the financial system.* FRB of New York Staff Report No. 977. https://dx.doi.org/10.2139/ssrn.3931516

Kahn, M. E., Mohaddes, K., Ng, R. N. C., Pesaran, M. H., Raissi, M., & Yang, J. C. (2021). Long-term macroeconomic effects of climate change: A cross-country analysis. *Energy Economics, 104,* 105624. https://doi.org/10.1016/j.eneco.2021.105624

Krueger, P., Sautner, Z., & Starks, L. (2020). The importance of climate risks for institutional investors. *The Review of Financial Studies, 33*(3), 1067–1111. https://dx.doi.org/10.2139/ssrn.3235190

Kruttli, M. S., Tran, B. R., & Watugala, S. W. (2019). *Pricing Poseidon: Extreme weather uncertainty and firm return dynamics.* Finance and Economics Discussion Series, 2019-054. https://doi.org/10.17016/feds.2019.054

Lamperti, F., Bosetti, V., Roventini, A., & Tavoni, M. (2019). *The public costs of climate-induced financial instability.* LEM Papers Series 2019/42, Laboratory of Economics and Management (LEM), Sant'Anna School of Advanced Studies. https://ideas.repec.org/p/ssa/lemwps/2019-42.html

Lamperti, F., Bosetti, V., Roventini, A., Tavoni, M., & Treibich, T. (2021). Three green financial policies to address climate risks. *Journal of Financial Stability*, *54*, 100875. https://doi.org/10.1016/j.jfs.2021.100875

Lang, Q., Ma, F., Mirza, N., & Umar, M. (2023). The interaction of climate risk and bank liquidity: An emerging market perspective for transitions to low carbon energy. *Technological Forecasting and Social Change*, 191, 122480. https://doi.org/10.1016/j.techfore.2023.122480

Le, A., Tran, T. P., & Mishra, A. V. (2023). Climate risk and bank stability: International evidence. *Journal of Multinational Financial Management*, *70–71*, 100824. https://doi.org/10.1016/j.mulfin.2023.100824

Lee, C. C., Wang, C. W., Thinh, B. T., & Xu, Z. T. (2022). Climate risk and bank liquidity creation: International evidence. *International Review of Financial Analysis*, *82*, 102198. https://doi.org/10.1016/j.irfa.2022.102198

Lee, S., & Alam, M.Z. (2024). The impact of climate risk on bank profitability through liquidity creation channel: empirical evidence from G7 countries. *Journal of Asset Management*, *25*, 726–739. https://doi.org/10.1057/s41260-024-00384-x

Liu, Z., He, S., Men, W., & Sun, H. (2024). Impact of climate risk on financial stability: Cross—country evidence. *International Review of Financial Analysis*, *92*, 103096. http://dx.doi.org/10.1016/j.irfa.2024.103096

Liu, Y., Wang, J., Wen, F., & Wu, C. (2024). Climate policy uncertainty and bank systemic risk: A creative destruction perspective. *Journal of Financial Stability*, *73*, 101289. https://doi.org/10.1016/j.jfs.2024.101289

Mertzanis, C., Marashdeh, H., Kampouris, I., & Atayah, O. (2025). Managing environmental finance in the digital era: Evidence from green bonds. *Journal of Environmental Management*, *373*, 123434. https://doi.org/10.1016/j.jenvman.2024.123434

Mésonnier, J. S. (2019). *Banks' climate commitments and credit to brown industries: new evidence for France*. Working Papers 743, Banque de France. https://ideas.repec.org/p/bfr/banfra/743.html

Monasterolo, I. (2020). *Climate change and the financial system*. https://dx.doi.org/10.2139/ssrn.3479380

Monasterolo, I., Battiston, S., Janetos, A. C., & Zheng, Z. (2017). Vulnerable yet relevant: The two dimensions of climate-related financial disclosure. *Climatic Change*, *145*, 495–507. https://doi.org/10.1007/s10584-017-2095-9

Mueller, I., & Sfrappini, E. (2022). *Climate change-related regulatory risks and bank lending*. ECB Working Paper No. 2022/2670. https://dx.doi.org/10.2139/ssrn.4144358

Network for Greening the Financial System (NGFS). (2019, June). *A call for action: Climate change as a source of financial risk. First comprehensive report*. Network for Greening the Financial System. https://www.ngfs.net/system/files/import/ngfs/medias/documents/ngfs_first_comprehensive_report_-_17042019_0.pdf

Network for Greening the Financial System (NGFS). (2020, June). *Guide to climate scenario analysis for central banks and supervisors.* Network for Greening the Financial System. https://www.ngfs.net/system/files/import/ngfs/medias/documents/ngfs_guide_scenario_analysis_final.pdf

Nguyen, Q., Diaz-Rainney, I., & Kuruppuarachchi, D. (2023). In search of climate distress risk. *International Review of Financial Analysis, 85*, 102444. https://doi.org/10.1016/j.irfa.2022.102444

Nieto, M. J. (2019). Banks, climate risk and financial stability. *Journal of Financial Regulation Compliance, 27*(2), 243–262. https://doi.org/10.1108/JFRC-03-2018-0043

Numan, U., Ma., B., Sadiq, M., Bedru, H. D., & Jiang, C. (2023). The role of green finance in mitigating environmental degradation: Empirical evidence and policy implications from complex economies. *Journal of Cleaner Production, 400*, 136693. https://doi.org/10.1016/j.jclepro.2023.136693

Oehmke, M., & Opp, M. (2023). *Green capital requirements.* Swedish House of Finance Research Paper No. 22–16. http://dx.doi.org/10.2139/ssrn.4040098

Ojea-Ferreiro, J., Reboredo, J. C., & Ugolini, A. (2024). Systemic risk effects of climate transition on financial stability. *International Review of Financial Analysis, 96*(B). 103722. https://doi.org/10.1016/j.irfa.2024.103722

Painter, M. (2020). An inconvenient cost: The effects of climate change on municipal bonds. *Journal of financial Economics, 135*(2), 468–482. https://doi.org/10.1016/j.jfineco.2019.06.006

Pankratz, N. M. C., & Schiller, C. (2023). *Climate change and adaptation in global supply-chain networks.* FEDS Working Paper No 2022–56. https://dx.doi.org/10.17016/FEDS.2022.056

Paulet, E., Parnaudeau, M., & Relano, F. (2015). Banking with ethics: Strategic moves and structural changes of the banking industry in the aftermath of the subprime crisis. *Journal of Business Ethics, 131*(1), 199–207. https://doi.org/10.1007/s10551-014-2274-9

Reghezza, A., Altunbas, Y., Marquez-Ibanez, D., Rodriguez d´Acri, C., & Spaggiari, M. (2022). Do banks fuel climate change? *Journal of Financial Stability, 62*, 101049. https://doi.org/10.1016/j.jfs.2022.101049

Rezai, A., Taylor, L., Foley, & D. (2018). Economic growth, income distribution, and climate change. *Ecological Economics, 146*, 164–172. https://doi.org/10.1016/j.ecolecon.2017.10.020

Rising, J., Tedesco, M., Piontek, F., & Stainforth, D. (2022). The missing risks of climate change. *Nature, 610*, 643–651. https://doi.org/10.1038/s41586-022-05243-6

Roncoroni, A., Battiston, S., Escobar-Farfán, L. O. L., & Martinez-Jaramillo, S. (2021). Climate risk and financial stability in the network of banks and investment funds. *Journal of Financial Stability, 54*, 100870. https://doi.org/10.1016/j.jfs.2021.100870

Rudebusch, G. D. (2021). Climate change is a source if financial risk. *FRBSF Economic Letter*, *3*, 1–6. http://refhub.elsevier.com/S1057-5219(24)00814-7/rf0295

Safiullah, M., Nurul-Kabir, M., & Dulal-Miah, M. (2021). Carbon emission credit ratings. *Energy Economics*, *100*, 105330. https://doi.org/10.1016/j.eneco.2021.105330

Shabir, M., Jiang, P., Shahab, Y., Wang, W., Isik, Ö., & Mehroush, I. (2024). Diversification and bank stability: Role of political instability and climate risk. *International Review of Economics & Finance*, *89*(B), 63–92. https://doi.org/10.1016/j.iref.2023.10.009

Spinaci, S. (2021). *Green and sustainable finance—briefing*. European Parliamentary Research Service, European Parliament. https://www.europarl.europa.eu/RegData/etudes/BRIE/2021/679081/EPRS_BRI(2021)679081_EN.pdf

Stolbova, V., Monasterolo, I., & Battiston, S. (2018). A financial macro-network approach to climate policy evaluation. *Ecological Economics*, *149*, 239–253. https://doi.org/10.1016/j.ecolecon.2018.03.013

Tong, L., Jabbour, C., Belgacem, S., Najam, H., & Abbas, J., (2022). Role of environmental regulations, green finance, and investment in green technologies in green total factor productivity: Empirical evidence from Asian region. *Journal of Cleaner Production*, *380*(2), 134930. https://doi.org/10.1016/j.jclepro.2022.134930

Wang, B., & Zhao, W. (2022). Interplay of renewable energy investment efficiency, shareholder control and green financial development in China. *Renewable Energy*, *199*, 192–203. https://doi.org/10.1016/j.renene.2022.08.122

Wang, C., Wang, C., Long, H., Zaremba, A., & Zhou, W. (2024). Green bond credit spreads and bank loans in China. *International Review of Financial Analysis*, *94*, 103300. https://doi.org/10.1016/j.irfa.2024.103300

Wu, B., Wen, F., Zhang, Y., & Huang, Z. (2024). Climate risk and the systemic risk of banks: A global perspective. *Journal of International Financial Markets, Institutions & Money*, *95*, 102030. https://doi.org/10.1016/j.intfin.2024.102030

Wu, Q., Yan, D., & Umair, M. (2023). Assessing the role of competitive intelligence and practices of dynamic capabilities in business accommodation of SMEs. *Economic Analysis and Policy*, *77*, 1103–1114. https://doi.org/10.1016/j.eap.2022.11.024

Xiong, Y., & Dai, L. (2023). Does green finance investment impact on sustainable development: Role of technological innovation and renewable energy. *Renewable Energy*, *214*, 342–349. https://doi.org/10.1016/j.renene.2023.06.002

Yip, A. W. H., & Bocken, N. M. P. (2018). Sustainable business model archetypes for the banking industry. *Journal of Cleaner Production*, *174*, 150–169. https://doi.org/10.1016/j.jclepro.2017.10.190

Zhang, H., Liu, J., Guo, Q., Zhang, X., & Hu, X. (2025). The impact of climate policy uncertainty on urban climate risk: Evidence from 274 cities in China.

Sustainable Cities and Society, *119*, 106097. https://doi.org/10.1016/j.scs.2024.106097

Zhou, T., Chen, G., Su, Y., Yang, T., & Ding, J. (2025). Green bond underwriting, financial openness, and profitability of commercial Banks. *International Review of Financial Analysis*, *99*, 103900. https://doi.org/10.1016/j.irfa.2024.103900

CHAPTER 3

A Note on the Employment Dynamics of Credit-Constrained Small- and Medium-sized Enterprises

Ioannis Vlassas and Christos Kallandranis

3.1 Introduction

There has been a growing literature deriving from capital market imperfections (Modigliani and Miller 1958) and the impact of financial constraints in defining investment decisions of firms. Under capital market imperfections, the perfect substitutability outcome between internal and external funds collapses due to ex ante and ex post informational asymmetries between borrowers and lenders. The gap in cost is referred to as External Finance Premium, and external funds are more expensive for a firm relative to internal funds (Townsend 1979; Greenwald et al. 1984; Myers and Majluf 1984; Bernanke and Gertler 1990; Kiyotaki and Moore 1997). As a result, asymmetric information problems intensify financial

I. Vlassas • C. Kallandranis (✉)
Department of Accounting and Finance, University of West Attica, Athens, Greece
e-mail: ivlassas@uniwa.gr; chriskal@uniwa.gr

E. Scannella and J. Williams (eds.), *Trends, Issues, and Challenges in Banking and Finance*, Palgrave Macmillan Studies in Banking and Financial Institutions,
https://doi.org/10.1007/978-3-031-96066-6_3

constraints, raising loan costs or restricting firms from accessing funds due to credit rationing (Stiglitz and Weiss 1981; Greenwald et al. 1984).

Such a deviation from the paradigm of perfect capital markets is even more amplified for the small- and medium-sized enterprises (SMEs hereafter) relying on bank credit when internal funds are scarce or alternatives are unavailable due to their size and informational opacity, which limits access to capital markets (e.g. Petersen and Rajan 1994; Berger and Udell 1998; Berger and Frame 2007; Moro et al. 2015; Kallandranis et al. 2023 etc.).

Within this context, any reduced ability of potential borrowers to access credit was treated as an issue that could harm the SMEs' investment opportunities. However, the employment factor has been largely overlooked. Fixed investment considerations can extend to the impact of financial distress on employment, given both capital and labor are quasi-fixed (Drakos and Kallandranis 2005a). Indeed, capital and employment jointly produce aggregate output. Financial frictions (credit rationing) via the easiness of access to credit can affect the real economy via the investment channel. Credit market frictions interlink with the labor market, magnifying employment volatility. This relationship significantly affects real economic activity, yet only a few studies have explored this issue (e.g., Campello et al. 2010; Benmelech et al. 2011; Ferrando and Muelier 2015; Gerlach et al. 2015; Gomez 2019; Vlassas et al. 2024, etc.).

In general, credit rationing may influence the hiring decisions of businesses for a variety of reasons. To begin with, it is important to note that labor may not be the only variable factor in the production process of firms (Oi 1962; Hamermesh and Pfann 1996). This is because certain processes, including employee training and employment, involve fixed or quasi-fixed cost components. Furthermore, when there is a discrepancy between labor costs and liquidity (cash flow), organizations will be compelled to fund the cost deficits through the production process (Greenwald and Stiglitz 1988). This may result in workforce reductions when financing is insufficient. Indirectly, credit rationing's impact on investment also affects employment (Benmelech 2011), as firms constrained in investment adjust employment to compensate for reduced capital.

The article examines the impact of credit restrictions on employment dynamics using data from the survey on the access to finance of enterprises (SAFE) across 18 Eurozone countries from 2014 to 2022. It focuses on whether enterprises requiring funding have changed their staff count in the past 6 months following loan rejections. The study uses investment theory to understand labor dynamics, stating that short-term labor demand is influenced by changes in employment decision-makers' financial profiles. The hypothesis is that potential borrowers use their financial situations and economic outlook as a surrogate for banks' assessment of their applications, thereby using the economic sentiment indicator (ESI) as a predictive measure.

Our main results suggest that credit rationing has a strong and statistically significant negative effect on employment decisions of firms. Moreover, micro and small firms face the highest threat, signifying the importance of SME-specific policies to alleviate their financial problems. Finally, the index capturing future prospects has a positive effect on employment growth, signaling that a more positive sentiment in the macroeconomic environment positively affects the probability of SMEs to increase their labor.

The remainder of the chapter is organized as follows. Sect. 3.2 contains analytical information about the data and the variables used for our analysis. Sect. 3.3 analyzes the results of the model. Finally, Sect. 3.4 concludes.

3.2 Data and Methodology

To assess the correlation between credit rationing and employment, we utilize the SAFE. The SAFE survey provides insights into recent improvements in enterprises' financial conditions and delineates trends in the demand for and availability of external borrowing. The survey primarily analyzes the behavior of SMEs, incorporating numerous categorical variables such as size, age, nation, and industry, thereby offering a comprehensive picture of SME conduct across various aspects.

For our analysis, we utilize data spanning 16 waves, from the second half of 2014 to the first half of 2022. As our research is primarily focused on analyzing firms in need of external financing, we utilize question Q7A of the SAFE survey, which inquires information from firms about their applications for bank finance in the last 6 months. We thus create a dichotomous variable that measures whether the *i*-th firm is in need of finance or otherwise.

The study examines the impact of credit rationing on enterprises' employment choices over the past 6 months, using the SAFE survey Question Q2i. The inquiry examines whether firms have increased, decreased, or maintained their employment levels. The study also explores the relationship between credit market conditions and labor market dynamics, focusing on actual employment outcomes to understand the direct influence of credit rationing on employment choices.

According to the preceding analysis, our dependent variable (*Ei*) is of a dichotomous nature, where *i* symbolizes the *i*-th firm of our sample as follows:

$$Ei = \begin{cases} 1 \text{ if firm needed credit, and their employment increased the last 6 months} \\ 0 \text{ otherwise} \end{cases}$$

3.2.1 Main Explanatory Variable

The key explanatory variables in our model include a measure of credit rationing. Question Q7B of the SAFE Survey is utilized to indicate debtors with credit rationing and favorable adjustments in bank cash flow. Question 7 comprises two sections. Initially, companies are enquired if they requested a bank loan within the past 6 months (Q7A). Subsequently, if a firm applies for a loan, they are further enquired about the outcome of their loan application (Q7B). The existing literature on credit rationing (Ferrando and Muelier 2015; Gerlach et al. 2015; Gomez 2019) defines a firm as credit-constrained when a bank denies its loan application, when it obtains only a fraction of the necessary funds (typically less than 75%), or when it rejects the lender's loan offer due to high interest rate costs. In accordance with the prevailing literature (Ferrando and Muelier 2015; Gerlach et al. 2015; Gomez 2019), a firm is designated as a credit rationed borrower (CR) if it receives less than 75% of its requested amount.

$$CRi = \begin{cases} 1 \text{ if firm needs credit, applied for a loan and received less than 75\% of requested amount} \\ 0 \text{ otherwise} \end{cases}$$

3.2.2 Control Variables

Research has extensively examined factors that can affect a company's employment growth, with size being the predominant theme (Campello et al. 2010; Duygan et al. 2015; Popov and Rocholl 2015; Berg 2018; Gomez 2019; Farinha et al. 2021). Larger enterprises typically have enhanced resources to withstand economic shocks and exhibit reduced vulnerability to informational asymmetries, making them more adaptable in modifying employment levels in response to substantial economic fluctuations. Firm age is also an important consideration in employment decisions, as a lengthy operational history mitigates informational asymmetries, enhancing prospects for bank financing (Ferrando and Mulier 2015; Gerlach et al. 2015; Berg 2018; Gomez 2019).

Dummy variables for significant balance sheet metrics are included to reflect each firm's perspective and their potential impacts on hiring decisions. A high debt-to-asset ratio may indicate financial restrictions, leading to cost-cutting or demonstrating adept financial leverage (Herrando and Carrascal 2008; Giroud and Mueller 2015). Profitability and turnover metrics indirectly affect employment by influencing investment and research and development (R&D), promoting employment expansion (Benmelech et al. 2011).

A firm's credit history is also considered, as entities with a deteriorating credit outlook can lead to declining ratings, stricter loan requirements, and employment changes (Bottazzi et al. 2014; Cowling et al. 2016). Ownership can influence employment decisions, but privately held companies may face greater financial constraints due to increased asymmetry of information (Freel et al. 2012). Finally, fixed investments clarify employment dynamics, as companies with liquidity challenges may forgo fixed asset investments (Hernando and Carrascal 2008). Detailed definitions of variables used in our models are presented in Table 3.1.

To analyze the effect of credit rationing on employment, we utilize a pooled panel probit model with robust standard errors. The first model is defined as follows:

$$\text{Prob}(E_{i,c,t} = 1 \mid N = 1) = \beta_0 + credit\ access_{i,c,t} + \sum_{k=1}^{N} \theta_k \cdot Controls_{i,c,t} + \varepsilon_{i,c,t} \quad (3.1)$$

where i, c, t represent the firm, country, and time (survey waves), respectively. In line with the aforementioned definitions, we denote as $E_{i,c,t}$ the probability of a firm to increase its employment given than it needs a bank loan ($N = 1$). The core variable (credit rationing) denoted as $credit\ access_{i,c,t}$ stands for the effect of limited access to financing on employment decisions made by firms. $Controls_{i,c,t}$ is a vector of contemporaneous firm-level control variables analyzed in the previous section. Fixed effects on the country, sector, ownership, and time level are also included in the models.

Table 3.1 Definition of variables

Variable	*Definition*	*Expected sign*
Dependent variable		
Employment	1, if a firm needs external financing and increased their employment; 0, otherwise.	n/a
Main explanatory variables		
Credit rationed	1, if a firm needs external financing and applies but receives less than 75% of requested funds; 0, otherwise	+/−
Firm-specific controls		
Age	Categorical variable equal to 1 if the firm is 10 years old or more; 2 if the firm is between 5 and 10 years old; 3 if the firm is between 2 and 5 years old; 4 if the firm is less than 2 years old.	+/−
Size	Categorical variable equal to 1 for micro firms (1–9 employees); 2 for small firms (10–49 employees); 3 for medium-sized firms (50–249 employees)	+
Ownership	Categorical variable equal to 1 if the firm is family-owned; 2 if business associates; 3 if venture capital firms or business angels; 4 if natural person-one owner only; 5 if public shareholders.	+/−
Activity	Categorical variable equal to 1 if the firm belongs to the construction sector; 2 if the firm belongs to the wholesale or retail trade sector; 3 if the firm belongs to the services sector; 4 if the firm belongs to the transport sector.	+/−
Profit	Dummy variable equal to 1 if the firm's profits increased in the past 6 months; 0 otherwise.	+
Turnover	Dummy variable equal to 1 if the firm's turnover increased in the past 6 months; 0 otherwise.	+
Leverage	Dummy variable equal to 1 if the firm's leverage increased in the past 6 months; 0 otherwise.	+/−
Credit history	Dummy variable equal to 1 if the firm's credit history increased in the past 6 months; 0 otherwise.	+
Fixed investment	Dummy variable equal to 1 if the firm's increased fixed investment in the past 6 months; 0 otherwise.	+

3.3 Empirical Results

3.3.1 Baseline Results

In Table 3.2, the marginal effects from probit models with credit rationing as the main explanatory variable are displayed. The first column tests solely the effect of credit rationing on employment dynamics, while the rest

Table 3.2 Credit-rationed firms and employment

Variables	*(1)* *Model 1*	*(2)* *Model 2*	*(3)* *Model 3*
Credit rationed	−0.0277***	−0.0196***	−0.0198***
	(0.00765)	(0.00677)	(0.00676)
Turnover		0.200***	0.200***
		(0.00386)	(0.00387)
Profit		0.0363***	0.0361***
		(0.00440)	(0.00440)
Fixed investments		0.115***	0.115***
		(0.00364)	(0.00364)
Debt to assets		0.0329***	0.0331***
		(0.00391)	(0.00391)
Size		0.0762***	0.0762***
		(0.00235)	(0.00235)
Age		−0.0194***	−0.0194***
		(0.00333)	(0.00333)
ESI			0.00135***
			(0.000511)
Credit history		0.0431***	0.0429***
		(0.00394)	(0.00394)
Observations	48,748	48,748	48,748
Controls	No	Yes	Yes
Country FE	Yes	Yes	Yes
Time FE	Yes	Yes	Yes
Sector FE	Yes	Yes	Yes

Standard errors in parentheses
*** $p<0.01$, ** $p<0.05$, * $p<0.1$

columns gradually introduce the aforementioned control variables along with the two metrics of economic sentiment.

In the baseline model (Model 1), the probability of employment growth decreases by 2.7% when a firm is classified as credit rationed. This effect drops to 1.9% (Model 2) when the control variables are included. The signs of the marginal effects align with predictions stated in Table 3.2. For example, if profitability and turnover, key indicators of internal cash flow, increased in the last 6 months, this leads to a higher probability of employment growth. Furthermore, the structural characteristics of a firm, such as age and size, significantly influence its employment decisions. Not surprisingly, we observe that smaller firms, on average, demonstrate lower levels of employment growth, consistent with prior literature findings (Campello et al. 2010; Duygan et al. 2015; Popov and Rocholl 2015; Giroud and Mueller 2015; Farinha et al. 2021), while for age, a negative relationship is reported. Additionally, a rising debt-to-assets ratio over the last 6 months positively impacts employment probability, signaling effective financial leverage. Finally, a similar positive impact is reported for fixed investments (as increased production capacities might require additional labor) and credit history (from its indirect effects on loans).

These results strengthen our initial hypothesis and coincide with existing literature on the adverse effect of credit rationing on employment (Gerlach et al. 2015; Gomez 2019). Failure to obtain necessary external funds can lead to internal cash flow issues and indirect effects on labor costs and decisions. Ultimately, the negative impact of credit rationing on employment growth highlights the importance of addressing financial constraints to create new job opportunities.

3.3.2 Proxying for Business Cycle Effects

Potential borrowers, in addition to their financial circumstances, do also consider the prevailing and anticipated economic conditions in their decision-making process, part of which is the investment in labor. For this reason, we incorporate in our analysis, the ESI, to capture for the business cycle effect which enables us to consider the interaction between macroeconomic sentiment and firm-specific limitations. The ESI is an essential indicator for assessing the actions of credit-constrained enterprises, especially regarding their hiring choices. The ESI serves as a composite indicator of business and consumer confidence, reflecting variations in economic attitude that affect lending accessibility and risk assessment by lenders and companies. For credit-constrained enterprises, whose decision-making is highly responsive to external economic situations, the ESI as a forward-looking indicator offers essential insights about their employment trends and investment activities (Bhamra et al. 2010; Drakos & Kallandranis 2005b; Pindado and Sánchez 2017).

When sentiment indicators are included, the main equation is transformed as follows:

$$\text{Prob}(E_{i,c,t}=1 \mid N=1)=\beta_0+\textit{credit access}_{i,c,t}+\sum_{k=1}^{N}\theta_k\cdot \textit{Controls}_{i,c,t}+\textit{ESI}_{c,t}+\varepsilon_{i,c,t}$$

The results are reported in Table 3.2, in column 3. The impact of credit rationing remains unchanged with the addition of sentiment variables, underscoring the enduring influence of restricted access to funding on job choices; hence, ESI favorably influences employment growth. Despite the existence of credit rationing, SMEs may be motivated to augment their employment when they recognize a favorable economic climate.

3.4 Conclusion

The research investigates the impact of credit rationing on employment growth, focusing on SMEs. Using the pooled panel dataset of SAFE, the study found that credit rationing negatively impacted enterprises' employment decisions. The findings suggest that companies may decrease staff recruitment when they fail to obtain their desired loan amount. The study provides critical insights and policy implications for policymakers aiming to foster economic growth and corporate sustainability. Historically, literature has primarily focused on investments, overlooking the influence of credit outcomes on work choices.

Policymakers should adopt a more holistic approach that considers both supply and demand dynamics in formulating counter-employment initiatives. They can help SMEs reduce their dependence on bank lending by enhancing access to alternative capital sources, such as equity capital. Specialized policies, such as credit guarantee programs, tax incentives, and interest rate subsidies, are essential strategies for fostering firm expansion along with initiatives with the aim to mitigate the negative impacts of information on employment choices of financially restricted enterprises.

References

Benmelech, E., Bergman, N. K., & Seru, A. (2011). *Financing labor* (No. w17144). National Bureau of Economic Research.

Berg, T. (2018). Got rejected? Real effects of not getting a loan. *The Review of Financial Studies, 31*(12), 4912–4957.

Berger, A. N., & Udell, G. F. (1998). The economics of small business finance: The roles of private equity and debt markets in the financial growth cycle. *Journal of Banking & Finance, 22*(6–8), 613–673.

Berger, A. N., & Frame, W. S. (2007). Small business credit scoring and credit availability. *Journal of Small Business Management, 45*(1), 5–22.

Bernanke, B., & Gertler, M. (1990). Financial fragility and economic performance. *Quarterly Journal of Economics, 105*, 97–114.

Bhamra, H. S., Kuehn, L. A., & Strebulaev, I. A. (2010). The aggregate dynamics of capital structure and macroeconomic risk. *The Review of Financial Studies, 23*(12), 4187–4241.

Bottazzi, G., Secchi, A., & Tamagni, F. (2014). Financial constraints and firm dynamics. *Small Business Economics, 42*, 99–116.

Campello, M., Graham, J. R., & Harvey, C. R. (2010). The real effects of financial constraints: Evidence from a financial crisis. *Journal of Financial Economics, 97*(3), 470–487.

Cowling, M., Liu, W., Minniti, M., & Zhang, N. (2016). UK credit and discouragement during the GFC. *Small Business Economics, 47*, 1049–1074.

Drakos, K., & Kallandranis, C. (2005a). Firm-specific attributes of financing constraints: The case of Greek listed firms. *Journal of Investment Management and Financial Innovations*, 2, 98–110.

Drakos, K., & Kallandranis, C. (2005b). Investment and cash flow: Evidence from Greek listed companies. *Applied Economics Quarterly, 51*(4), 323–344.

Duygan-Bump, B., Levkov, A., & Montoriol-Garriga, J. (2015). Financing constraints and unemployment: Evidence from the Great Recession. *Journal of Monetary Economics, 75*, 89–105.

Farinha, L., Kokas, S., Tsoukas, S., & Sette, E. (2021). Real effects of imperfect bank-firm matching. https://ssrn.com/abstract=4180054

Ferrando, A., & Mulier, K. (2015). The real effects of credit constraints: Evidence from discouraged borrowers in the euro area. *Journal of Corporate Finance, 73*, 102171. https://doi.org/10.1016/j.jcorpfin.2022.102171

Freel, M., Carter, S., Tagg, S., & Mason, C. (2012) The latent demand for bank debt: Characterizing discouraged borrowers. *Small Business Economics, 38*, 399–418.

Gerlach-Kristen, P., O'Connell, B., & O'Toole, C. (2015). Do credit constraints affect SME investment and employment? *The Economic and Social Review, 46*(1, Spring), 51–86.

Giroud, X., & Mueller, H. M. (2015). *Firm leverage and unemployment during the great recession* (No. w21076). National Bureau of Economic Research.

Gómez, M. G. P. (2019). Credit constraints, firm investment and employment: Evidence from survey data. *Journal of Banking & Finance, 99*, 121–141.

Greenwald, B., Stiglitz, J., & Weiss, A. (1984). Information imperfections and macroeconomic fluctuations. *American Economic Review, 74*, 194–199.

Greenwald, B. C., & Stiglitz, J. E. (1988). Pareto inefficiency of market economies: search and efficiency wage models. *The American Economic Review, 78*(2), 351–355.

Hamermesh, D. S., & Pfann, G. A. (1996). Adjustment costs in factor demand. *Journal of Economic Literature, 34*(3), 1264–1292.

Hernando, I., & Martínez-Carrascal, C. (2008). The impact of financial variables on firms' real decisions: Evidence from Spanish firm-level data. *Journal of Macroeconomics, 30*(1), 543–561.

Kallandranis, C., Anastasiou, D., & Drakos, K. (2023). Credit rationing prevalence for Eurozone firms. *Journal of Business Research, 158*, 113640.

Kiyotaki, N., & Moore, G. (1997). Credit cycles. *Journal of Political Economy, 105*, 211–248.

Modigliani, F., & Miller, M. H. (1958). The cost of capital, corporation finance and the theory of investment. *The American Economic Review, 48*(3), 261–297.

Moro, A., Fink, M., & Maresch, D. (2015). Reduction in information asymmetry and credit access for small and medium-sized enterprises. *Journal of Financial Research, 38*(1), 121–143.

Myers, S., & Majluf, N. (1984). Corporate financing and investment decisions when firms have information that investors do not have. *Journal of Financial Economics, 13*, 187–221.

Oi, W. Y. (1962). Labor as a quasi-fixed factor. *Journal of Political Economy, 70*(6), 538–555.

Petersen, M. A., & Rajan, R. G. (1994). The benefits of lending relationships: Evidence from small business data. *The Journal of Finance, 49*(1), 3–37.

Pindado, E., & Sánchez, M. (2017). Researching the entrepreneurial behaviour of new and existing ventures in European agriculture. *Small Business Economics, 49*, 421–444.

Popov, A. A., & Rocholl, J. (2015). Financing constraints, employment, and labor compensation: evidence from the subprime mortgage crisis. *ECB Working Paper No. 1821.*

Stiglitz, J. E., & Weiss, A. (1981). Credit rationing in markets with imperfect information. *The American Economic Review, 71*(3), 393–410.

Townsend, R. M. (1979). Optimal contracts and competitive markets with costly state verification. *Journal of Economic Theory, 21*(2), 265–293.

Vlassas, I., Kallandranis, C., Ballis, A., Glyptis, L., & Thanh, L. M. (2024). What else lies behind the credit rationing? Exploring the issue of employment. *Journal of Asia Business Studies, 18*(4), 865–885.

CHAPTER 4

Managerial Social Capital and Firm Risk

Evidence from the United Kingdom

Omar Al-Bataineh, Abdullah Iqbal, and Timothy King

4.1 Introduction

Social capital is one of the three pillars of sustainable development, and one understood to influence many aspects of societal functioning, including within the business environment. Yet, extant literature has only recently begun to consider the implications of social capital for firm outcomes, with a recent interdisciplinary research highlighting social capital as a key driver

O. Al-Bataineh
Department of Business Administration, The Hashemite University, Jordan
e-mail: omar.bataineh@hu.edu.jo

A. Iqbal
Kent Business School, University of Kent, Canterbury, UK
e-mail: a.iqbal@kent.ac.uk

T. King (✉)
School of Accounting and Finance, University of Vaasa, Vaasa, Finland
e-mail: timothy.king@uwasa.fi

E. Scannella and J. Williams (eds.), *Trends, Issues, and Challenges in Banking and Finance*, Palgrave Macmillan Studies in Banking and Financial Institutions,
https://doi.org/10.1007/978-3-031-96066-6_4

of corporate financial decisions, including capital structure, cash holdings, trade credit, corporate social responsibility (CSR), gender diversity, chief executive officer (CEO) pay, and dividend policy decisions (Renneboog and Zhao 2011; Hasan et al. 2017; Huang and Shang 2019; Hasan et al. 2020; Hossain et al. 2021; Javakhadze and Shelton 2022; Andriosopoulos and Deepty 2022), and that social capital can help mitigate unethical corporate behaviors, such as tax avoidance (Hasan et al. 2017), political and market competition risks (Andriosopoulos and Deepty 2022), and insider trading (Chung et al. 2023), as well as improving firms' access to external capital (Cheng et al. 2017).

In this chapter, we adopt a structural definition of social capital (SSC) (Bhandari and Bhuyan 2023) and apply network theory (Ferris et al. 2017b) to examine the implications of managerial social capital (MSC) for firm risk. Our MSC measure is defined based on a network centrality measure (El-Khatib et al. 2015) and defined based on the social network capital of executive and nonexecutive board members gained through network ties (Renneboog and Zhao 2011). In this way, our measure expands on the network centrality algorithm used in prior work (e.g., El-Khatib et al. 2015), in the sense we expand the focus from the network ties of CEOs to also consider those of the entire top management team (TMT).

We set our study in an important institutional environment—the United Kingdom (Renneboog and Zhao 2011; Horton et al. 2012), a collectivist society with high levels of social capital, and where there is ongoing debate regarding the effectiveness of the UK Corporate Governance Code (CGC), we conjecture that MSC should play an important role in determining firm risk-taking, and argue that strategic firm choices that involve risk should not ignore the social capital dimension (Hasan et al. 2020).

Theoretically MSC could be associated with lower or higher risk. On the one hand, MSC could be associated with lower firm risk. MSC, facilitated by network ties, can constitute important resources that can promote access to valuable resources, including information relevant to making better informed risk-taking choices (Javakhadze et al. 2016). For example, socially connected directors may be better positioned to monitor and discipline managerial risk-taking; one important reason being that social ties helps reduce asymmetrical information in labor markets, thereby facilitating access to more outside employment opportunities and thus lowering career concerns (Berger et al. 2013; Ferris et al. 2019). Consistent with these arguments, board social capital can positively influence shareholder value in cross-border acquisitions (Basuil and Datta 2017), while the extent of executive and director social connections are associated with reductions in the costs and breadth of legal interventions (Javakhadze et al. 2016) and firms' costs of equity (Ferris et al. 2017b). Moreover, social capital can help mitigate political and market competition risks (Andriosopoulos and Deepty 2022) as well as unethical corporate behaviors, such as tax avoidance (Hasan et al. 2017).

On the other hand, MSC could be associated with higher firm risk. Social ties can exacerbate agency costs, affording managers and directors greater power (Brass and Burkhardt 1993), which could lead to higher managerial risk-taking as naturally risk-averse managers increase risk-taking in response to greater outside employment options (Ferris et al. 2019). Moreover, due to changes in risk appetite higher MSC could promote undesirable behaviors and firm outcomes, including excessive real earnings management (Griffin et al. 2021). Such arguments are consistent with the notion that membership of a group or network can alter the risk preferences of individuals within it toward greater appetite for risk, through the pooling of individual risks (Ferris et al. 2017a, 2017b; Ferris et al. 2019).

We begin by investigating the effects of MSC on firm risk using an unbalanced panel of UK Financial Times Stock Exchange 350 Index (FTSE 350) firms between 2006 and 2017. Employing the system-generalized method of moments (GMM) estimator to address potential endogeneity concerns regarding the relationship between MSC and firm risk, we find that MSC is negatively associated with both idiosyncratic and total risk measures. This effect is economically meaningful. For example, a one-unit increase in MSC (using a standard deviation of 2.276) is associated with a 1.65% reduction in idiosyncratic risk. Our main results therefore appear consistent with the idea that senior managers working in firms operating in a high trust setting (the United Kingdom) are less likely to take on risk and pursue private benefits (Huang and Shang 2019).

We further consider CSR as an alternative measure of social capital, which could convey a different effect to MSC on firm risk (Lins et al. 2017; Amin et al. 2020). Importantly, we also demonstrate that our main results for MSC continue to hold even when controlling for CSR. We infer from these results that the impact of social capital on firm performance is complex and that future research should not ignore the potential influence of CSR. In doing so, we help address the lack of consensus regarding the nature of the relationship between corporate governance and CSR across different institutional contexts (Zaman et al. 2022). Pertinently, while our measure of MSC is closely aligned to a structural definition of social capital and based on network theory (Ferris et al. 2017b), CSR is more closely linked to a cognitive definition of social capital (CSC) (Sacconi and Antoni 2009). Recent interdisciplinary studies establish a link between CSR and social capital (Jha and Cox 2015, Lins et al. 2017) Amin et al. 2020) with Lins et al (2017) going as far to suggest that CSR performance can even be viewed as a form of firm-level social capital. Unlike our finding of a negative relationship between MSC and firm-risk measures, we show that CSR (firms' composite CSR scores) is positively associated with both firm-specific and total risks. This is interesting from the perspective of recent findings of an inverse relationship between CSR and firm risk in the case of US firms (Albuquerque et al. 2019). We consider this result likely to be reflective of differences in the institutional environment within the United Kingdom as well as the role and levels of social capital in the United Kingdom; for instance, larger MSC networks may encourage risk-taking through the pooling of individual risks (Ferris et al. 2017a, 2017b; Ferris et al. 2019).

Finally, we present a battery of further tests, and demonstrate that our results are robust to a battery of robustness tests, including use of an industry-adjusted indicator of MSC, controlling for the presence of a firm's risk management committee, a potential moderating effect from board of directors' (BoD) national diversity mix, and alternative estimations of firm risk.

Our study makes several contributions. First, while we are not the first to consider the risk implications of social capital per se, we go further than much prior work by considering social capital ties beyond those of the firm CEO to all board members—thereby deriving a more holistic measure of a firm's social capital. Importantly, while prior studies focus on CEOs' social connections (El-Khatib et al. 2015; Ferris et al. 2017a; Ferris et al. 2019), by contrast, we expand the algorithm used in these studies to capture (CEO) MSC, to compute a MSC measure that captures the social connections of CEOs plus other top executives and non-executive members of the corporate board. We argue this is important given that non-executive board members are understood to contribute valuable resources through their professional and social connections (Amin et al. 2020). In this way, our study departs from the nascent literature to date (El-Khatib et al. 2015; Ferris et al. 2017a; Ferris et al. 2019).

Second, we study the implications of MSC for firm-risk outcomes in a unique non-US setting, with the United Kingdom characterized by high social capital in the business environment. Our focus helps address the lack of non-US evidence regarding the role of MSC on firm outcomes and contributes to our understanding of the links between corporate governance and CSR in different institutional contexts (Zaman et al. 2022). Although prior research on MSC has almost exclusively focused on the United States (Lins et al. 2017; Ferris et al. 2017a; García-Feijóo et al. 2021), studying the effects of social capital in UK firms is of particular interest for at least several reasons. First, the levels and implications of managerial networked connections (social capital) may vary significantly in the United Kingdom compared to the United States, attributable to differences in governance, culture, ownership structure, and regulation (Renneboog and Zhao 2011; Goergen et al. 2019; Hasan et al. 2020). Second, the strength and extent of social capital in the United Kingdom are much higher than in the United States (Renneboog and Zhao 2013; Elsayed et al. 2022; The Social Capital Index 2023). These observations could lead to different corporate risk management decisions under the social capital perspective, and consequently differences in firm outcomes, including funding costs (Meng and Yin 2019; Renneboog and Zhao 2013; Filatotchev et al. 2018). Third, although social capital embodies the concept of trust, high social capital is not necessarily indicative of high societal trust. Notably, in the United Kingdom, reported trust in other people has remained quite stable over time but other dimensions of social capital have not—introducing a potential and unusual disconnect between social capital levels and trust (Ortiz-Ospina and Roser 2016).

Third, we go further than prior work by addressing important endogeneity concerns regarding the relationship between MSC and firm risk-taking by using the system-GMM estimator and argue that fixed effects are insufficient to fully address endogeneity concerns. In terms of existing studies, Ferris et al. (2017a) show that CEO social capital, under the structural definition, is associated with reductions in firm risk. However, they do not consider the social capital of other executives or directors, which may also play important, yet potentially different, roles. Consequently, such findings may not be generalizable.

The remainder of the chapter proceeds as follows: Sect. 4.2 introduces the study setting, reviews relevant literature, and develops the study hypotheses; Sect. 4.3 presents the empirical framework and describes the data and variables; Sect. 4.4 presents and discusses the study results; Sect. 4.5 presents tests of robustness; Sect. 4.6 concludes the chapter.

4.2 Study Setting and Literature Review

4.2.1 UK Institutional Setting

This study adopts the empirical setting of the United Kingdom (Renneboog and Zhao 2011; Horton et al. 2012), where corporate governance rules have been revised globally after the 2007–2009 financial crisis, with a focus on prudent risk-taking. During the crisis, the UK government implemented a £500 billion rescue package to bail out firms, and subsequently, more attention has been given to the roles of BoD and senior managers in shaping firm risk-taking (Erkens et al. 2012) The UK's 2010 CGC stresses a board's fiduciary responsibilities in helping identify and manage substantive risks that affect a firm's operations, while the Financial Reporting Council (FRC) issued a report in 2011 clarifying the boards' tasks in risk management, including risk classification and crisis management. This report highlights the importance of considering cultural settings and risk-taking together, which is an under-investigated area in corporate finance literature. Furthermore, although the UK CGCs acknowledge the relationship between risk-taking and cultural settings, further research is needed, particularly concerning the roles played by social capital (Abdelbadie and Salama 2019; Elsayed et al. 2022). More specifically, the impact of social capital as a board attribute in risk-taking decisions have been subject to little research (Mathew et al. 2016; Elsayed et al. 2022).

Under UK governance mechanisms, firms are expected to voluntarily follow governance recommendations or justify why they do not, which may depart from shareholders' best interests. Javakhadze et al. (2016) argue that MSC works as a disciplinary mechanism which reduces agency problems between investors and insiders due to the potentially negative consequences of loss of managerial reputation. Similarly, Hirshleifer and Thakor (1992) demonstrate that managers ignore risky investments because of the pressure of reputation building. Accordingly, directors with high social capital may be expected to play a significant role to protect shareholder interests. In this vein, high MSC could reduce firm risk through the building of a reputation for honest dealing (Kandori 1992; Harjoto and Wang 2020), whereby managers and directors have incentives to protect their reputations in external labor markets (Fama and Jensen 1983; Harjoto and Wang 2020). In support, Elsayed et al. (2022) show that, in the case of UK firms, social capital created by boards of directors and senior managers through their social and managerial networks can help protect companies from the risk of bankruptcy.

There are also likely to be notable differences in the roles played by social capital in UK firms compared to US firms, which is important given that a majority of prior work on MSC has focused on the US setting (Lins et al. 2017; Ferris et al. 2017a; Gupta et al. 2018; Hoi et al. 2019; García-Feijóo 2021; Griffin et al. 2021). First, there are differences in governance, culture, ownership structure, and regulation (Renneboog and Zhao 2011; Goergen et al. 2019; Hasan et al. 2020). For example, the Higgs Report (2003) shows that the US regulatory body overemphasizes the monitoring role of nonexecutive directors while ignoring their prospective contribution to wealth creation. Accordingly, putting the expected monitoring role of non-executives and the reputation concern in an environment that implements the role of "follow or explain" for corporate governance regulations compared to the rigid view of nonexecutives like in the United States may result in key differences in relations between MSC and firm risk (Elsayed et al. 2022). Second, levels of social capital are much higher in the United Kingdom compared to the United States (Renneboog and Zhao 2013; Elsayed et al. 2022, The Social Capital Index 2023), which could result in a greater effect attributable to MSC on firm risk-taking. Third, although social capital embodies the concept of trust, high social capital is not necessarily indicative of high societal trust. Notably, in the United Kingdom, reported trust in other people has remained quite stable over time but other dimensions of social capital have not—introducing a potential and unusual disconnect between social capital levels and trust (Ortiz-Ospina and Roser 2016).

4.2.2 *Social Capital and Risk-taking*

The concept of social capital has received much attention over the last couple of decades and has grown to become one of the influential topics in the social sciences (Putnam et al. 1994; Nahapiet and Ghoshal 1998; Woolcock 1998; Dasgupta 2005; Lins et al. 2017; Hasan et al. 2020; Javakhadze and Shelton 2022).

Prior literature emphasizes that social capital has value through the strength and number of social ties within networks. Such social networks can be formed to the extent that allows social relationships to acquire significant information and control (Bourdieu 1986a, 1986b, 1989; Bourdieu and Wacquant 1992; Larcker et al. 2013; Goergen et al. 2019; García-Feijóo et al. 2021). Consistent with this, Lin (1999) suggests that social capital theory can be defined as a set of resources embedded in a social network. Accordingly, subsequent research measures social capital based on the network theory by applying centrality measures (Freeman 1979; Wasserman and Faust 1994), which infers that social capital can be measured by observing social network characteristics (Wasserman and Faust 1994; Javakhadze et al. 2016).

There is no one-encompassing definition of social capital. Instead, social capital can have different meanings which determines how best to measure it. At a micro-level, it can be defined as representing the resources embedded in people's social networks (Lin 2002), or at a macro-level, as "*resources embedded in a social structure that are accessed and/or mobilized in purposive actions*" (Lin 2002, p. 29). Prior literature that examines MSC refers to both macro-level and micro-level aspects of social capital. While the macro-social capital definition is community-based and focuses on civic norms, trust, membership of associations, and voluntary works (Scrivens and Smith 2013; Huang and Shang 2019), the micro-level focuses on the SSC that is rooted in social networking between nodes, and these nodes may reflect firms, individuals, etc. (Wasserman and Faust 1994; El-Khatib et al. 2015; Fracassi 2017). However, both definitions have similarities, in that social capital represents a source of competitive advantage for its participants. For instance, micro-level social capital has an embedded asset value through the connections between network participants, whereas macro-level social capital offers a competitive advantage as means of public good (Javakhadze et al. 2016; Lins et al. 2017; Hasan et al. 2020).

Although social capital definitions vary, it is useful to differentiate between the two sources of social capital most relevant for studies of corporations: SSC (Bourdieu 1986b, 1989; Bourdieu and Wacquant 1992; Lin 1999), which is closely related to agents such as BoD (Tuugi et al. 2014; Javakhadze et al. 2016); and CSC (Coleman 1988; Putnam et al. 1994; Sacconi and Antoni 2009, 2011), which captures the environment in which the firms operate. In other words, SSC is generally defined at a micro-social level, whereas CSC is defined at a macro-social level (e.g., Javakhadze et al. 2016; Hasan et al. 2020). Unlike SSC, CSC is more closely associated with investments in CSR, as CSR can be used to emphasize the beliefs and fiduciary duties of the BoD and managers to a firm's stakeholders (Sacconi and Antoni 2009; Endrikat et al. 2021).

Previous research investigates the impact of social capital on various corporate finance policies, including capital structure (Huang and Shang 2019), risk-taking (Ferris et al. 2019), and firm performance (Larcker et al. 2013; Zona et al. 2018), and from differing perspectives. The first perspective is referred to as managerial opportunism and is based on agency theory (Jensen and Meckling 1976). Here, social capital is considered to impede firm performance by facilitating managerial opportunistic behavior (Fich 2005; Perry and Peyer 2005). Seemingly consistent with this view, Ferris et al. (2017a) focus on CEO social capital and find that the relationship between MSC and risk-taking decisions is positive, yet can also be value-enhancing. Moreover, they also argue that this relationship is influenced by country-specific factors. Although these studies are informative as to how social capital may impact firm risk-taking behavior, they do not explore the potentially important role played by executives other than the CEO and the wider corporate board.

Resource dependence theory (RDT) posits that senior managers and BoD can constitute important resources through the strength of their human and social capital (Hillman and Dalziel 2003; Endrikat et al. 2021). While human capital refers to managers' and directors', for example, expertise, experience, and reputation, social capital refers to the provision of resources through networks and/or relationships (Tian et al. 2011). Considering this, social capital may influence firm policies in several ways.

Social capital can work as an information channel, whereby valuable information is transmitted through social networks. For example, Javakhadze et al. (2016) argue that social capital plays an important role in asset pricing by providing useful information to market participants through social networks that help alleviate information asymmetries. For instance, board directors can help provide legitimacy, contribute to advice and counsel senior managers, act as channels for information exchange between external institutions and firms, and help in the development of firm strategies (Hillman and Dalziel 2003; Endrikat et al. 2021). This is important because in imperfect capital markets seeking information from financial markets implies searching costs and the fear of contractual failure. Similarly, social capital can also play an important role through trust, which is a social capital mechanism that facilitates reliability and repeatability in transactions, thereby lowering transaction costs (Hasan et al. 2020; Pasiouras and Samet 2022). Trust, built through social capital, can help to promote compliance with cooperative norms (Coleman 1988; Hossain et al. 2021), efficient allocation of resources (Lins et al. 2017), and access to valuable firm resources including external capital (Javakhadze et al. 2016). At the macro-level, social capital can promote economic and financial growth (Dasgupta 2005; Hasan et al. 2020), while at the micro-level, García-Sánchez and Noguera-Gámez (2017) argue that as every business transaction necessitates trust, social capital allows agents to operate even in markets characterized by high asymmetric information.

Agency theory identifies that conflicts of interest are rooted in the principal–agent relationship (Jensen and Meckling 1976; Fama and Jensen 1983). It also argues that nonexecutive directors are rather motivated to perform a monitoring role than insiders, and therefore they can exert a more positive influence in conditioning managerial behavior (Tian et al. 2011; Amin et al. 2020). One reason for this stems from the fact that independent directors are more cautious to protect shareholder interests and to protect their reputations in director labor markets (Fama and Jensen 1983). Thus, firm risk-taking may be moderated by the managerial reputation view, whereby the reputation effect underpins the monitoring role; such arguments can be extended to different board members, that is, those with high levels of social capital (Diamond 1989; Kandori 1992). Consistent with these arguments, Akbar et al. (2017) report that the presence of non-executive directors on corporate boards mitigates risk-taking in financial firms, whereas board size has no significant effect. These results imply that managers are more risk-averse when they face higher reputational and employment risks. Relatedly, Javakhadze et al. (2016) argue that MSC works as a disciplinary mechanism that reduces agency problems between shareholders and insiders due to reputation loss consequences. Finally, Hirshleifer and Thakor (1992) suggest that managers may ignore riskier investments because of reputation concerns. Thus, social capital is related to the reputation and monitoring effects, which play a significant role in determining firms' risk-taking decisions (Fracassi and Tate 2012; Ferris et al. 2019; Harjoto and Wang 2020; Hasan et al. 2020).

A further perspective, based on RDT (Pfeffer and Salancik 1978), is that social capital can contribute to firm performance through the relaxing of resource constraints (Pfeffer and Salancik 1978; Mizruchi 1996; Zona et al. 2018). Indeed, these contrasting perspectives yield very different expectations regarding the effects of MSC on firm outcomes, and, in the context of the BoD, whether social capital will, for example, enhance the performance of executives and non-executive directors (Fama 1980; Adams et al. 2010). Alternatively, social capital can encourage directors to act in self-interest that deviates from that of shareholders and other key stakeholders (Adams and Ferreira 2007).

Given that opposing arguments can be made for the impact of social capital on risk-taking, especially as we capture the social capital of both executive and non-executive members of the BoD, we specify the following hypotheses:

***H1a**: The relationship between MSC and risk-taking is negative.*
***H1b**: The relationship between MSC and risk-taking is positive.*

4.2.3 Controlling for Corporate Social Responsibility

According to Uphoff (2000), social capital can be classified into cognitive (norms, values, attitudes, and beliefs) or structural (roles, rules, precedents, and procedures) perspectives. He argues that SSC is linked with different forms of social organization and a wide range of networks which contribute to cooperation, and particularly to mutually beneficial collective action (MBCA), while the CSC is derived from ideas and mental processes, bolstered by ideological and cultural backgrounds that support cooperative behavior and MBCA.

Stakeholder theory (Freeman 1984; Jones 1995) and risk management theory postulate that CSR stimulates moral capital or represents a relationship-based intangible asset that provides the firm with a form of insurance-like protection (Godfrey 2005). Accordingly, by defining CSR as a social capital measure, Lins et al. (2017) expand the scope of CSR as insurance against firm-specific risk (Godfrey 2005; Dunbar et al. 2020). In support, Lins et al. (2017) find that firms with high social capital, built up through CSR activities, hold an advantage during crisis periods where trust is lacking. They use CSR as a social capital measure by considering four explicit social capital dimensions: (a) personal relationships; (b) social networks; (c) civic engagements; and (d) trust and cooperative norms. As illustrated in Scrivens and Smith (2013), this definition can be described under structural or cognitive social capital (Putnam et al. 1994; Andriosopoulos and Deepty 2022). However, Lins et al. (2017) do not distinguish clearly between CSC and SSC (Javakhadze et al. 2016; Hasan et al. 2020).

Krishna and Uphoff (2002) highlight some similarities between both levels of social capital, in that they can both stimulate a willingness and are associated with the mechanism, to pursue commonly advantageous collective actions. These mutual benefits evolve from social relationships, roles, and networks that motivate cooperative behavior, and from values, norms, and other cognitive functions that motivate people to work collectively to obtain shared rewards. Yet, it is arguably not logical to use SSC and CSC interchangeably. For example, Krishna and Uphoff (2002) show that the set of norms and forms of interactions between people can vary across different cultures, so what might motivate people from specific cultures to work together for the shared benefit may not work in another.

Accordingly, as the present study seeks to examine the relationship between social capital and risk-taking, CSR is employed as an additional proxy for social capital (Lins et al. 2017) that is more aligned with the CSC perspective (Sacconi and Antoni 2009), and which may convey a differential effect on firm risk. Prior studies on the association between social capital indexed through CSR and risk-taking present two contrasting outcomes. To illustrate, social capital is characterized by management's ability to transfer information to stakeholders, which can reduce information asymmetries and agency costs, such as between shareholders and management (Jiraporn et al. 2014; Lins et al. 2017). Accordingly, from one point of view, the firm's management might use CSR to improve its reputation, but this may, or may not, be consistent with shareholder objectives—especially if these are more based on short-term investment horizons. Yet, there is growing support for the notion that the use of CSR enhances the firm's image in the long run by fostering social capital (Dunbar et al. 2020). For instance, Dunbar et al. (2020) argue that firms should improve (reduce) CSR performance by increasing (lowering) CEO risk-taking incentives, according to what they term the "risk capacity hypothesis." Comparably, Jiraporn et al. (2014) argue that a positive association between CSR and a firm's risk-taking can result from building long-term trust within society. They show that "moral capital" can convey positive reputational effects that help offset negative valuations, and subsequent penalties by stakeholders, following firms' misbehaviors, as well as reducing the vulnerabilities of firms to adverse incidents. They support the "risk mitigation view" where CSR works as "insurance-like" protection (e.g., Godfrey et al. 2009; El Ghoul et al. 2011).

Nevertheless, and consistent with the earlier discussion regarding the use of CSR as a proxy for CSC, firms working in a socially responsible way can become more trustworthy, and better at civic engagement, which can lead to higher valuations (Hasan et al. 2020). Consequently, CSC pays off as a means of reciprocal moral obligation. Consistent with this, Dunbar et al. (2020) show that firms that act to enrich their CSR performance can increase their capacity to assume more risk, given that higher CSR performance (cognitive capital) can provide insurance-like protection to firms.

4.3 Research Design

4.3.1 *Sample Construction and Data*

The sample consists of UK FTSE 350 index firms between 2006 and 2017 for which data are available on the social connections and biographical characteristics of firm executive and non-executive directors from BoardEx. The sample begins in 2006 because BoardEx coverage is poor prior to this year. We also require data on firm characteristics, which are sourced from Thomson Datastream. BoardEx data are matched with Datastream data using the corporate International Securities Identification Number (ISIN) code, with each match carefully verified by all study authors. The final unbalanced panel dataset includes 4,325 firm-year observations for 333 unique firms. To mitigate the potential influence of outliers, we winsorize all variables at the 1st and 99th percentiles (Javakhadze et al. 2016). Appendix A1 provides details of all the study variables, including definitions and data sources.

4.3.2 *Dependent Variables*

Risk-taking is commonly measured using the standard deviation of a performance measure over a specific time. When examining the influence of MSC on firm risk, idiosyncratic (or unsystematic) risk is of particular interest given that it captures the proportion of total risk that directly stems from the decision-making and actions of senior managers and the BoD (Jin 2002). In contrast, systematic risk is more abstracted from the decisions of firm insiders as it captures the volatility of the firm's cash flows to business cycles and is beyond the direct influence of firms' management. Therefore, we focus on idiosyncratic risk[1] as our main measure of

[1] In this study, firm-specific risk and idiosyncratic risk are used interchangeably.

firm risk-taking, which accounts for more than 80% of total risk, and use total risk as our second measure (Goyal and Santa-Clara 2003). We estimate firm-specific risk and total risk using the capital asset pricing model (CAPM), and we use the market model for additional tests of robustness.[2] We require at least 175 daily observations for all models to estimate the idiosyncratic risk, which is measured as the annualized standard deviation of the residuals of each of these models.[3]

4.3.3 Measuring Managerial Social Capital

The main variable of interest in our study is MSC. This measure captures the size/degree centrality of senior executive and non-executive directors' social networks, and it is based on an SSC perspective (Lin, 1999; Burt 1992). Accordingly, we define the SSC between agents as an asset embedded in social networks that can be utilized through connections between agents (Lin 1999; Burt 2000). An individual is considered as being highly connected if they have strong connections with other agents in the network (i.e., sample firms).

Following prior work (Fracassi and Tate 2012; Javakhadze et al. 2016; Fracassi 2017), we collect the number of connections for all agents in a specific firm to compute a firm-level measure of social capital. These connections are the summation of connections from (a) *current employment*, where two agents are connected through working together in the same firm; (b) *past employment*, where two agents are connected from previously working in the same firm (distinct from current employment); (c) *educational network*, where two agents attended the same higher education institution within a 1-year overlap;[4] and (d) *other social activities*, which represent the total number of connections between two agents if they hold a membership at the same social and charitable organization(s), including football clubs, golf clubs, charities, and other social organizations at the same time. However, to ensure connections are "active,"

[2] In robustness tests, we use alternative models to estimate risk including the Fama and French (1993) model (FF3), a momentum factor as in Carhart (1997), and the Fama and French (2016) four-factor model (FF4). Our main results remain unchanged.

[3] For brevity, we do not present these models here given that these are fairly standard in finance literature.

[4] We also ran analyses where we alternatively specified a 2-year overlap and obtained very similar results.

we only consider connections through educational networks and other social activities, if the agents also have connections from current or previous employment.

To compute the MSC measure, we aggregate all connections to capture the firm-level social capital from 2006 to 2017 as follows:

$$MSC_{it} = \sum_{n=1}^{i} \left(CEC_{it} + PEC_{it} + EDC_{it} + OSAC_{it} \right) \tag{4.1}$$

where MSC is the managerial social capital measure; CEC represents current employment connections; PEC captures previous employment connections; EDC represents connections through education; OSAC captures the other social activity connections; and subscripts i and t represent the firm and time, respectively. In further analyses we also use an alternative industry-adjusted measure of MSC (ADJ-MSC), which we calculate as the difference between the MSC at time for firm and the industry average value of the MSC, excluding the sample firm to have an unbiased industry-average measure of MSC. For further details on all these variables, please refer to Appendix A1.

Moreover, in additional analyses we consider CSR as an alternative proxy for social capital that is more closely aligned with the CSC perspective (Sacconi and Antoni 2009). Our preferred CSR measure is based on the composite Refinitiv ESG scores for each firm-year, sourced from Datastream (Javakhadze et al. 2016). A higher score indicates a firm has higher CSR performance.[5]

Recent studies confirm a strong association between CSR and social capital (Javakhadze et al. 2016; Lins et al. 2017; Andriosopoulos and Deepty 2022). In line with Lins et al. (2017), we argue that CSC and SSC are not mutually exclusive and that CSC can facilitate reciprocal flow of norms, information, and other social attributes across social network participants. In this respect, our use of CSR helps facilitate a more holistic treatment of the effect of social capital on corporate risk-taking (Lins et al. 2017; Andriosopoulos and Deepty 2022).

[5] For further details on the scores and methodology, please see https://www.refinitiv.com/en/sustainable-finance/esg-scores

4.3.4 *Control Variables*

Motivated by prior literature we include a vector of control variables. Beginning with firm characteristics, we include: (a) return on assets (ROA), measured as the ratio of net income to total assets; (b) firm size (FSIZE), using the natural logarithm of total assets; (c) the turnover ratio (TURN), which captures the relative efficiency of use of a firm's assets (Pae et al. (2018), computed as the ratio of firm sales to total assets; (d) financial leverage (DEBTR) (Adams et al. 2005), computed as the ratio of total debt to total assets (Huang and Shang 2019); (e) firm dividend payout (DIVTOASS), the ratio of total dividends to total assets, which could influence managerial investment, as it implies greater or less access to retained capital; (f) *Tobin's Q*[6] which captures the extent of a firm's growth opportunities (Huang and Shang 2019), calculated as total shares outstanding multiplied by the stock price plus total liabilities divided by total assets; (g) finally, given that established firms may differ in operations and risk, we also include control for firm age (FAGE), measured as the natural logarithm of years since a firm was incorporated (Cao et al. 2006; Akbar et al. 2017).

We also account for board and governance characteristics. We first control for board size (BSIZE), which captures the total number of directors on the corporate board (Fracassi 2017). Previous studies provide conflicting results regarding optimal board size. For instance, Pathan (2009) shows that smaller boards are associated with both higher total and idiosyncratic risks, while Cheng (2008) finds that firms with larger boards go for less risky investments. Next, we control for the extent of board independence (NED), measured as the ratio of the number of nonexecutive directors to the total board size (Cheng 2008). Jensen and Meckling (1976) suggest that the existence of independent directors on the board can mitigate agency conflicts, while Cheng (2008) adds that because independent directors bring more heterogeneous views this can moderate board decision-making and lead to more stable performance. In a similar vein, Fama (1980) suggests that independent directors can provide effective monitoring given their reputation concerns and independence from management. The audit committee may also play an important monitoring role. For example, Younas et al. (2019) show that audit committee

[6] In unreported analyses, we repeat all our main analyses using Total Q (Peters and Taylor, 2017) and obtain very similar results.

quality can mitigate excessive risk-taking and that firms with higher social capital pay lower audit fees than firms with low social capital. We, therefore, control for the size of the audit committee (ASIZE), which is measured as the total number of directors sitting on the audit committee. Finally, as previous studies suggest that the presence of females on the board may influence firm risk, although the direction of this influence is unclear (Adams and Ferreira 2003; Berger et al. 2014), we control for a potential gender effect (GEN), computed as the percentage of female directors relative to board size.

4.3.5 Descriptive Statistics

Table 4.1 presents summary statistics for the final sample of 322 FTSE 350 firms from 2006 to 2017.

Firm-specific (idiosyncratic) risk is computed as the residual value from the capital assets pricing model (CAPM) or the market model and is denoted as IDO-CAPM or IDO-MKT, respectively. In robustness checks, we also compute firm risk as the residual value calculated from the Fama–French (1993) three-factor model (IDO-FF3), and the Fama–French (2016) four-factor model (IDO-FF4). The mean value of IDO-CAPM is 0.29, which is similar to those of IDO-MKT, IDO-FF3, and IDO-FF4 measures. The mean value of idiosyncratic risk is comparable to that found for the United States (Chakraborty et al. 2019). The mean value for MSC (ADJ-MSC) is 5.04 (0.424) with a standard deviation of 2.276 (2.480). Control variables are also in line with those reported in the extant literature for both the United Kingdom and the United States.

Appendix A3 presents the evolution of social capital and corporate risk-taking over the sample period. As shown in the table, MSC and ADJ-MSC exhibit declining trends, which we interpret as tentative evidence of the tendency of UK firms to follow the CGC of 2010—the recommendation for FTSE 350 firms is that over 50% of board directors are independent.[7] However, corporate risk-taking variables (IDO-MKT, IDO-CAPM, IDO-FF3, IDO-FF4, and TRISK) have a very similar mean and standard deviation values, suggesting no discernible time trends in firm risk, except for the global financial crisis (GFC) period where risk is more pronounced.

[7] Section (B.1.2) of the UK CGC 2010 states that "*Except for smaller companies, at least half the board, excluding the chairman, should comprise non-executive directors determined by the board to be independent*" (UK Corporate Governance Code, 2010, p. 9).

Table 4.1 Summary statistics

Variables	*Number*	*Mean*	*SD*	*Percentile*					*Maximum*	*Minimum*	*Skewness*	*Kurtosis*
				p5	*p25*	*p50*	*p75*	*p95*				
IDO-CAPM	4102	0.289	0.176	0.113	0.179	0.248	0.341	0.604	2.486	0.045	2.920	19.397
IDO-MKT	4102	0.289	0.176	0.113	0.179	0.248	0.341	0.604	2.486	0.045	2.920	19.397
TRISK	4102	0.325	0.179	0.147	0.214	0.284	0.380	0.662	2.488	0.054	2.796	17.735
ADJ-MSC	4241	0.424	2.480	−5.052	−0.944	0.552	2.014	4.403	6.877	−5.641	−0.360	3.200
MSC	4241	5.040	2.276	0.000	3.951	5.308	6.561	8.114	11.790	0.000	−0.607	3.337
ROA	4115	0.048	0.105	−0.118	0.013	0.050	0.095	0.203	0.300	−0.428	−1.479	8.827
FSIZE	4115	13.639	1.879	11.183	12.339	13.295	14.577	17.224	20.512	10.599	1.157	4.781
TURN	4101	0.782	0.787	0.020	0.100	0.600	1.170	2.410	3.530	−0.070	1.243	4.260
DEBTR	4115	0.187	0.165	0.000	0.050	0.157	0.280	0.521	0.720	0.000	0.971	3.588
DIVTA	4089	0.026	0.026	0.000	0.008	0.019	0.033	0.079	0.141	0.000	1.994	7.931
FAGE	4216	3.561	0.786	2.303	2.944	3.434	4.331	4.771	4.852	1.792	−0.003	1.943
Q	4109	1.144	0.811	0.275	0.731	0.907	1.328	2.759	4.976	0.075	2.274	9.644
BSIZE	3941	2.023	0.318	1.609	1.792	2.079	2.197	2.565	2.773	1.386	0.107	2.444
ASIZE	4001	1.402	0.338	1.099	1.099	1.386	1.609	1.946	2.197	0.000	−0.821	5.659
NED	3203	0.706	0.321	0.300	0.500	0.636	0.857	1.333	1.800	0.200	1.087	4.293
GEN	3941	0.130	0.121	0.000	0.000	0.130	0.200	0.330	0.500	0.000	0.679	2.952
Variables used in the further analysis												
IDO-FF3	4102	0.279	0.172	0.108	0.174	0.239	0.331	0.571	2.481	0.043	3.007	20.667
IDO-FF4	4102	0.279	0.171	0.108	0.173	0.238	0.331	0.570	2.481	0.043	3.009	20.724
CSR	2,279	45.047	17.233	17.2	31.78	44.87	56.89	74.61	91.91	3.02	0.142	2.433
RSKCOM	4325	0.0377	0.190	0	0	0	0	0	1	0	4.855	24.573
NATMIX	3,673	0.709	.453	0	0	1	1	1	1	0	−0.924	1.85449

This table provides summary statistics for the variables employed in this paper. The data form an unbalanced panel of UK FTSE 350 firms between 2006 and 2017. It is worth noting that the variables' descriptions and system of measurement correspond to the criteria specified in Appendix A1.

SD, standard deviation

In particular, the highest risk mean values were reported in 2008 and 2009, which likely reflects the consequences of the GFC (Pathan 2009).

4.4 Results

4.4.1 Econometric Framework

Our empirical framework seeks to provide a more rigorous treatment of potential endogeneity, which could affect the relationship between MSC and firm risk-taking, compared to prior related work (Mathew et al. 2016; Elsayed et al. 2022). Notably, in a dynamic estimation model a lagged dependent variable and fixed effects might be correlated, which would yield biased estimations of the Ordinary Least Squares (OLS) estimator. In other words, fixed effects would be suitable only if the unobserved individual effect is time-invariant. If this assumption does not hold, it is important to use another technique to address the endogeneity concerns. Moreover, endogeneity could arise from omitted factors, which may result in correlation across explanatory variables and with the error term and result in inconsistent OLS and fixed-effect estimates (Abdallah et al. 2015).

We mitigate such concerns by applying the dynamic panel generalized method of moments estimator (known as system-GMM), as recommended by Arellano and Bond (1991). This technique has several advantages. First, it helps mitigate simultaneity concerns, which may arise in our setting as we combine risk-taking variables with other financial variables concurrently. For example, if managers were to adjust firm debt levels to address a potential insolvency concern, then it would misrepresent the actual risk level in the firm. Second, it helps in accounting for unobservable heterogeneity and in mitigating dynamic endogeneity. As considered by Wintoki et al. (2012), this source of endogeneity is usually ignored in corporate governance research, yet it may have a significant influence on observed results. Pertinently, if financial variables are influenced by previous corporate risk-taking observations, dynamic endogeneity would be present in model specifications. Therefore, applying the system-GMM estimator allows us to better control for potential sources of endogeneity, which could bias the results and lead to inaccurate conclusions regarding the influence of MSC on firm risk.

The system-GMM estimator has the effect of first transforming all explanatory variables (regressors) by differencing; it then builds on the assumption that the first instrumental variables differences are exogeneous and not correlated with the fixed effects; finally, it includes additional instruments to improve efficiency. Accordingly, we employ lags of the dependent variable (firm risk) to control for the dynamic effect of prior firm risk-taking on current firm risk, as well as other lagged regressors in our model.[8]

We estimate the effects of MSC on firm risk based on the following model estimated using system-GMM:

$$y_{it} = \alpha_{it} + y_{it-1} + y_{it-2} + \beta_1 \mathrm{MSC}_{it} + \beta_2 \mathrm{control}_{it} + \theta x_{it} + \mu_i + \varepsilon_{it} \qquad (4.2)$$

where y_{it} is the dependent variable, which is either the idiosyncratic risk or total risk, y_{it-1} represents the first and y_{it-2} the second lags, of firm risk respectively. MSC *represents* the MSC measure. Controlit represents the full vector of our control variables as detailed in Sect. 4.3.4 and Appendix A1. We also include year and industry dummies θx_{it}, which are treated as exogenous variables in the model. Finally, $\varepsilon_{\mathrm{it}}$ captures the unobserved firm effect, while denotes the error term.

4.4.2 *Managerial Social Capital and Corporate Risk-taking*

Table 4.2 presents the results of the baseline estimations. In models (1a) and (1b) the dependent variable is idiosyncratic firm risk estimated using the CAPM model (IDO-CAPM). In models (2a) and (2b), the dependent variable is total firm risk (TRISK), which is also estimated based on this model.[9]

Managerial social capital is negative and highly significant in all models, which infers that higher MSC is associated with both lower firm-specific and total risk. More specifically, and consistent with the hypothesis H1a, this suggests that firms with socially well-connected executive and non-executive directors are associated with a lower appetite for firm risk. This result is arguably most consistent with the managerial reputation model, according to which managers may forgo risky investments and directors exert greater control, because of reputational and career concerns (Hirshleifer and Thakor 1992; Ferris et al. 2017b; Gupta et al. 2018).

[8] We follow the guidance of Wintoki et al. (2012) in determining the correct number of lags. Specifically, the first and second lags of the dependent variable are used throughout to ensure a sufficient number of lags to capture the dynamic effect under the system-GMM.

[9] As we discuss in Sect. 4.5.3 we also reproduce our results but using the market model to estimate firm idiosyncratic and total risks.

The effect of MSC on risk-taking (i.e., idiosyncratic risk and total risk) is economically meaningful. For example, model (1b) indicates that increasing MSC from the 25th percentile to 75th percentile is associated with an 0.065 (2.61 × −0.025) reduction in idiosyncratic risk, where 2.610 represents the interquartile range of MSC as reported in Table 4.1 (6.561 − 3.951 = 2.610), and −0.025 is the coefficient estimate in model (1b). The reported coefficient in model (1b) further implies that a firm with an MSC value in the 75th percentile is associated with 1.66 times [(−0.025 × 6.561)/(−0.025 × 3.951)] lower idiosyncratic risk than firms in the 25th percentile of the distribution. Stated differently, an increase in MSC by one unit (using a standard deviation of 2.276 from Table 4.1) would result in decreasing idiosyncratic risk by 1.65% (ln2.276 × 0.025/ln0.289 = −0.0165, where 0.289 is the mean value of idiosyncratic risk estimated using the market model).

Regarding financial control variables, ROA has a highly significant and negative effect on risk-taking in all cases. This suggests that more profitable firms have lower firm-specific and total risks (Pástor and Pietro 2003; Cheng 2008; Mathew et al. 2016). We also find some tentative evidence that larger firms (FSIZE) have higher total risk (models 2a and 2b). The positive and significant coefficients for TURN in models 1a and 1b infer that higher asset turnover is associated with higher firm-specific risk. Previous literature provides very limited evidence regarding the effect of asset turnover on firm risk-taking. The positive relationship we find might reflect the fact that more active firms which utilize their assets effectively are exposed to higher firm-specific risk compared to less active firms, although this does not impact total risk (Pae et al. 2018). Consistent with prior studies, we also find that leverage (DEBTR) is positively associated with both idiosyncratic and total risks (Adams et al. 2005; Akbar et al. 2017). Moreover, more mature firms, based on firm age (FAGE), have lower idiosyncratic and total risks (Cao et al. 2006; Akbar et al. 2017).

In terms of governance variables, board size (BSIZE) has a negative and significant effect on both idiosyncratic and total risks—especially so in the case of total risk. This infers that larger UK boards are more effective in mitigating firm and managerial risk-taking (e.g., Cheng 2008; Pathan 2009; Mathew et al. 2016). Consistent with our earlier conjecture that boards with a higher percentage of NED should be better monitors of managerial risk-taking, we observe a significant and negative association between the proportion of non-executive directors and both firm-specific and total risks (Pathan 2009; Mathew et al. 2016; Akbar et al. 2017).

Finally, we report test statistics that highlight the validity of the system-GMM estimator at the bottom of Table 4.2 (and subsequent tables). Wintoki et al. (2012) argue that while it is expected that the first differences AR(1) exhibit serial correlation, this should not be the case in the second difference AR(2). The results suggest that we have no serial correlation in the second difference.[10] Additionally, the Hansen test of over-identification indicates that the instruments used are valid.

4.4.3 *Corporate Social Responsibility and Firm Risk*

In this section, we reexamine the relations between social capital and firm risk, using CSR as alternative social capital measure that captures a firm's CSR performance, and one more closely aligned with a CSC perspective (Sacconi and Antoni 2009). We reestimate our models by employing the CSR indicator measure as our dependent variable (Lins et al. 2017). We collect this CSR variable for our sample firms from the Thomson Reuters ESG database, which provides a composite equally weighted indicator of a firm's CSR performance.[11] Such data have emerged as a key measure of CSR in corporate finance literature (Cheung 2016; Duque-Grisales and Aguilera-Caracuel 2019).

The results, shown in columns 1a and 1b of Table 4.3, illustrate that the relationship between CSR and both idiosyncratic risk (columns 1) and total risk (column 2) is significant and positive (in contrast to the negative relationship between MSC and firm risk). Such collective behavior can be explained under the cushioning hypothesis, which predicts more risk-taking in collectivistic countries and is reflective of CSR being more closely aligned with a CSC perspective of social capital than an SSC definition (Sacconi and Antoni 2011). The intuition behind this prediction is that managerial decision-makers working in these environments, which are characterized by relatively high "social solidarity," may be more receptive to risk-taking compared to managers working in countries characterized by weak social solidarity (Schneider et al. 2017). We consider that this positive effect of the CSC indicator (i.e., CSR), which is different from the negative effect we documented earlier for our main social capital measures, is interesting and that future research should pay attention to both SSC and CSC dimensions.

[10] For brevity, we only report the AR(2).

[11] For a detailed overview of this variable, we kindly refer the reader to https://www.esade.edu/itemsweb/biblioteca/bbdd/inbbdd/archivos/Thomson_Reuters_ESG_Scores.pdf

Table 4.2 The relationship between MSC and firm risk

	Idiosyncratic risk (IDO-CAPM)		*Total risk (TRISK)*	
	Model (1a)	*Model (1b)*	*Model (2a)*	*Model (2b)*
MSC	-0.0263***	-0.0250***	-0.0325***	-0.0319***
	(-2.639)	(-2.673)	(-2.709)	(-2.680)
ROA	-0.555***	-0.500**	-0.509**	-0.435**
	(-2.871)	(-2.581)	(-2.432)	(-2.066)
FSIZE	0.0226	0.0207	0.0308*	0.0269*
	(1.411)	(1.356)	(1.86)	(1.781)
TURN	0.0703**	0.0713**	0.0472	0.0515
	(2.3)	(2.035)	(1.486)	(1.548)
DEBTR	0.449**	0.440**	0.435**	0.431**
	(2.518)	(2.496)	(2.135)	(2.083)
DIVTOASS	-0.302	-0.596	-0.0308	-0.0509
	(-0.330)	(-0.705)	(-0.0326)	(-0.0551)
FAGE	-0.0170**	-0.0114*	-0.0178*	-0.0135
	(-2.317)	(-1.665)	(-1.819)	(-1.488)
Q	-0.00271	0.00587	0.0186	0.0295
	(-0.0968)	-0.216	-0.419	-0.704
BSIZE	-0.237*	-0.252**	-0.374***	-0.367***
	(-1.950)	(-2.251)	(-3.202)	(-3.126)
ASIZE	0.0387	0.0444	0.0231	0.0281
	(1.071)	(1.217)	(0.624)	(0.74)
NED	-0.233**	-0.230**	-0.382***	-0.361***
	(-2.120)	(-2.377)	(-2.969)	(-2.948)
GEN	0.00391	0.00574	0.0501	0.0359
	(0.0505)	(0.0756)	(0.573)	(0.41)
$Risk_{(t-1)}$	0.470***	0.476***	0.456***	0.460***
	(7.326)	(7.711)	(6.937)	(7.033)
$Risk_{(t-2)}$	-0.0926**	-0.0937**	-0.0669*	-0.0649*
	(-2.296)	(-2.286)	(-1.887)	(-1.849)
Constant	0.459	0.529	0.747**	0.844**
	(1.327)	(1.533)	(2.059)	(2.274)
Observations	2512	2511	2513	2513
No. of firms	322	322	322	322
F-statistic	32.18***	28.04***	41.07***	31.32***
AR(2)	0.413	0.417	0.336	0.333
Hansen test (*p*-value)	0.432	0.352	0.648	0.628
Industry FE	NA	Yes	NA	Yes
Year FE	Yes	Yes	Yes	Yes

This table presents the results of multivariate analyses using the dynamic panel generalized method of moments estimator. The dependent variables are idiosyncratic risk or total risk estimated using the CAPM model. The reported *p*-values are enclosed in parentheses, while the *t*-statistics are based on robust standard errors. The symbols ***, **, and * signify significance levels of 1%, 5%, and 10%, respectively. AR(2) represents the tests for second-order serial correlation in the first-differenced residuals, under the null of no serial correlation. Hansen's test of over-identification is under the null that all instruments are valid. Risk(t–1) and Risk(t–2) are the first and second lags of the dependent variable, respectively. Further details on variable definitions and measurements can be found in Appendix A1.

Table 4.3 Corporate social responsibility and firm risk

	Idiosyncratic risk (IDO-CAPM): CSR	*Total risk (TRISK-CAPM): CSR*	*Idiosyncratic risk (IDO-CAPM): CSR and MSC*	*Total risk (TRISK-CAPM): CSR and MSC*
	Model (1a)	*Model (1b)*	*Model (2a)*	*Model (2b)*
			−0.00839*	−0.00783*
			(−1.845)	(−1.783)
CSR	0.0337**	0.0341**	0.0432**	0.0385**
	(2.145)	(2.038)	(2.428)	(2.222)
ROA	−0.521***	−0.478***	−0.518***	−0.483***
	(−3.286)	(−3.111)	(−3.289)	(−3.364)
FSIZE	−0.0132***	−0.0103***	−0.0134**	−0.0118**
	(−2.859)	(−2.597)	(−2.439)	(−2.311)
TURN	0.0247**	0.0234**	0.0215*	0.0203*
	(2.062)	(2.210)	(1.930)	(1.822)
DEBTR	0.105**	0.0825	−0.00727	−0.0405
	(2.118)	(1.424)	(−0.0942)	(−0.564)
DIVTOASS	0.164	0.165	−0.0838	−0.118
	(0.503)	(0.441)	(−0.303)	(−0.414)
FAGE	−0.00291	−0.00120	−0.00150	0.000596
	(−0.663)	(−0.275)	(−0.237)	(0.103)
Q	−0.00997	−0.0119	−0.00197	−0.000248
	(−0.820)	(−0.901)	(−0.207)	(−0.0274)
BSIZE	0.0151	0.0192	0.000168	0.0152
	(0.373)	(0.440)	(0.00415)	(0.347)
ASIZE	−0.00694	−0.00519	0.0456	0.0519
	(−0.301)	(−0.236)	(1.463)	(1.431)
NED	0.0148	0.0124	0.0368	0.0500
	(0.394)	(0.340)	(0.597)	(0.852)
GEN	0.116*	0.131**	0.0977	0.0648
	(1.674)	(1.981)	(1.193)	(0.773)
Risk $_{(t-1)}$	0.590***	0.610***	0.0432**	0.0385**
	(9.015)	(8.543)	(2.428)	(2.222)
Risk $_{(t-2)}$	−0.000323	0.00286	−0.00839*	−0.00783*
	(−0.00620)	(0.0528)	(−1.845)	(−1.783)
Constant	0.345***	0.332**	0.126	0.0301
	(2.994)	(2.567)	(0.631)	(0.158)
Observations	1,334	1,334	1,334	1,334
Number of firms	313	313	313	313
F-statistic	36.39***	43.06***	28.76***	35.23***
AR(2)	0.674	0.248	0.747	0.282
Hansen (*p*-value)	0.618	0.502	0.69	0.619
Industry FE	Yes	Yes	Yes	Yes
Year FE	Yes	Yes	Yes	Yes

This table presents the results of multivariate analyses using the dynamic panel generalized method of moments estimator. The dependent variables are idiosyncratic risk or total risk estimated using the CAPM model. We proxy for cognitive social capital (CSC) using CSR. Models 1a and 1b use CSR as an alternative proxy for social capital, while columns 2a and 2b include MSC while controlling for CSR, to explore the possibility that CSR and MSC capture different dimensions of social capital. The reported *p*-values are enclosed in parentheses, while the *t*-statistics are based on robust standard errors. The symbols ***, **, and * signify significance levels of 1%, 5%, and 10%, respectively. AR(2) represents the tests for second-order serial correlation in the first-differenced residuals, under the null of no serial correlation. Hansen's test of over-identification is under the null that all instruments are valid. Risk(t−1) and Risk(t−2) are the first and second lags of the dependent variable, respectively. Further details on variable definitions and measurements can be found in Appendix A1.

4.4.4 *Managerial Social Capital and Firm Risk-taking: Controlling for Corporate Social Responsibility*

Here we extend the previous analyses (in columns 1a and 1b of Table 4.3) that looked at the effect of firm CSR on risk, by re-examining the relationship between MSC and firm risk, while controlling for CSR. Although CSR can be thought of as an alternative social capital measure (Lins et al. 2017), it arguably reflects different aspects of social capital and is more consistent with a CSC perspective than an SSC one (in contrast to MSC). It can be argued that managers and directors with high levels of *both* structural and cognitive social capitals are "resource-rich" and can provide valuable access to resources for firms as well as play important roles in monitoring managerial effort and behavior, in addition to the advice and counsel they provide. Yet the impact on risk-taking according to both perspectives may differ. Such a view is also supported under RDT (Pfeffer and Salancik 1978).

Given this, in Table 4.3 columns 2a and 2b we consider the effects of both MSC while controlling for CSR, which is a social capital proxy more closely aligned with a CSC perspective (Sacconi and Antoni 2010). We continue to find that MSC has a significant negative effect on risk-taking decisions. Moreover, the effect of CSR on firm-risk measures continues to be positive. These results confirm the importance of our MSC construct as a social capital measure that more closely captures structural social capital, while also providing interesting evidence that CSR represents a different dimension of social capital, and one more consistent with a cognitive definition. Taken together, we consider that these results suggest that future researchers should account for both dimensions.

4.5 Robustness Checks

In unreported tests, which are all available upon request, we conduct a battery of robustness checks to probe the reliability of our main findings.

4.5.1 *Controlling for a Firm's Risk Management Committee*

A relevant concern is that the impact of MSC on firm risk may be attenuated by the presence of a firm risk committee. For example, it could be argued that because the risk committee is responsible for setting and implementing and observing firm risk management policies, this could enhance monitoring—especially as this committee is independent of the BoD. Motivated by these concerns, we repeat our analyses but with the inclusion of RSKCOM. a dummy variable equal to one if a firm has a risk committee or zero otherwise (Akbar et al. 2017).

The results indicate that the effects of MSC and ADJ-MSC are similar. We continue to find significant and negative coefficients for both measures, implying that social capital helps in reducing firms' idiosyncratic and total risks. Our main results are therefore robust to controlling for the potential effect of the risk management committee.

4.5.2 *Industry-adjusted Managerial Social Capital*

In additional analyses, we depart from prior work by considering an industry-adjusted measure of MSC (ADJ-MSC) to further account for a differential impact of MSC based on industry context. Industry "norms" are understood to often influence the strategic decisions of firms. In considering an industry-adjusted measure, we help mitigate the possibility that our main findings are driven by specific industries, although our main results do account for industry and year fixed effects.

In Appendix A2, we show how our sample firms are distributed according to industry and over time. The highest representation of firms is from the financial sector, followed by the industrial sector, which equates to 37.66% and 23.40% of the total sample, respectively. This lends support to our inclusion of financial firms in social capital studies (Mizruchi 1996; Engelberg et al. 2012; Javakhadze et al. 2016).

To implement our empirical tests, we repeat the analyses from Table 4.2 but instead use the industry-adjusted MSC measure (ADJ-MSC) as our main variable of interest. Despite our conjecture that the results for industry-adjusted MSC may differ, we do not find any evidence to substantiate it. Contrarily and consistent with our baseline results, we find that the effect of industry-adjusted social capital on the firm's risk-taking decision is also negative and statistically significant. Noteworthy, however, is the size of parameter estimates being slightly smaller, which suggests that industry differences matter.

4.5.3 Controlling for Corporate Board Nationality Mix

The UK corporate sector is characterized by the diversity of the BoD nationality mix. For instance, the 2021 UK Spencer Stuart Board Index shows that foreign directors (those who have a citizenship that differs from that of the firm) account for 34% of all board members, and on average, four members of the board are from different nationalities, where 81% of boards have a minimum one foreign member.[12]

While general board diversity has been associated with increased diffusion of knowledge and information transfer between senior managers and board members, similarly, BoD nationality diversity has been put forward as an important factor influencing firm performance (Estélyi and Nisar 2016). BoD nationality diversity has been associated with changes in firm outcomes, such as earnings management (Du et al. 2017) and both increases (Estélyi and Nisar 2016) and decreases in firm performance (García-Meca et al. 2015; Estélyi and Nisar 2016). For example, García-Meca et al. (2015) show that foreign board members participate actively in the board meetings of UK firms and that there is a positive relationship between UK board nationality diversity and firm operating performance. Conversely, Estélyi and Nisar (2016) find the opposite using the same UK setting.

Accordingly, here, we control for the nationality mix of the BoD as one important aspect of board diversity that may influence relations between social capital dimensions and firm risk-taking, although the direction of the effect is unclear. The BoD nationality mix measure we employ is constructed as follows: First, we extract the nationality mix variable from the BoardEx data and then standardize it using board size (i.e., the total number of directors on the board). Next, we create a dummy variable (NATMIX) that takes a value of 1 if the nationality mix variable is greater than the mean value and zero otherwise. In our sample, the mean value of the nationality mix in the BoD is about 38%.[13]

[12] For more details and information, we refer the interested reader to https://www.spencerstuart.com/research-and-insight/uk-board-index/diversity.

[13] Note: this is the mean of the national mix variable for the study sample; however, the standardized form of the variable is about 71% (from Table 4.1 the NATMIX mean is 0.709).

The results demonstrate that the nationality mix measure (NATMIX) has a significant and positive effect on firm idiosyncratic and total risk. This positive association seems consistent with findings by Guney et al. (2020) that, according to the RDT, firms with more foreign directors can benefit from a wide number of opportunities. These include receiving more investments from foreign investors, exposure to diversified skills, and easier expansion into foreign markets.

We further consider whether BoD nationality mix can moderate the effect of social capital on risk-taking by including interactions between social capital (MSC and CSR) with the BoD nationality mix. The results reveal that the negative relationship between MSC and risk-taking intensifies when we include the interaction term (MSC*NATMIX). Similarly, results for the interaction between CSR and BoD nationality mix (MSC*NATMIX) indicate that BoD nationality mix intensifies the positive effect of CSR on firm risk. The overall results infer that while the main results for MSC and CSR on firm risk do not change in significance or sign, BoD nationality mix can intensify their effect.

4.5.4 *Alternative Ways of Calculating Firm Risk*

We also run several tests of robustness in which we calculate firm risk using Fama–French three (FF3) and four (FF4) factor models and rerun our main regressions. The results remain very similar to the main results based on the market model and CAPM. Therefore, we conclude that our estimation of the effect of social capital on firm risk is not driven by the choice of methodology to estimate risk.

As a final test of robustness, we rerun the baseline regressions as well as all the robustness tests in this section but estimating idiosyncratic and total risk using the market model as an alternative to the CAPM. We find our results continue to hold and are very similar in both magnitude and statistical significance levels.

4.6 Conclusion

Social capital plays important roles throughout society including within the corporate environment. Understanding how the social capital of managers can influence corporate risk-taking is important in order to better understand the factors that can result in heterogeneity in firms' risk-taking. In this study, we contribute new evidence on the relationship between

MSC and corporate risk-taking in the context of UK firms using a rich sample of FTSE 350 index firms over the period 2006–2017.

Our main analyses explore how MSC impacts firms' idiosyncratic and total risks. We employ the system-GMM estimator to help mitigate endogeneity concerns regarding a potentially endogenous relationship between social capital and firm risk. We find consistently that MSC is negatively associated with both idiosyncratic and total risk measures and demonstrate that this effect is economically meaningful. While MSC closely embodies a structural social capital definition, we also expand the analyses to consider firms' CSR as an alternative measure of firm social capital, and one more aligned with the cognitive social capital dimension. We find, interestingly, that CSR is associated with an increase in both measures of firm risk. We consider that this result can be explained according to the cushioning hypothesis, which predicts more risk-taking in collectivistic countries such as the UK and is also reflective of CSR being more closely aligned with a CSC perspective of social capital than the SSC definition (Sacconi and Antoni 2010).

Finally, our study is not without its limitations. First, although we explore the effect of social capital on corporate risk-taking by considering several risk measures and social capital indicators, other variables such as ownership structure, ethnicity, and political connections may also play a role. Future research could build on our work and explore these dimensions, in addition to, as noted earlier, delving further into the origins of social ties. Finally, it would be interesting to explore the role of MSC during times of crisis, such as during the COVID-19 pandemic, as extant interdisciplinary research suggests that boards and directors should matter most during crisis periods.

Appendices

Appendix A1: Variable Descriptions and Data Sources

Variable	*Name*	*Source*	*Variable description*
Idiosyncratic risk	IDO-MKT	Authors' calculation	Idiosyncratic risk volatility estimated based on the market model.
Idiosyncratic risk	IDO-CAPM	Authors' calculation	Idiosyncratic risk volatility estimated based on the capital asset pricing model.
Total risk	TRISK	Authors' calculation	Standard deviation of the daily stock returns (annualized).

(Continued)

Appendix A1 (Continued)

Variable	*Name*	*Source*	*Variable description*
Managerial social capital	MSC	Authors' calculation based on BoardEx data	Natural logarithm of a firm's aggregate social connections for each executive and non-executive corporate board member from current employment, previous employment, education, and social activity. This is computed using NodeXL software. The measure is based on the aggregate sum of the following dimensions (Javakhadze et al. 2016): *Current employment (CE)*: Two individuals are socially connected if they work in the same company and set together either on the BOD's or on the top management group, and this includes the traditional interlocking where two firms may have a common director and connections where individuals from two firms setting together in a third firm; *Previous employment (PE)*: Two individuals are socially connected if they work concurrently with each other in the past in the same firm either on the BOD's or in the top management group; *Education (ED)*: Two individuals are socially connected if they attend the same school and graduated within 1 year of each other; *Other activities (OA)*: Two individuals are socially connected if they have a membership in clubs, organizations, or charities for at least 1 year.
Adjusted managerial social capital	ADJ-MSC	Authors' calculation	The MSC adjusted to industry excluding the focal firm
Return on assets	ROA	DataStream	The ratio of net income to total assets *(winsorized)*.
Firm size	FSIZE	DataStream	Natural logarithm (total assets) *(winsorized)*.
Turnover ratio	TURN	DataStream	Asset turnover is measured as ratio of annual sales to total assets *(winsorized)*.
Debt ratio	DEBTR	DataStream	Short-term debt and long-term debt divided by book value of total assets *(winsorized)*.
Dividends to assets	DIVTOASS	DataStream	Total dividends (common and preferred) to total assets *(winsorized)*.

Variable	*Name*	*Source*	*Variable description*
Tobin's Q ratio	Q	DataStream	Tobin's Q measured as the number of shares outstanding times stock price plus total liabilities divided by total assets *(winsorized)*.
Firm age	FAGE	DataStream/ gov.uk	Number of years since incorporation of the firm *(winsorized)*.
Board size	BSIZE	BoardEx	Total number of directors sitting on the board *(winsoried)*.
Board independence	NED	BoardEx	The ratio of the number of independent directors to the number of all directors *(winsorized)*.
Audit committee size	ASIZE	BoardEx	Total number of directors sitting on the audit committee *(winsorized)*.
Female director	GEN	BoardEx	The ratio of number of female directors to the total number of directors *(winsorized)*.
Nationality mix	NATMIX	BoardEx	The nationality mix variable from BoardEx divided by the board size; then a dummy variable has been created that equals one if NATMIX > mean and zero otherwise.
Industry dummy	SIC	DataStream	A dummy for each micro-sector
Year dummy	YEAR		A dummy variable for each year based on the Industry Classification Benchmark (ICB) (FTSE Factsheet 2018)
Unsystematic risk	IDO-FF3	Authors' calculation based on DataStream	Idiosyncratic risk volatility estimated based on Fama–French three-factor model.
Unsystematic risk	IDO-FF4	Authors' calculation	Idiosyncratic risk volatility estimated based on Fama–French four-factor model.
Corporate social responsibility	CSR	DataStream	Composite corporate social responsibility score
Risk committee	RSKCOM	BoardEx	Firm risk committee represented by a dummy that equals one if the firm has a risk committee, zero otherwise

The table details the variable names, calculations, and sources of all variables.

Appendix A2: Distribution of Sample Firms by Industry and Year

Industry	*Code*	*2006*	*2007*	*2008*	*2009*	*2010*	*2011*	*2012*	*2013*	*2014*	*2015*	*2016*	*2017*	*Frequency*	*Percentage*
Oil and Gas	1	8	8	8	8	8	8	8	8	9	9	9	9	100	2.31%
Basic materials	1000	13	13	13	13	13	13	13	13	13	13	13	13	156	3.61%
Industrials	2000	84	84	84	84	84	84	84	84	85	85	85	85	1012	23.40%
Consumer goods	3000	28	28	28	28	28	28	28	28	28	28	28	28	336	7.77%
Healthcare	4000	11	11	11	11	11	11	11	11	11	11	11	11	132	3.05%
Consumer services	5000	54	54	54	54	54	54	54	54	54	54	54	54	648	14.98%
Telecommunications	6000	4	4	4	4	4	4	4	4	4	4	4	4	48	1.11%
Utilities	7000	5	5	5	5	5	5	5	5	5	5	5	5	60	1.39%
Financials	8000	134	135	136	136	136	136	136	136	136	136	136	136	1629	37.66%
Technology	9000	17	17	17	17	17	17	17	17	17	17	17	17	204	4.72%
Total		358	359	360	360	360	360	360	360	362	362	362	362	4325	100.00%

The table shows the distribution of FTSE350 (sample) firms by industry and over time. Industry names and codes are as reported according to the Industry Classification Benchmark (ICB) (FTSE Factsheet 2018).

Appendix A3: The Evolution of Managerial Social Capital and Risk Over Time

		2006	*2007*	*2008*	*2009*	*2010*	*2011*	*2012*	*2013*	*2014*	*2015*	*2016*	*2017*
MSC	Mean	5.822	5.634	5.674	5.628	5.593	5.506	5.397	5.148	4.930	4.511	3.882	2.787
	Diff	–	−0.188	0.040	−0.046	−0.035	−0.087	−0.109	−0.249	−0.218	−0.419	−0.629	−1.095
	% diff		−0.032	0.007	−0.008	−0.006	−0.016	−0.020	−0.046	−0.042	−0.085	−0.139	−0.282
	St. Dev.	1.785	1.757	1.744	1.841	1.907	2.024	2.128	2.282	2.336	2.366	2.438	2.445
ADJ-MSC	Mean	1.209	1.020	1.059	1.013	0.978	0.891	0.782	0.533	0.312	−0.108	−0.737	−1.831
	Diff	–	−0.189	0.039	−0.046	−0.035	−0.087	−0.109	−0.249	−0.221	−0.420	−0.629	−1.094
	% diff		−0.156	0.038	−0.043	−0.035	−0.089	−0.122	−0.318	−0.415	−1.346	5.824	1.484
	St. Dev.	2.045	2.034	2.028	2.110	2.171	2.278	2.318	2.475	2.529	2.547	2.609	2.606
IDO-MKT	Mean	0.234	0.263	0.471	0.422	0.267	0.285	0.261	0.232	0.234	0.246	0.298	0.239
	Diff	–	0.029	0.208	−0.049	−0.155	0.018	−0.024	−0.029	0.002	0.012	0.052	−0.059
	% diff		0.124	0.791	−0.104	−0.367	0.067	−0.084	−0.111	0.009	0.051	0.211	−0.198
	St. Dev.	0.090	0.125	0.207	0.216	0.130	0.171	0.200	0.107	0.112	0.145	0.167	0.181
IDO-CAPM	Mean	0.234	0.263	0.471	0.422	0.267	0.285	0.261	0.232	0.234	0.246	0.298	0.239
	Diff	–	0.029	0.208	−0.049	−0.155	0.018	−0.024	−0.029	0.002	0.012	0.052	−0.059
	% diff		0.124	0.791	−0.104	−0.367	0.067	−0.084	−0.111	0.009	0.051	0.211	−0.198
	St. Dev.	0.090	0.125	0.207	0.216	0.130	0.171	0.200	0.107	0.112	0.145	0.167	0.181
IDO-FF3	Mean	0.226	0.256	0.451	0.407	0.261	0.278	0.255	0.227	0.227	0.240	0.278	0.233
	Diff	–	0.030	0.195	−0.044	−0.146	0.017	−0.023	−0.028	0.000	0.013	0.038	−0.045
	% diff		0.133	0.762	−0.098	−0.359	0.065	−0.083	−0.110	0.000	0.057	0.158	−0.162
	St. Dev.	0.090	0.124	0.198	0.207	0.129	0.169	0.200	0.107	0.111	0.144	0.165	0.179

(Continued)

Appendix A3 (Continued)

		2006	*2007*	*2008*	*2009*	*2010*	*2011*	*2012*	*2013*	*2014*	*2015*	*2016*	*2017*
IDO-FF4	Mean	0.225	0.255	0.450	0.405	0.261	0.277	0.254	0.226	0.226	0.239	0.278	0.233
	Diff	–	0.030	0.195	–0.045	–0.144	0.016	–0.023	–0.028	0.000	0.013	0.039	–0.045
	% diff		0.133	0.765	–0.100	–0.356	0.061	–0.083	–0.110	0.000	0.058	0.163	–0.162
	St. Dev.	0.090	0.090	0.123	0.198	0.207	0.128	0.168	0.200	0.107	0.111	0.144	0.164
TRISK	Mean	0.263	0.307	0.546	0.466	0.306	0.339	0.289	0.254	0.254	0.278	0.336	0.247
	Diff	–	0.044	0.239	–0.080	–0.160	0.033	–0.050	–0.035	0.000	0.024	0.058	–0.089
	% diff	–	0.167	0.779	–0.147	–0.343	0.108	–0.147	–0.121	0.000	0.094	0.209	–0.265
	St. Dev.	0.086	0.121	0.205	0.222	0.123	0.163	0.196	0.100	0.105	0.138	0.164	0.178

This table presents descriptive statistics for social capital and firm risk measures over time. It reports the mean, mean difference, percentage (%) difference, and standard deviation for MSC, ADJ-MSC, IDO-MKT, IDO-CAPM, IDO-FF3, IDO-FF4, and TRISK variables over the sample period. Variable definitions and measurements are as given in Appendix A1.

References

Abdallah, W., Goergen, M., & O'Sullivan, N. (2015). Endogeneity: How failure to correct for it can cause wrong inferences and some remedies. *British Journal of Management, 26*, 791–804.

Abdelbadie, R. A., & Salama, A. (2019). Corporate governance and financial stability in US banks: Do indirect interlocks matter? *Journal of Business Research, 104*, 85–105.

Adams, R., & Ferreira, D. (2003). *Diversity and incentives: Evidence from corporate boards.* Unpublished working paper, University of Stockholm.

Adams, R. B., Almeida, H., & Ferreira, D. (2005). Powerful CEOs and their impact on corporate performance. *Review of Financial Studies, 18*, 1403–1432.

Adams, R. B., & Ferreira, D. (2007). A theory of friendly boards. *Journal of Finance, 62*, 217–250.

Adams, R. B., Hermalin, B. E., & Weisbach, M. S. (2010). The role of boards of directors in corporate governance: A conceptual framework and survey. *Journal of Economic Literature*, 48, 58–107.

Akbar, S., Kharabsheh, B., Poletti-Hughes, J., & Shah, S. Z. A. (2017). Board structure and corporate risk taking in the UK financial sector. *International Review of Financial Analysis, 50*, 101–110.

Albuquerque, R., Koskinen, Y., & Zhang, C. (2019). Corporate social responsibility and firm risk: Theory and empirical evidence. *Management Science, 65*(10), 4451–4469.

Amin, A., Chourou, L., Kamal, S., Malik, M., & Zhao, Y. (2020). It's who you know that counts: Board connectedness and CSR performance. *Journal of Corporate Finance, 64*, 101662.

Andriosopoulos, D., & Deepty, S. T. (2022). Can social capital and reputation mitigate political and market competition risk? *European Journal of Finance*, 1–38.

Arellano, M., & Bond, S. (1991). Some tests of specification for panel data: Monte Carlo evidence and an application to employment equations. *Review of Economic Studies*, 58, 277–297.

Basuil, D. A., & Datta, D. K. (2017). Value creation in cross-border acquisitions: The role of outside directors' human and social capital. *Journal of Business Research, 80*, 35–44.

Berger, A. N., Kick, T., Koetter, M., & Schaeck, K. (2013). Does it pay to have friends? Social ties and executive appointments in banking. *Journal of Banking & Finance*, 37, 2087–2105.

Berger, A. N., Kick, T., & Schaeck, K. (2014). Executive board composition and bank risk taking. *Journal of Corporate Finance, 28*, 48–65.

Bhandari, A., & Bhuyan, M. N. H. (2023). Social capital and capital allocation efficiency. *Journal of Business Finance & Accounting, 50*, 1439–1466.

Bloch, F., Genicot, G., & Ray, D. (2008). Informal insurance in social networks. *Journal of Economic Theory, 143*, 36–58.

Bourdieu, P. (1986a). Distinction: A social critique of the judgment of taste (2de2). *Distinction: A Social Critique of the Judgment of Taste*, 169–193.

Bourdieu, P. (1986b). The forms of capital. In J. G. Richardson (ed.), *Handbook of Theory and Research for the Sociology of Education* (pp. 241–258). Greenwood Press.

Bourdieu, P. (1989). Social space and symbolic power. *Sociological Theory, 7*, 14–25.

Bourdieu, P., & Wacquant, L. J. (1992). *An invitation to reflexive sociology*. University of Chicago Press.

Brass, D. J., & Burkhardt, M. E. (1993). Potential power and power use: An investigation of structure and behavior. *Academy of Management Journal, 36*, 441–470.

Burt, R. (1992). *Structural holes: The social structure of competition*. Harvard University Press.

Cao, C., Simin, T., & Zhao, J. (2006). Can growth options explain the trend in idiosyncratic risk ? *Review of Financial Studies, 21*, 2599–2633.

Carhart, M. M. (1997). On persistence in mutual fund performance. *The Journal of Finance, 52*(1), 57–82.

Chakraborty, A., Gao, L. S., & Sheikh, S. (2019). Managerial risk taking incentives, corporate social responsibility and firm risk. *Journal of Economics and Business, 101*, 58–72.

Cheng, C. A., Wang, J., Zhang, N., & Zhao, S. (2017). Bowling alone, bowling together: Is social capital priced in bank loans? *Journal of Accounting, Auditing & Finance, 32*, 449–479.

Cheng, S. (2008). Board size and the variability of corporate performance. *Journal of Financial Economics, 87*, 157–176.

Cheung, A. (2016). Corporate social responsibility and corporate cash holdings. *Journal of Corporate Finance, 37*, 412–430.

Chung, S. G., Lee, J., & Park, S. H. (2023). Does social capital mitigate managerial self-dealing? Evidence from insider trading. *Journal of Accounting, Auditing & Finance*, 0, 0148558X231167202.

Coleman, J. S. (1988). Social capital in the creation of human capital. *American Journal of Sociology, 94*, S95–S120.

Dasgupta, P. (2005). Economics of social capital. *Economic Record, 81*, S2–S21.

Degli Antoni, G., & Sacconi, L. (2011). *Modeling cognitive social capital and corporate social responsibility as preconditions for sustainable networks of relations. Social capital, corporate social responsibility, economic behaviour and performance*. Springer.

Diamond, D. W. (1989). Reputation acquisition in debt markets. *Journal of Political Economy, 97*, 828–862.

Du, X., Jian, W., & Lai, S. (2017). Do foreign directors mitigate earnings management? Evidence from China. *International Journal of Accounting, 52*, 142–177.

Dunbar, C., Li, F., & Shi, Y. (2020). CEO risk-taking incentives and corporate social responsibility. *Journal of Corporate Finance*, 101714.

Duque-Grisales, E., & Aguilera-Caracuel, J. (2019). Environmental, social and governance (ESG) scores and financial performance of multilatinas: Moderating effects of geographic international diversification and financial slack. *Journal of Business Ethics*, 1–20.

El Ghoul, S., Guedhami, O., Kwok, C. C. Y., & Mishra, D. R. (2011). Does corporate social responsibility affect the cost of capital? *Journal of Banking & Finance*, *35*, 2388–2406.

El-Khatib, R., Fogel, K., & Jandik, T. (2015). CEO network centrality and merger performance. *Journal of Financial Economics*, *116*, 349–382.

Elsayed, M., Elshandidy, T., & Ahmed, Y. (2022). Corporate failure in the UK: An examination of corporate governance reforms. *International Review of Financial Analysis*, *82*, 102165.

Endrikat, J., De Villiers, C., Guenther, T. W., & Guenther, E. M. (2021). Board characteristics and corporate social responsibility: A meta-analytic investigation. *Business & Society*, *60*(8), 2099–2135.

Engelberg, J., Gao, P., & Parsons, C. A. (2012). Friends with money. *Journal of Financial Economics*, *103*, 169–188.

Erkens, D. H., Hung, M., & Matos, P. (2012). Corporate governance in the 2007–2008 financial crisis: Evidence from financial institutions worldwide. *Journal of Corporate Finance*, *18*, 389–411.

Estélyi, K. S., & Nisar, T. M. (2016). Diverse boards: Why do firms get foreign nationals on their boards? *Journal of Corporate Finance*, *39*, 174–192.

Fama, E. F. (1980). Agency problems and the theory of the firm. *Journal of Political Economy*, *88*, 288–307.

Fama, E. F., & French, K. R. (1993). Common risk factors in the returns on stocks and bonds. *Journal of Financial Economics*, *33*(1), 3–56.

Fama, E. F., & French, K. R. (2016). Dissecting anomalies with a five-factor model. *Review of Financial Studies*, *29*, 69–103.

Fama, E. F., & Jensen, M. C. (1983). Separation of ownership and control. *Journal of Law and Economics*, *26*, 301–325.

Ferris, S. P., Javakhadze, D., & Rajkovic, T. (2017a). CEO social capital, risk-taking and corporate policies. *Journal of Corporate Finance*, *47*, 46–71.

Ferris, S. P., Javakhadze, D., & Rajkovic, T. (2017b). The international effect of managerial social capital on the cost of equity. *Journal of Banking & Finance*, *74*, 69–84.

Ferris, S. P., Javakhadze, D., & Rajkovic, T. (2019). An international analysis of CEO social capital and corporate risk-taking. *European Financial Management*, *25*, 3–37.

Fich, E. M. (2005). Are some outside directors better than others? Evidence from director appointments by Fortune 1000 firms. *Journal of Business*, *78*, 1943–1972.

Filatotchev, I., Chahine, S., & Bruton, G. D. (2018). Board interlocks and initial public offering performance in the United States and the United Kingdom: An institutional perspective. *Journal of Management*, *44*, 1620–1650.

Fracassi, C. (2017). Corporate finance policies and social networks. *Management Science*, *63*, 2420–2438.

Fracassi, C., & Tate, G. (2012). External networking and internal firm governance. *Journal of Finance*, *67*, 153–194.

Freeman, L. C. (1979). Centrality in social networks conceptual clarification. *Social Networks*, *1*, 215–239.

Freeman, R. (1984). *Strategic management: A stakeholder approach* (Latest edition). Pitman.

Gao, Z., Li, L., & Lu, L. Y. (2021). Social capital and managers' use of corporate resources. *Journal of Business Ethics*, *168*, 593–613.

García-Feijóo, L., Hossain, M. M., & Javakhadze, D. (2021). Managerial social capital and dividend smoothing. *Journal of Corporate Finance*, *66*, 101811.

García-Meca, E., García-Sánchez, I. M., & Martínez-Ferrero, J. (2015). Board diversity and its effects on bank performance: An international analysis. *Journal of Banking & Finance*, *53*, 202–214.

García-Sánchez, I.-M., & Noguera-Gámez, L. (2017). Integrated information and the cost of capital. *International Business Review*, *26*, 959–975.

Godfrey, P. C. (2005). The relationship between corporate philanthropy and shareholder wealth: A risk management perspective. *Academy of Management Review*, *30*, 777–798.

Godfrey, P. C., Merrill, C. B., & Hansen, J. M. (2009). The relationship between corporate social responsibility and shareholder value: An empirical test of the risk management hypothesis. *Strategic Management Journal*, *30*, 425–445.

Goergen, M., Renneboog, L., & Zhao, Y. (2019). Insider trading and networked directors. *Journal of Corporate Finance*, *56*, 152–175.

Goyal, A., & Santa-Clara, P. (2003). Idiosyncratic risk matters! *Journal of Finance*, *58*, 975–1007.

Griffin, P. A., Hong, H. A., Liu, Y., & Ryou, J. W. (2021). The dark side of CEO social capital: Evidence from real earnings management and future operating performance. *Journal of Corporate Finance*, *68*, 101920.

Guney, Y., Karpuz, A., & Komba, G. (2020). The effects of board structure on corporate performance: Evidence from East African frontier markets. *Research in International Business and Finance*, *53*, 101222.

Gupta, A., Raman, K., & Shang, C. (2018). Social capital and the cost of equity. *Journal of Banking & Finance*, *87*, 102–117.

Harjoto, M. A., & Wang, Y. (2020). Board of directors network centrality and environmental, social and governance (ESG) performance. *Corporate Governance: The International Journal of Business in Society*, *20*, 965–985.

Hasan, I., He, Q., & Lu, H. (2020). The impact of social capital on economic attitudes and outcomes. *Journal of International Money and Finance, 108*, 102162.

Hasan, I., Hoi, C.-K., Wu, Q., & Zhang, H. (2017). Does social capital matter in corporate decisions? Evidence from corporate tax avoidance. *Journal of Accounting Research, 55*, 629–668.

Hasan, M. M., & Habib, A. (2020). Social capital and payout policies. *Journal of Contemporary Accounting & Economics, 16*, 100183.

Horton, J., Millo, Y., & Serafeim, G. (2012). Resources or power? Implications of social networks on compensation and firm performance. *Journal of Business Finance & Accounting, 39*, 399–426.

Hillman, A. J., & Dalziel, T. (2003). Boards of directors and firm performance: Integrating agency and resource dependence perspectives. *Academy of Management Review, 28*, 383–396.

Hillman, A. J., Withers, M. C., & Collins, B. J. (2009). Resource dependence theory: A review. *Journal of Management, 35*, 1404–1427.

Hirshleifer, D., & Thakor, A. V. (1992). Managerial conservatism, project choice, and debt. *The Review of Financial Studies, 5*, 437–470.

Hoi, C. K. S., Wu, Q., & Zhang, H. (2019). Does social capital mitigate agency problems? Evidence from Chief Executive Officer (CEO) compensation. *Journal of Financial Economics, 133*(2), 498–519.

Hossain, A. T., Hossain, T., & Kryzanowski, L. (2021). Social environment and corporate payouts. *European Journal of Finance, 27*, 1413–1437.

Huang, K., & Shang, C. (2019). Leverage, debt maturity, and social capital. *Journal of Corporate Finance, 54*, 26–46.

Javakhadze, D., Ferris, S. P., & French, D. W. (2016). Social capital, investments, and external financing. *Journal of Corporate Finance, 37*, 38–55.

Javakhadze, D., & Shelton, A. (2022). Executive social connections and gender pay gaps. *Journal of Corporate Finance, 73*, 102169.

Jensen, M. C., & Meckling, W. H. (1976). Theory of the firm: Managerial behavior, agency costs and ownership structure. *Journal of Financial Economics, 3*, 305–360.

Jha, A., & Cox, J. (2015). Corporate social responsibility and social capital. *Journal of Banking & Finance, 60*, 252–270.

Jin, L. (2002). CEO compensation, diversification, and incentives. *Journal of Financial Economics, 66*, 29–63.

Jiraporn, P., Jiraporn, N., Boeprasert, A., & Chang, K. (2014). Does corporate social responsibility (CSR) improve credit ratings? Evidence from geographic identification. *Financial Management, 43*, 505–531.

Jones, T. M. (1995). Instrumental stakeholder theory: A synthesis of ethics and economics. *Academy of Management Review, 20*, 404–437.

Kandori, M. (1992). Social norms and community enforcement. *Review of Economic Studies, 59*, 63–80.

Krishna, A., & Uphoff, N. (2002). Mapping and measuring social capital through assessment of collective action to conserve and develop watersheds in Rajasthan, India. In R. Puttnam (Author), C. Grootaert, & T. Van Bastelaer (eds.), *The role of social capital in development: An empirical assessment* (pp. 85–124). Cambridge University Press. doi:10.1017/CBO9780511492600.005

Larcker, D. F., So, E. C., & Wang, C. C. (2013). Boardroom centrality and firm performance. *Journal of Accounting and Economics, 55*, 225–250.

Lin, N. (1999). Social networks and status attainment. *Annual Review of Sociology, 25*, 467–487.

Lin, N. (2002). *Social capital: A theory of social structure and action*. Cambridge University Press.

Lins, K. V., Servaes, H., & Tamayo, A. (2017). Social capital, trust, and firm performance: The value of corporate social responsibility during the financial crisis. *Journal of Finance, 72*, 1785–1824.

Mathew, S., Ibrahim, S., & Archbold, S. (2016). Boards attributes that increase firm risk –evidence from the UK. *Corporate Governance, 16*, 233–258.

Meng, Y., & Yin, C. (2019). Trust and the cost of debt financing. *Journal of International Financial Markets, Institutions and Money, 59*, 58–73.

Mizruchi, M. S. (1996). What do interlocks do? An analysis, critique, and assessment of research on interlocking directorates. *Annual Review of. Sociology, 22*, 271–298.

Nahapiet, J., & Ghoshal, S. (1998). Social capital, intellectual capital, and the organizational advantage. *Academy of Management Review, 23*, 242–266.

Ortiz-Ospina, E., & Roser, M. (2016). *Trust*. Published online at OurWorldInData.org. Retrieved from: https://ourworldindata.org/trust [Online Resource].

Pae, Y., Bae, S. C., & Lee, N. (2018). Idiosyncratic volatility and cash flow volatility: New evidence from S&P 500. *International Review of Financial Analysis, 56*, 127–135.

Pasiouras, F., & Samet, A. (2022). Social capital and the cost of bank equity: Cross-country evidence. *Journal of Banking & Finance*, 141, 106535.

Pástor, Ľ., & Pietro, V. (2003). Stock valuation and learning about profitability. *Journal of Finance, 58*, 1749–1789.

Pathan, S. (2009). Strong boards, CEO power and bank risk-taking. *Journal of Banking & Finance, 33*, 1340–1350.

Perry, T., & Peyer, U. (2005). Board seat accumulation by executives: A shareholder's perspective. *Journal of Finance, 60*, 2083–2123.

Peters, R. H., & Taylor, L. A. (2017). Intangible capital and the investment-q relation. *Journal of Financial Economics, 123*, 251–272.

Pfeffer, J., & Salancik, G. R. (1978). *The external control of organizations: A resource dependence approach*. Harper and Row Publishers.

Putnam, R. D., Leonardi, R., & Nanetti, R. Y. (1994). *Making democracy work: Civic traditions in modern Italy*. Princeton University Press.

Renneboog, L., & Zhao, Y. (2011). Us knows us in the UK: On director networks and CEO compensation. *Journal of Corporate Finance*, 17, 1132–1157.

Renneboog, L., & Zhao, Y. (2013). The Governance of Director Networks'. In Mike Wright, et al. (eds), *The Oxford Handbook of Corporate Governance* (online ed., Oxford Academic, July 1, 2013). https://doi.org/10.1093/oxfordhb/9780199642007.013.0009, accessed May 3, 2023.

Rosenstein, S., & Wyatt, J. G. (1994). Shareholder wealth effects when an officer of one corporation joins the board of directors of another. *Managerial and Decision Economics, 15*, 317–327.

Sacconi, L., & Antoni, G. (2009). *A theoretical analysis of the relationship between social capital and corporate social responsibility: Concepts and definitions, knowledge in the development of economies.* Edward Elgar Publishing.

Sacconi, L., & Antoni, G. (2011). *Social capital, corporate social responsibility, economic behaviour and performance.* Palgrave Macmillan.

Sánchez-Ballesta, J. P., & Yagüe, J. (2022). Social capital and earnings management in small and medium firms. *Accounting Forum, 46*, 191–214.

Schneider, C. R., Fehrenbacher, D. D., & Weber, E. U. (2017). Catch me if I fall: Cross-national differences in willingness to take financial risks as a function of social and state "cushioning." *International Business Review, 26*, 1023–1033.

Scrivens, K., & Smith, C. (2013). Four Interpretations of Social Capital: An Agenda for Measurement. http://ina.bnu.edu.cn/docs/20140604161123289293.pdf (accessed May 12, 2023).

The Social Capital Index. (2023). Available from: https://solability.com/the-global-sustainable-competitiveness-index/the-index/social-capital#:~:text=The%20Social%20Capital%20Index%202022%20-%20Key%20Observations&text=The%20USA%2C%20due%20to%20comparable,reflecting%20the%20deteriorating%20social%20fabric, accessed September 20, 2023.

The UK Corporate Governance Code (2010) Available at: https://www.ecgi.global/publications/codes/the-uk-corporate-governance-code.

Tian, J., Haleblian, J., & Rajagopalan, N. (2011). The effects of board human and social capital on investor reactions to new CEO selection. *Strategic Management Journal, 32*, 731–747.

Tuugi, C., Andrew, P., & John, P. (2014). Board ties and the cost of corporate debt. *Financial Management, 43*, 533–568.

Uphoff, N. (2000). Understanding social capital: Learning from the analysis and experience of participation. In P. Dasgupta & I. Serageldin (eds.), *Social capital: A multifaceted perspective* (pp. 215–249). World Bank.

Wasserman, S., & Faust, K. (1994). *Social network analysis: Methods and applications.* Cambridge University Press. https://doi.org/10.1017/CBO9780511815478, accessed May 3, 2023.

Wintoki, M. B., Linck, J. S., & Netter, J. M. (2012). Endogeneity and the dynamics of internal corporate governance. *Journal of Financial Economics, 105*, 581–606.

Woolcock, M. (1998). Social capital and economic development: Toward a theoretical synthesis and policy framework. *Theory and Society*, *27*, 151–208.

Younas, Z. I., Klein, C., Trabert, T., & Zwergel, B. (2019). Board composition and corporate risk-taking: A review of listed firms from Germany and the USA. *Journal of Applied Accounting Research*, *20*, 526–542.

Young, C. S., & Tsai, L. C. (2008). The sensitivity of compensation to social capital: Family CEOs vs. nonfamily CEOs in the family business groups. *Journal of Business Research*, *61*(4), 363–374.

Zaman, R., Jain, T., Samara, G., & Jamali, D. (2022). Corporate governance meets corporate social responsibility: Mapping the interface. *Business & Society*, *61*(3), 690–752.

Zona, F., Gomez-Mejia, L. R., & Withers, M. C. (2018). Board interlocks and firm performance: Toward a combined agency–resource dependence perspective. *Journal of Management*, *44*, 589–618.

CHAPTER 5

Are Investors More Reactive to Simultaneous Changes in Chief Executive Officer and Chair Positions?

Myriam García-Olalla, Eleuterio Vallelado, and Jonathan Williams

5.1 Introduction and Literature Review

The board of directors, a pivotal entity in a company, is responsible for controlling, advising, monitoring, and replacing the top management, including the chief executive officer or CEO (Jensen 1993). In this

M. García-Olalla
Department of Business Administration, Universidad de Cantabria, Santander, Spain
e-mail: myriam.garcia@unican.es

E. Vallelado
Department of Financial Economics and Accounting, Universidad de Valladolid, Valladolid, Spain
e-mail: evallelado@uva.es

J. Williams
Discipline of Finance and Accounting, Surrey Business School, University of Surrey, Guildford, UK
e-mail: jon.williams@surrey.ac.uk

E. Scannella and J. Williams (eds.), *Trends, Issues, and Challenges in Banking and Finance*, Palgrave Macmillan Studies in Banking and Financial Institutions,
https://doi.org/10.1007/978-3-031-96066-6_5

context, the interpersonal relationships among the board members and between them and the senior management become relevant to explain the company's effectiveness in reaching its goals (Canals 2024).

Moreover, when analyzing the replacement of the CEO, it is necessary to consider whether this is accompanied by the renewal of the Chair of the board. This question garners importance from an agency-theoretic perspective which favors splitting the roles of CEO and Chair between two people because separation contributes to better monitoring of the CEO to improve firm performance (Harris and Helfat 1998). The proximity between the CEO and the board's directors is crucial in shaping the CEO–board relationship. While proximity increases over the CEO's tenure, it could facilitate entrenchment which is known to have positive and negative features (Berger et al. 2023).

The issue of whether to combine the CEO and Chair positions in one person or separating the functions in two persons is a topic that is far from settled. The ongoing debate around this issue attests to its complexity and significance, which underlines its depth. A leadership perspective contends that combining the CEO and Chair positions reflects a collaborative approach to corporate governance that contributes to the authority of the CEO–Chair in making critical decisions (Harris and Helfat 1998). In contrast, separation of the positions is considered important to ensure greater board control (Jensen 1993), although Krause (2017) demonstrates that different people in the roles of CEO and Chair can combine collaboration and control between the management and the board.

The CEO has great influence on the company´s business. Several empirical studies show that CEOs with high ability exert a positive effect on firm valuation (Hayes and Schaefer 1999; Demerjian et al. 2012), improve firm performance (Bertrand and Schoar 2003), modify the capital structure (Staneva 2024), and implement higher innovation activities (Bonsall et al. 2017; Chen et al. 2015). However, in a world where the CEO and Chair tend to be separated, the Chair position assumes greater importance given the critical role that chairs play in developing successful companies.

Upper echelons theory suggests that managerial characteristics affect firm performance through the strategic decisions executives make (Hambrick and Mason 1984; Hambrick 2007). Building upon Simon's (1957) concept of bounded rationality, this theory suggests that CEOs and Chairs are limited in their ability to access, process, and use information. Nguyen et al. (2023) show evidence suggesting that managerial ability is not only an essential factor for firm performance, but its role becomes particularly significant when firms are operating in crisis periods. Then, different management styles explain various corporate policy choices and, consequently, firm performance (see, e.g., Dyreng et al. 2010; Benmelech and Frydman 2015; Schoar and Zuo 2016; Law and Mills 2017). Hence, the lack of a standard measure which values the roles of CEO and Chair further motivates our research.

If the CEO and the Chair work together, why would a company decide to replace the CEO, the Chair, or both simultaneously? A wide literature analyzes the causes and consequences of CEO replacement. However, no studies investigate the simultaneous turnover of the CEO and the Chair when there is a separation between the two roles.

Larcker et al. (2022) find that companies are slow to terminate an underperforming CEO, are caught flat-footed following sudden CEO departures, and are unprepared to identify a viable successor. Dewally and Peck (2010) document that the vast majority (more than 92%) of directors leave the board without criticizing the firm's management even following their exit. Prior research has examined CEO replacements to elicit a more direct impact of managerial ability on firm performance (see, e.g., Bonsall et al. 2017). As Chemmanur and Fedaseye (2018) and Von Meyerinck et al. (2023) point out, a paucity of evidence exists on the consequences of CEO turnover in the functioning or dynamics of the board. However, CEO replacement can result from disputes on the board; in such situations, CEO replacement is often accompanied by other changes in the composition of the board (Marshall 2010). It follows that directors' involvement in CEO turnovers is assessed by the market and affects the reputation of the directors, in particular, the reputation of the Chair who hired the replaced CEO.

Rarely does a firm publicly state that the CEO has been fired (Larcker et al. 2022). Thus, we must use other signals in announcements to understand the reasons for replacing the CEO. One signal is if the replacement of the CEO is accompanied at the same time by the replacement of other board members, especially the Chair. Thus, it is not unusual for firms to announce a CEO replacement and information about another important events concomitantly to manage stakeholder impressions (Graffin et al. 2011). Along the same lines of analysis, Bae et al. (2023) show the market reaction to CEO replacement is lower when companies make other announcements simultaneously, such as the successor's name, to reduce investors' uncertainty. However, the announcement of several changes in the board, including that of the CEO and the Chair, can induce uncertainty for investors and manifests through adverse abnormal reactions in stock price returns (Decressin et al. 2024). Additionally, Florou (2005) argues that Chair replacement is associated with board restructuring.

A priori poor performance explains the decision to replace the CEO (Brickley 2003). However, Weel (2011) finds that manager quality does not reliably predict turnover and that many other variables exert a moderating effect. Alolah (2024) find the complexity of compensation arrangements is inversely related to CEO turnover following episodes of poor performance. It supports an agency-based perspective that it is unlikely a powerful CEO will be replaced after poor performance. Other reasons are suggested to increase or decrease the probability of a CEO being replaced, such as better corporate governance (Weisbach 1988; Mobbs 2013; Chen et al. 2019); high reliance on bank loans (Ozelge and Saunders 2012; Akins et al. 2020); better investor protection (Defond and Hung 2004); over-investment (Hornstein 2013); increasing in firm idiosyncratic risk (Bushman et al. 2010); corporate social responsibility (Cooper 2017; Colak et al. 2024; Chulkov and Wang 2023); environmental, social, and governance issues—ESG (Burke 2022; Colak et al. 2024); misconduct (Ertugrul and Krishnan 2011; Hazarika et al. 2012; Chyz and Gaertner 2018; Cline et al. 2018); or media exposure of poor performance in the financial press (Farrell and Whidbee 2002). On the other hand, corporate director networks; political connections (Liu 2014; Cao et al. 2017); investor myopia (Goyal and Low 2019); high economic policy uncertainty (Frye and Pham 2020); and corporate culture (Fiordelisi and Ricci 2014) reduce the probability of CEO turnover.

Announcing the replacement of the CEO and additional changes in board composition, namely the change in the Chair, indicates a more profound change in the company than merely replacing the CEO, including possible forced CEO turnover. CEO turnover is a noteworthy firm event (Mackey 2008; Hambrick and Quiqley 2014), which theory suggests may be informative about the state of the firm and the industry in which it operates (Eisfeldt and Kuhnen 2013). If investors recognize this, they should react accordingly because CEO turnover is a disruptive event for the company and provides opportunities for other companies (Burchard et al. 2021). Firm performance is the dominant predictor of CEO turnover (Kaplan and Minton 2012; Jenter and Kanaan 2015; Farrell and Whidbee 2003; Weisbach 1988; Mobbs 2013), and evidence suggests that industry performance also influences the decision to forcibly terminate a CEO (see,

Kaplan and Minton 2012; Eisfeldt and Kuhnen 2013; Jenter and Kanaan 2015; Peters and Wagner 2014). If industry performance does determine CEO turnover, investors can use this information to value not just the firm making the announcement but also peer firms (Desir et al. 2024). Besides, success in CEO nominations is also related to the company's leadership development process, including senior managers and those who report to them (Canals 2024).

We should consider the relationship between the CEO turnover, the Chair's replacement, and the incoming external CEO. CEO turnover is a board decision that may not have uniform support among board members which could trigger the stepping-down of those who disagree (Von Meyerinck et al. 2023). Florou (2005) reports that the Chair is six times more likely to be replaced when the CEO is dismissed and four times more likely to be penalized if she/he appointed the departing CEO. Similarly, Weisbach (1988) notes that board structure affects CEO turnover. Besides, better-performing CEOs acquire more bargaining power with the board over time (Pan et al. 2015). Ferri et al. (2023) argue that the ways in which boards select new appointees matter because CEOs often nominate people from their network whom they know and trust.

Desir et al. (2024) argue that appointing an external or outside replacement provides a reinforcing signal of a Chair–CEO mismatch. The newly demanded skillset differs substantially from the managerial skills previously employed. Braendle (2005) contends that changing the firm's culture also requires changing the CEO and the board, in the same way that if a soccer team wants to change its dynamic, it should change the coach and the players. Hence, hiring an external CEO triggers a substantial amount of information transfer to industry peers than do turnovers and internal or inside replacements.

Most papers on this topic examine market reactions to CEO turnovers. Hermalin and Weisbach (2003) argue that stock price reaction should be negative if the CEO is fired based on private information but positive if the CEO is fired based on public information. Whether an announcement includes several replacements simultaneously, it could be considered a signal of an abrupt managerial change, which could induce company shareholders to question the value of their shares and favor a significant sell-off (Florou 2005). However, the company might decide to retain a departing CEO on the board or even to become the new Chair. Such cases reduce the negative impact to investors of the simultaneous departure of the CEO and Chair (Akins et al. 2020).

Generally, there is no consensus on how markets should react to CEO turnovers. Furtado and Karan (1990) suggest that the conflicting empirical results arise from multiple factors, such as whether the turnover is voluntary or forced, the presence of concurrent earnings' releases, and perceived differences between internal and external successions. Clayton et al. (2005) add that reactions to announcements of CEO changes can be decomposed into an information effect, which tends to be harmful, and a natural positive effect. Furtado and Rozeff (1987), Weisbach (1988), Bonnier and Bruner (1989), and Huson et al. (2004) report significantly positive stock price reactions to news of CEO turnovers. However, Pukthuanthong et al. (2018) report the opposite finding that the market considers CEO turnover as a manifestation of severe problems within the firm, while Khanna and Poulsen (1995) find negative abnormal stock returns. To emphasize the lack of consensus, Warner et al. (1988) find the effects of turnover announcements to be insignificant. Finally, Guenzel and Malmendier (2020) caution that market discipline does not ensure the firing of biased decision-makers because the board members charged with firing a biased CEO are also subject to bias in evaluating the CEO.

Building on the extant literature, we shall delve deeper into investors' reactions to announcements of turnover in firms' top management teams. Specifically, we examine how markets react to announcements that a company simultaneously replaces the CEO and the Chair. In doing so, we shall answer the following research questions:

- Does the market react differently when the Chair changes compared to the CEO?
- How do investors react to simultaneous changes in the CEO and the Chair?

To provide answers, we apply event study methods to a sample of 915 nonfinancial companies from 28 European countries.

5.2 Data and Methodology

From BoardEx, we identify 915 nonfinancial companies with 2,644 CEO and/or Chair announcements from 2002 to 2021. Table 5.1 describes the announcements regarding the position replaced, the movement (in or out of the board), and the number of positions affected. Around 50% of our sample announcements consider only one board movement; 887 out of 1,316 concern the Board Chair, and 469 the CEO. Interestingly, of the single movement information, the majority refers to the Chair to indicate

Table 5.1 Number of announcements

Type of announcement	*Quantity*
CEO In (CEOI)	264
CEO Out (CEOO)	205
Chair In (CHI)	400
Chair Out (CHO)	447
Announcements of one change	1,316
CEOI+CEOO	126
CEOI+CHI	133
CEOI+CHO	15
CEOO+CHI	78
CEOO+CHO	87
CHI+CHO	655
Announcements of two changes	1,094
CEOI+CEOO+CHI	79
CEOI+CEOO+CHO	35
CEOI+CHI+CHO	80
CEOO+CHI+CHO	40
Announcements of three changes	234
Total announcements	2,644
Announcement about the CEO, Chair, or both	
Includes at least CEO	1,142
Only includes CEO	595
Includes at least Chair	2,049
Only includes Chair	1,502
Includes both CEO and Chair	547
Announcements about entry or exit	
Only about the incoming position	797
Only about the outgoing position	739
Includes both incoming and outgoing	1,108

the Chair's departure; for CEOs, most of these announcements concern the name of the incoming CEO.

Over 40% of our sample announcements communicate two names. By far, the most common announcement is the combination of the names of the departing Chair and her/his replacement. In combined announcements on CEOs, the most common is the simultaneous announcement of the names of the incoming new CEO and the new Chair.

Our sample also includes announcements with three movements which constitute around 9% of our sample. Here, the most common announces the arrival of the new CEO and substitutes the old Chair for new. A minor number of announcements include over three movements, but the number is low for empirical analysis. In brief, our sample includes more announcements about the Chair than the CEO, whereas 547 announcements contain news about both the CEO and the Chair.

The companies that released the announcements are from 28 European countries. Table 5.2 shows that there are more announcements in Germany. Table 5.3 shows that over the period we collect announcements; there are more announcements in 2020. Finally, Table 5.4 reports the proportion of announcements by the months of the year. It shows there are more announcements in February, March, and April.

Table 5.2 Announcements by country

Countries	*% announcements*	*Number of companies*
Austria	2.36%	21
Belgium	2.55%	31
Croatia	0.37%	2
Cyprus	0.20%	1
Czech Republic	0.09%	1
Denmark	4.11%	41
Estonia	0.06%	1
Finland	5.76%	50
France	11.83%	128
Germany	23.98%	183
Greece	0.45%	4
Hungary	0.03%	2
Iceland	0.11%	2
Ireland	4.23%	24
Italy	1.45%	30
Luxembourg	0.74%	8
Malta	0.17%	1
The Netherlands	7.41%	47
Norway	6.21%	56
Poland	0.28%	8
Portugal	0.20%	7
Romania	0.09%	2
Russia	1.39%	15
Slovenia	0.03%	1
Spain	2.87%	39
Sweden	10.56%	119
Switzerland	7.97%	79
UK	4.51%	12

Table 5.3 Announcements by year

Year	*% of announcements*
2002	0.11%
2003	0.48%
2004	1.11%
2005	2.30%
2006	2.41%
2007	4.31%
2008	4.68%
2009	6.90%
2010	5.14%
2011	7.38%
2012	4.97%
2013	3.69%
2014	5.39%
2015	4.48%
2016	6.56%
2017	7.86%
2018	7.72%
2019	7.89%
2020	9.39%
2021	7.24%

Table 5.4 Announcements by month of the year

Month	*% of announcements*
January	8.31%
February	12.74%
March	17.17%
April	11.80%
May	9.31%
June	5.96%
July	4.23%
August	4.60%
September	5.33%
October	6.84%
November	5.56%
December	8.14%

We use the event study methodology to analyze investors' responses to information regarding the turnover of companies' top management. While event studies are common in the fields of business and finance, they have been extended to other disciplines, such as management, to check whether any extraordinary profitability arises for the company shareholders as the consequence of new information about a specific event or occurrence entering the market. Event studies analyze the reaction of stock price returns to the arrival of new information as it might change the expected value of affected companies and cause abnormal returns (MacKinlay 1997). The underlying idea is that changes in a company's market value around an event date can be interpreted as the net present value of future costs and profits associated with that event.

We analyze the evolution of stock prices before and after the date ($t = 0$) on which information concerning top management turnover is announced. This method is based on the efficient market hypothesis (Fama 1970), which assumes that changes in investors' expectations cause market reaction.[1] Like Bhagat and Romano (2007), we consider this methodology suitable as it offers a valuable way to evaluate the implications of corporate actions on the well-being of society by analyzing their impact on stock price returns.

To determine the impact of turnover announcements, we estimate the market model proposed by Sharpe (1963)[2] for each company's returns relative to the return of a stock market index represented by a global, regional, or local equity index, which is used as a benchmark. We estimate the following equations:

$$R_{it} = \alpha_i + \beta_i R_{mt} + \varepsilon_{it} \quad t = -240,\ldots-21 \tag{5.1}$$

$$E(R_{it}) = \alpha_i + \beta_i E(R_{mt}) \tag{5.2}$$

where:

R_{it} is the return of company i on day t.

[1] For instance, when new measures are announced and not only when those measures are implemented.

[2] Campbell et al. (1996) and Schäfer et al. (2016), among others, contend that empirical evidence affirms that the market model yields very robust results which suggests that using more complicated models of stock returns is unnecessary.

R_{mt} is the return on a representative market portfolio used as a benchmark (we use the MSCI World index for this purpose).

α and β are the model parameters.

ε_{it} is the error term, with $E(\varepsilon_{it}) = 0$.

$E(R_{it})$ is the expected return the model estimates for a particular company on a specific date based on the market model.

Next, we calculate abnormal returns (ARs) of company *i* following Eq. 5.3 which are assumed to reflect stock market reaction to the arrival of new information. We calculate AR as the actual return of the security (R_{it}*) minus the normal return ($E(R_{it})$) which is defined as the expected return conditioned by the event taking place. Positive AR values imply that the stock prices "abnormally" rise following an event, while negative values indicate a drop. Next, we compute the average abnormal return (AAR) across all the N companies in our sample on day t (Eq. 5.4):

$$\mathrm{AR}_{it} = R_{it}^* - E(R_{it}) \tag{5.3}$$

$$\mathrm{AAR}_t = \frac{1}{N}\sum_{i=1}^{N} \mathrm{AR}_{it} \tag{5.4}$$

To assess price reaction over a longer period, we sum the AR of company *i* in the event window (t_1, t_2) around the event date to derive cumulative abnormal return (CAR). Lastly, the AAR of N companies in the event window is aggregated (CAAR):

$$\mathrm{CAR}\,(t_1,\cdot t_2) = \sum_{t=t_1}^{t_2} \mathrm{AR}_{it} \tag{5.5}$$

$$\mathrm{CAAR}\,(t_1,t_2) = \frac{1}{N}\sum_{i=1}^{N} \mathrm{CAR}_i\,(t_1,t_2) = \sum_{t=t_1}^{t_2} \mathrm{AAR}_t \tag{5.6}$$

We estimate the model using daily returns calculated on the closing prices of each security and index listed in Thomson Eikon DataStream over 240 trading days and ending 21 days before the event date which is the date a turnover announcement became public ($t = 0$). We set the event date as the next working day in cases when announcements were made at the weekend. Therefore, the estimation period is (−240, −21).

We estimate CAR over different event windows around the event date. Consistent with others (e.g., McWilliams and Siegel 1997; Köster and

Pelster 2017), we contend that investors require time to evaluate accurately the announcement's impact on company performance. A critical issue in implementing an event study is the length of the event window, which should be determined by the nature of the event under analysis. The assumption of market efficiency is difficult to reconcile with using a long event window. Nevertheless, in some circumstances, it is reasonable to assume that information is revealed to investors slowly over a period, as in the case of management studies, where event windows are typically longer.

Hence, we choose event windows of different lengths that are short enough to avoid the problem of overlapping events, but long enough to capture the effect of turnover. We also consider the possibility of the market reacting to rumors or news before the event. Thus, the event window must include days prior to the announcement to account for the possibility of information leaks in addition to days following the event. To analyze reactions around event dates, the lengthiest event window we select ranges from 20 days before to 20 days after the event date, while the shortest is 1 day only (the event date). In addition, we report evidence of post-event reaction by analyzing windows from 1 to 10 days following announcements.

Subsequently, we calculate CAAR as the mean of the estimates for each of the windows. We verify the statistical significance of CAAR using parametric tests, such as the *T*-test and Patell's *Z*-test (Patell 1976), as well as nonparametric tests, such as the Corrado Rank and the Generalized Sign Test.

5.3 Results

We present the results from applying the event study to estimate the stock price reaction to company announcements regarding changes in the CEO and/or Chair. We divide the section into four parts: stock price reaction for the whole sample; stock market reaction to CEO announcements; stock market reaction to Chair announcements; and stock market reaction to simultaneous CEO and Chair announcements.

5.3.1 Investor's Reaction to Top Management Turnover Announcements

Table 5.5 presents CAAR following the announcement of top management changes (CEO or Chair) in the sample firms for each of the selected

Table 5.5 Market reaction to top management turnovers

Event window	*CAAR %*	*T-test*	*Patel Z*	*Corrado rank*	*Sign test*
(−20...20)	0.85	21.258**	-10.698	−0.7941	0.0992
(−5...5)	0.47	22.812**	-22.514**	-24.150**	-23.830**
(−1...1)	0.38	35.236***	-20.704**	-19.121*	-18.102*
(−3...0)	0.40	32.133***	0.2248	−0.5119	−0.1299
(0...0)	0.15	24.696**	0.3649	-11.004	-10.464
(0...1)	0.09	10.343	-37.360***	-26.760***	−0.6646
(0...10)	0.18	0.8529	-22.894**	-21.671**	-23.448**

***, **, and * indicate statistical significance at the 1%, 5%, and 10% level, respectively

windows around announcement dates. In total, we analyze a total of 2,644 announcements from a sample of 915 companies.

We provide empirical evidence on market reactions to changes in top management positions, specifically CEO or Chair. Our analysis indicates that, on average, the market reacts positively and statistically significantly to changes in top management. Irrespective of window length, we find positive reactions around event dates with ARs of 0.85% for long windows (−20, +20 days) and 0.38% for shorter 3-day windows (−1, +1 days). Focusing on the day of the announcement, we find positive returns of 0.15% which increases to 0.18% 10 days later. These results suggest the market reacts upon confirmation of the news, and in days prior to announcements possibly in response to rumors and/or leakages in information.

As we estimate the average of CAAR, it implies that not every company and announcement experience a positive reaction from shareholders. However, it is valid to assert there is a significantly positive effect on average. Our results are consistent with Furtado and Rozeff (1987), Weisbach (1988), Bonnier and Bruner (1989), and Huson et al. (2004) who report significantly positive stock price reactions to news about changes in companies' top management.

Our sample comprises various types of turnover depending on whether the changes in top management pertain to the CEO or the Chair. Additionally, for each case, we can differentiate between announcements of a CEO or Chair's departure, and announcements of the appointment of new executives. Hence, we next explore whether market reaction is sensitive to the type of announcement.

5.3.2 Investor's Reaction to CEO Change Announcements

Table 5.6 displays market reaction to changes in the CEO role distinguishing between reactions obtained from three subsamples: hiring a new CEO, that is, 264 announcements (CEO In); departure of CEO, 205 announcements (CEO Out); and replacement of one CEO with another (CEO In+CEO Out), 126 announcements.

We find a positive and significant investor reaction when companies announce the hiring of a new CEO across all windows. ARs range from 1.73% on announcement day to 4.04% in the lengthiest window (−20, +20 days). We find positive ARs of 2.22% in the short window covering 3 days prior to and the day of the announcement (−3, 0). Potentially, this result indicates information leakage. For the window (0, +1), that is, day of the announcement and the following day, we estimate a CAAR of 3.58%.

Table 5.6 Market reaction to CEO turnover

Event window	*CAAR %*	*T-test*	*Patel Z*	*Corrado rank*	*Sign test*
CEO In					
(−20...20)	4.04	34.639***	−0.0880	−0.7089	0.6350
(−5...5)	4.00	66.194***	21.973**	0.3198	0.1426
(−1...1)	3.80	120.407***	56.809***	11.222	0.7580
(−3...0)	2.22	61.056***	49.377***	13.993	0.1426
(0...0)	1.73	95.334***	72.943***	−0.1202	0.3888
(0...1)	3.58	139.214***	64.801***	0.4998	0.8811
(0...10)	2.95	48.799***	0.9162	-13.298	-14.576
CEO Out					
(−20...20)	-2.10	-17.147*	-26.583***	-13.152	-13.191
(−5...5)	-1.97	-31.103***	-45.932***	-21.411**	-15.985
(−1...1)	-1.46	-44.065***	-66.071***	-38.737***	-29.953***
(−3...0)	−0.87	-22.736**	-30.924***	-14.554	-13.191
(0...0)	−0.93	-48.704***	-64.384***	-42.549***	-34.144***
(0...1)	-1.44	-53.365***	-71.619***	-46.184***	-32.747***
(0...10)	-2.27	-35.771***	-43.292***	-27.680***	-27.160***
CEO In+CEO Out					
(-20...20)	1.13	0.7274	−0.0904	10.131	0.3467
(-5...5)	-1.52	-18.927*	−0.8878	0.0213	−0.3661
(−1...1)	-2.08	-49.594***	-31.558***	-11.732	-10.789
(−3...0)	-1.34	-27.698***	-17.465*	−0.2338	−0.0097
(0...0)	-1.50	-61.993***	-38.853***	−0.7237	-12.571
(0...1)	-2.31	-67.391***	-43.892***	-19.113*	-16.135
(0...10)	-1.77	-22.046**	−0.9843	−0.5285	−0.7225

***, **, and * indicate statistical significance at the 1%, 5%, and 10% level, respectively.

However, the results we observe following the departure of a CEO are markedly different. We find an adverse and significant market reaction across windows. ARs range from –0.93% on announcement day to –2.10% in the 40-day (–20, +20) window. For 3 days prior (–3, 0) CAAR is –0.87%, whereas for (0, +1) investor losses amount to –1.44%.

Analyzing only the announcements of a CEO replacement, namely, the departure of a CEO and their replacement by another person, we find investor reaction is also adverse and significant, especially in short windows. For example, we estimate ARs of –1.50% on the day of the announcement day, and –2.31% for announcement day and the following day (0, +1). Our results suggest the market reacts to the uncertainty associated with the change.

Clayton et al. (2005) suggest decomposing market reaction to announced CEO changes into an information effect, which tends to be negative (the firm's prospects are worse than previously believed), and a real effect, which is positive (the new CEO is expected to improve future firm performance). In our case, when the announcement concerns an incoming CEO, we find the real effect is more powerful than the information effect, suggesting that investors place trust in the abilities of the new CEO. However, the information effect of terminating the CEO becomes more relevant than the real effect, suggesting that investors evaluate the uncertainty associated with the departure of the CEO. Finally, if the announcement includes both names, the departing and the arriving CEO, investors are more prone to react negatively, which implies they consider the firm's prospects are worse than they expected before the announcement. There are several possible explanations for the negative reaction. Bae et al. (2023) attribute negative reaction to the outgoing CEO having exhibited superior performance. However, Hermalin and Weisbach (2003) attribute it to an increase in uncertainty about the company's future direction.

Our results support Jenter et al. (2024) in suggesting that CEOs are an essential determinant of shareholder value. Thus, investors' reaction indicates that shareholders know which CEOs improve performance and which do not.

5.3.3 Investor's Reaction to Changes in the Board Chair

Table 5.7 displays market reactions to changes in the Chair of the Board. We form the same subsamples as before. We have 400 announcements concerning the appointment of a new Chair (Chair In); 447

announcements relating to the departure of the current Chair (Chair Out); and 655 announcements of a departing Chair being replaced by new (Chair In+Chair Out).

We observe significant and positive reactions to the announcement of a new Chair's appointment both on the day of the announcement and in short windows surrounding it. Investors react more swiftly to these appointments compared to changes in the CEO. ARs range from 1.15% on event day (0, 0) to 0.45% the following day (0, +1). That we find ARs before the announcement (–3, 0) suggests information leakage or rumors.

Conversely, the resignation of the Chair triggers the opposite reaction in investors. The ARs are negative at –0.19% in the long window (–20, +20) and –0.26% on event day (0, 0).

Table 5.7 Market reaction to Chair turnover

Event window	*CAAR %*	*T-test*	*Patel Z*	*Corrado rank*	*Sign test*
Chair In					
(–20...20)	0.33	0.2761	0.3460	0.4019	–0.0362
(–5...–5)	–0.13	–0.7118	0.1659	0.5305	10.638
(–1...1)	0.27	0.8362	–28.118***	–29.380***	–38.362***
(–3...0)	1.14	30.736***	0.4614	–0.3903	–0.7362
(0...0)	1.15	62.072**	18.399*	0.0186	–0.7362
(0...1)	0.45	17.154*	–29.286***	–28.650***	–18.362*
(0...10)	0.69	11.264	–0.2541	–0.3550	–0.4362
Chair Out					
(–20...20)	–0.19	–0.1828	–16.566*	–12.059	0.2281
(–5...–5)	0.14	0.9007	19.126*	0.8364	0.7011
(–1...1)	–0.22	–0.8136	–12.883	0.0367	0.4173
(–3...0)	–0.16	–0.4968	–0.3577	–0.2322	11.741
(0...0)	–0.26	–16.667*	–13.425	–12.367	–0.2448
(0...1)	–0.22	–0.9936	–12.250	–0.1129	11.741
(0...10)	–0.16	–0.3120	–15.170	–14.678	–0.5286
Chair in + Chair Out					
(–20...20)	1.74	19.982**	21.666**	11.801	12.971
(–5...5)	0.66	14.534	0.2536	–0.7641	–0.2659
(–1...1)	–0.01	–0.0356	–0.0566	12.578	0.9064
(–3...0)	–0.07	–0.2676	0.0612	–0.4768	–0.0315
(0...0)	–0.01	–0.0889	19.209*	17.656*	10.627
(0...1)	–0.08	–0.4091	0.2032	17.165*	12.190
(0...10)	0.0045	0.9962	13.447	12.430	0.5156

***, **, and * indicate statistical significance at the 1%, 5%, and 10% level, respectively.

When analyzing the combined news of one Chair being replaced by another, investors react positively in the long window (–20, +20) with ARs of 1.74%. However, on the announcement day (0, 0) and the following day (0, +1), returns are small and negative.

Although the Chair is relevant to understanding a company's performance, particularly in more complex environments as well as in low-munificent environments (Withers and Fitza 2017), our results show that investors are not so well equipped to identify the value added by the Board Chair. If Jenter et al. (2024) affirm that shareholders know which CEOs improve performance and which do not, our results indicate that those company's shareholders are less informed about which Chairs improve performance.

We compare the magnitude and significance of market reaction to chair turnover with CEOs. Announcements about the CEO receive a clearer evaluation by investors than for the Chair. Our evidence shows that even though investors are responsive to changes in both positions, they are more reactive to CEO movements.

5.3.4 Investor's Reaction to Simultaneous Changes in CEO and Board Chair

We next analyze the combined effect of dual announcements, that is, one announcement concerning the CEO and the other the Chair. We create 4 subsamples as follows: 133 announcements where both a new CEO and a new Chair are appointed; 78 announcements involving the departure of the CEO alongside the appointment of a new Chair; 87 announcements where both the CEO and Chair depart; and 15 announcements of the departure of the Chair and appointment of a new CEO. However, we exclude the latter from our analysis due to the small number of events.

The simultaneous appointment of a Chair and a CEO results in a significant outcome primarily within the extended window of –20 to +20 days, where the CAAR is recorded at –0.66% (Table 5.8). However, if the appointment of a new Chair coincides with the departure of the CEO, the market reaction is positive with ARs of 4% in the extended window (–20, +20). When the announcement reveals that both executives are vacating their positions, investors interpret this news negatively across all windows. ARs range from –0.74% on announcement day (0, 0) to a cumulative –3.53% over 11 days from 5 days before to 5 days after the event (–5, +5).

Table 5.8 Market reaction to CEO and Chair turnover

Event window	*CAAR %*	*T-test*	*Patel Z*	*Corrado rank*	*Sign test*
CEO In+Chair In (133)					
(-20...20)	-0.66	-0.4353	-21.476**	-11.046	-0.2025
(-5...5)	0.49	0.6171	-0.8461	0.9368	0.8382
(-1...1)	0.40	0.9774	-0.4109	0.1814	0.6648
(-10...0)	0.05	0.0638	-13.708	0.3444	0.4913
(-3...0)	0.18	0.3693	-14.525	11.321	0.3179
(0...0)	0.30	12.735	0.4433	0.4106	-0.3760
(0...1)	0.13	0.3815	-10.678	-0.7719	0.3179
(0...10)	0.18	0.2284	-16.318	-0.5644	-0.7229
CEO Out+Chair In (78)					
(-20...20)	4.06	17.510*	15.104	20.686	0.8823
(-5...5)	-1.64	-13.628	-13.821	-10.940	-16.088
(-1...1)	-0.50	-0.7982	-0.4524	-0.3181	-0.0236
(-10...0)	0.75	0.6230	0.8789	13.925	13.352
(-3...0)	-0.39	-0.5401	-0.2269	-0.0470	-0.0236
(0...0)	0.02	0.0558	0.7656	11.975	0.4293
(0...1)	-0.50	-0.9799	-0.6056	0.0344	0.4293
(0...10)	-0.02	-0.0139	-0.3791	0.1378	0.4293
CEO Out+Chair Out (87)					
(-20...20)	-2.18	-11.254	-23.264**	-18.473*	-10.013
(-5...5)	-3.53	-35.204***	-51.078***	-39.945***	-29.311***
(-1...1)	-1.52	-29.043***	-45.602***	-38.882***	-25.023**
(-10...0)	-1.56	-15.599	-21.342**	-13.798	-0.3580
(-3...0)	-1.44	-23.861**	-33.225***	-23.070**	-16.446
(0...0)	-0.74	-24.340**	-30.718***	-27.553***	-22.878**
(0...1)	-1.34	-31.418***	-49.330***	-43.042***	-29.311***
(0...10)	-1.14	-11.390	-23.009**	-24.928*	-14.301

***, **, and * indicate statistical significance at the 1%, 5%, and 10% level, respectively.

The combined announcement of the departure of the CEO and the Chair creates an explicit negative market reaction. Our results concur with Pukthuanthong et al. (2018), who attribute the negative market reaction to severe problems within the firm. Additionally, Larcker et al. (2022) attribute the negative reaction to the fact that companies are often unprepared to identify a viable or permanent successor, which creates uncertainty among investors reacting negatively to the announcement that both the CEO and the Chair are to leave the company. In the same vein, Ertugrul and Krishnan (2011) attribute adverse market reaction to an early dismissal because late dismissals do not cause significant market reaction. Similarly, Jenter and Lewellen (2021) argue that negative reaction to the departure of top management is more likely to relate to the CEO and Chair being terminated because firms are not required to reveal the reason for the departure. Our results also confirm that the Chair is more likely to be replaced when the CEO is dismissed (Florou 2005). Finally, the simultaneous exit of the CEO and the Chair signals a change in the firm's culture because such turnovers affect the dynamics of the board. Thus, Braendle (2005) argues that to change the culture of the firm, one should change the CEO and the board.

5.4 Final Remarks

When the same person fulfills the positions of the CEO and the Chair, investors' reactions to the CEO's replacement cannot be differentiated from those of the Chair. However, if the two positions are separate, we can analyze investors' reactions to changes only in the CEO, only the Chair, or both simultaneously. We provide evidence that the market negatively values the simultaneous change in the CEO and Chair positions indicated by negative ARs around the announcement date. Our results suggest the simultaneous exit of the CEO and the Chair signals a forced turnover that could change the dynamics of the board and introduce uncertainty about the firm's prospects. As uncertainty increases, investors react negatively in comparison to cases when there is a planned and well-designed CEO turnover only. In this case, investors respond positively to the announcement of the new CEO.

The issue of combining or separating the CEO and Chair positions is not just about a collaborative board (Harris and Helfat 1998) under the leadership of one person or a control board (Jensen 1993) where separation of the roles of the CEO and Chair ensures greater board control. It also pertains to the uncertainty that replacing one or several top management positions can transmit to investors during top management turnover. Our research findings highlight the relevance of this issue, emphasizing its implications for corporate governance and investor reactions. The announcement of more than one replacement could be designed to introduce noise in the information to the investors and, in this way, manage their response (Graffin et al. 2011).

Poor performance is the most common reason for dismissing the CEO, the Chair, or both simultaneously. However, the literature highlights that various factors moderate the relevance of poor performance in top management turnover. It implies there is implicit information on how companies announce top management replacements and the number of turnovers they choose to address simultaneously. The market's reaction to such announcements helps incorporate this implicit information into stock prices. After analyzing 2,644 announcements of European non-financial companies from 2002 to 2021, we find that, on average, the market reacts positively to changes in top management. Our evidence supports the notion that investors perceive turnover as a vehicle to enhance firm performance.

Investors evaluate the announcement of hiring a new CEO positively but view negatively the departure of the incumbent CEO. If the announcement includes the departure of the incumbent and the name of the replacement, the market reaction indicates there is an increase in uncertainty due to the surprise arising from the news. Similarly, the market reacts positively if the company announces hiring a new Chair. However, if the announcement concerns dismissing the Chair, stock prices show negative ARs. Notwithstanding, our results show that market reaction is more relevant for CEOs than Chairs.

We conclude that investors react positively when the company makes announcements, including simultaneously hiring a new CEO and a new Chair. Such a positive reaction is stronger when the incumbent CEO's firing accompanies the new Chair's arrival. However, the announcement of the simultaneous departure of the CEO and the Chair creates a strong negative signal in the market. Investors seem to identify a change in the dynamics of the board for which they do not have enough information to identify as a positive change. Instead, investors identify such a movement as raising difficulties in the way the board makes decisions with no clear direction obvious.

This chapter is not an ending but a starting point to disentangle the question of how to explain the market reaction to changes in top management. Further research is warranted to explore the functioning of corporate boards as it affects decision-making, including the turnover of top management, notably the CEO and the Chair, who have the highest responsibilities within top management. Moreover, we suggest taking a closer look at the timing for companies to make turnover announcements, how often they make such announcements, the relevance of making one or several announcements each time, how boards deal with such changes, and what the final impact on company performance is.

References

Akins, B., De Angelis, D., & Gaulin, M. (2020). Debt contracting on management. *The Journal of Finance, 75*(4), 2095–2137. https://doi.org/10.1111/jofi.12893

Alolah, O. (2024). CEO compensation complexity: Optimal contracts or agency problems? *Journal of Financial Research, 47*(3), 789–821. https://doi.org/10.1111/jfir.12383

Bae, J., Joo, J. H., & Yu, J. (2023). CEO succession planning and market reactions to CEO turnover announcements. *Finance Research Letters, 58*, 103946. https://doi.org/10.1016/j.frl.2023.103946

Benmelech, E., & Frydman, C. (2015). Military CEOs. *Journal of Financial Economics, 117*(1), 43–59. https://doi.org/10.1016/j.jfineco.2014.04.009

Berger, P. G., Cai, W., & Qiu, L. (2023). *Dynamic CEO-board cultural proximity*. SSRN eLibrary. https://doi.org/10.2139/ssrn.4452390

Bertrand, M., & Schoar, A. (2003). Managing with style: The effect of managers on firm policies. *The Quarterly Journal of Economics, 118*(4), 1169–1208. https://doi.org/10.1162/003355303322552775

Bhagat, S., & Romano, R. (2007). Empirical studies of corporate law. In M. Polinski & S. Shavell (eds.), *Handbook of Law and Economics* (Vol. 2, pp. 945–1012). Elsevier. https://doi.org/10.1016/S1574-0730(07)02013-7.

Bonnier, K. A., & Bruner, R. F. (1989). An analysis of stock price reaction to management change in distressed firms. *Journal of Accounting and Economics, 11*, 95–106. https://doi.org/10.1016/0165-4101(89)90015-3

Bonsall IV, S. B., Holzman, E. R., & Miller, B. P. (2017). Managerial ability and credit risk assessment . *Management Science, 63*(5), 1425–1449. https://doi.org/10.1287/mnsc.2015.2403.

Braendle, U. C. (2005). *Replacement of executives and corporate culture*. SSRN eLibrary. https://papers.ssrn.com/sol3/papers.cfm?abstract_id=721442

Brickley, J. A. (2003). Empirical research on CEO turnover and firm performance : A discussion. *Journal of Accounting and Economics, 36*, 227–233.

Burchard, C. H., Proelss, J., Schäffer, U., & Schweizer, D. (2021). Bad news for announcers, good news for rivals: Are rivals fully seizing transition-period opportunities following announcers' top management turnovers? *Strategic Management Journal, 42*, 579–607. https://doi.org/10.1002/smj.3234.

Burke, J.J. (2022). Do Boards Take Environmental, Social, and Governance Issues Seriously? Evidence from Media Coverage and CEO Dismissals. *Journal of Business Ethics, 176*(4), 647–671. Doi:10.1007/s10551-020-04715-x

Bushman, R., Dai, Z., & Wang, X. (2010). Risk and CEO turnover . *Journal of Financial Economics, 96*(3), 381–398. https://doi.org/10.1016/j.jfineco.2010.03.001

Campbell, J. Y., Lo, A. W., & MacKinlay, C. (1996). *The econometrics of financial markets*. Princeton University Press. https://doi.org/10.2307/j.ctt7skm5

Canals, J. (2024). *The changing nature and functions of boards of directors.* IESE Business School Working Paper No. WP-1307-E. https://doi.org/10.2139/ssrn.4721856.

Cao, X., Pan, X., Qian, M., & Tian, G. G. (2017). Political capital and CEO entrenchment: Evidence from CEO turnover in Chinese non-SOEs. *Journal of Corporate Finance*, *42*, 1–14. https://doi.org/10.1016/j.jcorpfin.2016.11.003

Chemmanur, T. J., & Fedaseyeu, V. (2018). A theory of corporate boards and forced CEO turnover . *Management Science*, *64*, 4798–4817. https://doi.org/10.1287/mnsc.2017.2762

Chen, G. L., & Hambrick, D. C. (2012). CEO replacement in turnaround situations: Executive (mis)fit and its performance implications. *Organization Science*, *23*(1), 225–243. https://doi.org/10.1287/orsc.1100.0629

Chen, J., Goergen, M., Leung, W.S., & Song, W. (2019). CEO and director compensation, CEO turnover and institutional investors: Is there cronyism in the UK? *Journal of Banking and Finance*, *103*, 18–35. https://doi.org/10.1016/j.jbankfin.2019.03.019

Chen, Y., Podolski, E. J., & Veeraraghavan, M. (2015). Does managerial ability facilitate corporate innovative success? *Journal of Empirical Finance*, *34*, 313–326. https://doi.org/10.1016/j.jempfin.2015.08.002

Chulkov, D., & Wang, X. (2023). *The relationship between corporate social responsibility and types of CEO turnover : Evidence from US firms.* SSRN eLibrary. https://doi.org/10.2139/ssrn.4400083

Clayton, M. C., Hartzell, J. C., & Rosenberg, J. (2005). The impact of CEO turnover on equity volatility. *The Journal of Business*, *78*(5), 1779–1808. https://doi.org/10.1086/431442

Cline, B. N., Walkling, R. A., & Yore, A. S. (2018). The consequences of managerial indiscretions: Sex, lies, and firm value. *Journal of Financial Economics*, *127*, 389–415. https://doi.org/10.1016/j.jfineco.2017.11.008

Colak, G., Korkeamäki, T. P., & Meyer, N. O. (2024). ESG and CEO turnover around the world. *Journal of Corporate Finance*, *84*, 102523. https://doi.org/10.1016/j.jcorpfin.2023.102523

Cooper, E. (2017). Corporate social responsibility , gender, and CEO turnover . *Managerial Finance*, *43*(5), 528–544. https://doi.org/10.1108/MF-02-2016-0049

Decressin, Y., Kaplan, S. N., & Sorensen, M. (2024). *Have CEOs changed?* SSRN eLibrary. https://doi.org/10.2139/ssrn.4931800

DeFond, M. L., & Hung, M. (2004). Investor protection and corporate governance: Evidence from worldwide CEO turnover . *Journal of Accounting Research*, *42*(2), 269–312. https://doi.org/10.1111/j.1475-679X.2004.00138.x.

Demerjian, P., Lev, B., & McVay, S. (2012). Quantifying managerial ability: A new measure and validity tests. *Management Science*, *58*(7), 1229–1248. https://doi.org/10.1287/mnsc.1110.1487

Desir, R., Seavey, S. E., & Thevenot, M. (2024). Information transfer of CEO turnover : Evidence from firm-CEO mismatch. *Journal of Corporate Finance, 84*, 102509. https://doi.org/10.1016/j.jcorpfin.2023.102509.

Dewally, M., & Peck, S. W. (2010). Upheaval in the boardroom: Outside director public resignations, motivations, and consequences. *Journal of Corporate Finance, 16*(1), 38–52. https://doi.org/10.1016/j.jcorpfin.2009.01.002

Dyreng, S. D., Hanlon, M., & Maydew, E. L. (2010). The effects of executives on corporate tax avoidance. *The Accounting Review, 85*(4), 1163–1189. https://doi.org/10.2308/accr.2010.85.4.1163

Eisfeldt, A. L., & Kuhnen, C. M. (2013). CEO turnover in a competitive assignment framework. *Journal of Financial Economics, 109*(2), 351–372. https://doi.org/10.1016/j.jfineco.2013.02.020

Ertugrul, M., & Krishnan, K. (2011). Can CEO dismissals be proactive? *Journal of Corporate Finance*, 17(1), 134–151. https://doi.org/10.1016/j.jcorpfin.2010.09.005.

Fama, E. F. (1970). Efficient capital markets: A review of theory and empirical work. *The Journal of Finance, 25*(2), 383–417. https://doi.org/10.2307/2325486

Farrell, K. A., & Whidbee, D. A. (2002). Monitoring by the financial press and forced CEO turnover . *Journal of Banking & Finance, 26*(12), 2249–2276. https://doi.org/10.1016/S0378-4266(01)00183-2.

Farrell, K. A., & Whidbee, D. A. (2003). Impact of firm performance expectations on CEO turnover and replacement decisions. *Journal of Accounting and Economics, 36*(1–3), 165–196. https://doi.org/10.1016/j.jacceco.2003.09.001

Ferri, F., Ou, Z., & Wang, Y. (2023). *Searching for directors.* University of Miami Business School Research Paper No. 4572326. https://doi.org/10.2139/ssrn.4572326

Fiordelisi, F., & Ricci, O. (2014). Corporate culture and CEO turnover . *Journal of Corporate Finance, 28*, 66–82. 10.1016/j.jcorpfin.2013.11.009

Florou, A. (2005). Top director shake-up: The link between chairman and CEO dismissal. *Journal of Business Finance & Accounting, 32*(1–2), 97–128. https://doi.org/10.1111/j.0306-686X.2005.00589.x

Frye, M. B., & Pham, D. T. (2020). Economic policy uncertainty and board monitoring: Evidence from CEO turnovers. *Journal of Financial Research, 43*(4), 675–703. https://doi.org/10.1111/jfir.12222

Furtado, E. P. H., & Karan, V. (1990). Causes, consequences, and shareholder wealth effects of management turnover: A review of the empirical evidence. *Financial Management, 19*(2), 60–75. https://doi.org/10.2307/3665635.

Furtado, E. P. H., & Rozeff, M. S. (1987). The wealth effects of company initiated management changes. *Journal of Financial Economics, 18*(1), 147–160. https://doi.org/10.1016/0304-405X(87)90065-1

Goyal, V. K., & Low, A. (2019). Investor myopia and CEO turnover . *International Review of Finance, 19*(4), 759–786. https://doi.org/10.1111/irfi.12198.

Graffin, S. D., Carpenter, M. A., & Boivie, S. (2011). What's all that (strategic) noise? Anticipatory impression management in CEO succession. *Strategic Management Journal*, *32*(7), 748–770. https://doi.org/10.1002/smj.906.

Guenzel, M., & Malmendier, U. (2020). *Behavioral corporate finance: The life cycle of a CEO career* (NBER Working Paper No. 27635). National Bureau of Economic Research. https://doi.org/10.3386/w27635

Hambrick, D. C. (2007). Upper echelons theory: An update. *Academy of Management Review*, *32*(2), 334–343. https://doi.org/10.5465/amr.2007.24345254

Hambrick, D. C., & Mason, P. A. (1984). Upper echelons: The organization as a reflection of its top managers. *Academy of Management Review*, *9*(2), 193–206. https://doi.org/10.5465/amr.1984.4277628

Hambrick, D.C. & Quigley, T.J. (2014). Toward more accurate contextualization of the CEO effect on firm performance. *Strategic Management Journal*, *35*, 473–491. DOI: 10.1002/smj.2108

Harris, D., & Helfat, C. E. (1998). CEO duality, succession, capabilities and agency theory : Commentary and research agenda. *Strategic Management Journal*, *19*(9), 901–904. https://doi.org/10.1002/(SICI)1097-0266(199809)19:9<901::AID-SMJ2>3.0.CO;2-V

Hayes, R. M., & Schaefer, S. (1999). How much are differences in managerial ability worth? *Journal of Accounting and Economics*, *27*(2), 125–148.

Hazarika, S., Karpoff, J. M., & Nahata, R. (2012). Internal corporate governance, CEO turnover , and earnings management. *Journal of Financial Economics*, *104*(1), 44–69. https://doi.org/10.1016/j.jfineco.2011.10.011

Hermalin, B. E., & Weisbach, M. S. (2003). Boards of directors as an endogenously determined institution: A survey of the economic literature. *Economic Policy Review*, *9*(1), 7–26. https://doi.org/10.3386/w8161.

Hornstein, A. S. (2013). Corporate capital budgeting and CEO turnover . *Journal of Corporate Finance*, *20*, 41–58. https://doi.org/10.1016/j.jcorpfin.2012.11.003

Huson, M. R., Malatesta, P. H., & Parrino, R. (2004). Managerial succession and firm performance . *Journal of Financial Economics*, *74*(2), 237–275. https://doi.org/10.1016/j.jfineco.2003.08.002

Jensen, M. C. (1993). The modern industrial revolution, exit, and the failure of internal control systems. *The Journal of Finance*, *48*(3), 831–880. https://doi.org/10.1111/j.1540-6261.1993.tb04022.x

Jenter, D., & Kanaan, F. (2015). CEO turnover and relative performance evaluation. *The Journal of Finance*, *70*(5), 2155–2184. https://doi.org/10.1111/jofi.12282

Jenter, D., & Lewellen, K. (2021). Performance-induced CEO turnover . *The Review of Financial Studies*, *34*(2), 569–617. https://doi.org/10.1093/rfs/hhaa069

Jenter, D., Matveyev, E., & Roth, L. (2024), Good and Bad CEOs. *European Corporate Governance Institute – Finance Working Paper No. 935/2023*, https://ssrn.com/abstract=4523213 or http://dx.doi.org/10.2139/ssrn.4523213

Kaplan, S. N., & Minton, B. A. (2012). How has CEO turnover changed? characteristics and abilities matter? *International Review of Finance*, *12*(1), 57–87. https://doi.org/10.1111/j.1468- 2443.2011.01135.x

Khanna, N., & Poulsen, A. B. (1995). Managers of financially distressed firms: Villains or scapegoats? *The Journal of Finance*, *50*(3), 919–940. https://doi.org/10.1111/j.1540-6261.1995.tb04042.x

Köster, H., & Pelster, M. (2017). Financial penalties and bank performance . *Journal of Banking & Finance*, *79*, 57–73. https://doi.org/10.1016/j.jbankfin.2017.02.009

Krause, R. (2017). Being the CEO 's boss: An examination of board chair orientations. *Strategic Management Journal*, *38*(3), 697–713. https://doi.org/10.1002/smj.2500.

Larcker, D. F., Tayan, B., & Watts, E. M. (2022). *Firing and hiring the CEO: What does CEO turnover data tell us about succession planning*? Stanford Closer Look Series, Corporate Governance Research Initiative, Stanford University. Recuperado de https://www.gsb.stanford.edu/faculty-research/publications/firing-hiring-ceo-what-does-ceo-turnover-data-tell-us-about

Law, K. K., & Mills, L. F. (2017). Military experience and corporate tax avoidance. *Review of Accounting Studies*, *22*(1), 141–184. https://doi.org/10.1007/s11142-016-9373-z.

Liu, Y. (2014). Outside options and CEO turnover : The network effect. *Journal of Corporate Finance*, *28*, 201–217. https://doi.org/10.1016/j.jcorpfin.2014.03.004.

Mackey, A. (2008). The effect of CEOs on firm performance . *Strategic Management Journal*, *29*(12), 1357–1367. https://doi.org/10.1002/smj.708

MacKinlay, A. C. (1997). Event studies in economics and finance. *Journal of Economic Literature*, *35*(1), 13–39.

Marshall, C. D. (2010). Are dissenting directors rewarded? *SSRN Electronic Journal*. https://ssrn.com/abstract=1668642

McWilliams, A., & Siegel, D. (1997). Event studies in management research: Theoretical and empirical issues. *Academy of Management Journal*, *40*(3), 626–657. https://doi.org/10.5465/257056.

Mobbs, S. (2013). CEOs under fire: The effects of competition from inside directors on forced CEO turnover and CEO compensation. *Journal of Financial and Quantitative Analysis*, *48*(3), 669–698. https://doi.org/10.1017/S0022109013000318.

Nguyen, H. T., Pham, M. H., & Truong, C. (2023). Leadership in a pandemic: Do more able managers keep firms out of trouble? *Journal of Behavioral and Experimental Finance*, *37*, 100781. https://doi.org/10.1016/j.jbef.2022.100781.

Ozelge, S., & Saunders, A. (2012). The role of lending banks in forced CEO turnovers. *Journal of Money, Credit and Banking*, *44*(4), 631–659. https://doi.org/10.1111/j.1538-4616.2012.00504.x.

Pan, Y., Wang, T. Y., & Weisbach, M. S. (2015). Learning about CEO ability and stock return volatility. *The Review of Financial Studies, 28*(6), 1623–1666. https://doi.org/10.1093/rfs/hhv014.

Patell, J. M. (1976). Corporate forecasts of earnings per share and stock price behavior: Empirical test. *Journal of Accounting Research, 14*(2), 246–276. https://doi.org/10.2307/2490543.

Peters, F. S., & Wagner, A. F. (2014). The executive turnover risk premium. *Journal of Finance, 69*(4), 1529–1563. https://doi.org/10.1111/jofi.12166.

Pukthuanthong, K., Ullah, S., Walker, T. J., & Zhang, J. (2018). Conflict-induced forced CEO turnovers and firm performance . *Managerial Finance, 44*(9), 1134–1154. https://doi.org/10.1108/MF-06-2017-0227.

Schoar, A., & Zuo, L. (2016). Does the market value CEO styles? *American Economic Review, 106*(5), 262–266. https://doi.org/10.1257/aer.p20161031.

Sharpe, W. F. (1963). A simplified model for portfolio analysis. *Management Science, 9*(2), 277–293. https://doi.org/10.1287/mnsc.9.2.277

Simon, H. A. (1957). Models of man. Wiley.

Staneva, V. (2024). CEO turnovers and capital structure persistence. *Accounting & Finance, 64*(1), 693–721. https://doi.org/10.1111/acfi.13163.

ter Weel, B. (2011). Does manager turnover improve firm performance ? Evidence from Dutch soccer, 1986–2004. *De Economist, 159*(3), 279–303. https://doi.org/10.1007/s10645-010-9157-y.

von Meyerinck, F., Romer, J., & Schmid, M. (2023). *CEO turnover and director reputation*. European Corporate Governance Institute—Finance Working Paper No. 942/2023. https://www.ecgi.global/sites/default/files/working_papers/documents/ceoturnoveranddirectorreputation.pdf

Warner, J. B., Watts, R. L., & Wruck, K. H. (1988). Stock prices and top management changes. *Journal of Financial Economics, 20*, 461–492. https://doi.org/10.1016/0304-405X(88)90054-2.

Weisbach, M. S. (1988). Outside directors and CEO turnover . *Journal of Financial Economics, 20*(1–2), 431–460. https://doi.org/10.1016/0304-405X(88)90053-0.

Withers, M. C., & Fitza, M. A. (2017). Do board chairs matter? The influence of board chairs on firm performance . *Strategic Management Journal, 38*(6), 1343–1355. https://doi.org/10.1002/smj.2587.

CHAPTER 6

The Value Relevance of Banking Loans

A Comparison Between IFRS 9 and IAS 39 in European Banks

Federico Beltrame, Marco Boso, Gianni Zorzi, and Maurizio Polato

6.1 Introduction

In July 2014, the International Accounting Standards Board (IASB) completed its process of revising the accounting treatment of financial instruments by publishing the new accounting standard IFRS 9, which became mandatory in place of IAS 39, as of January 1, 2018.

In this chapter, we aim to investigate the value relevance of the aforementioned accounting standard IFRS 9, as in the ability to find a

F. Beltrame • M. Boso • G. Zorzi • M. Polato
Department of Economics and Statistics, University of Udine, Udine, Italy
e-mail: federico.beltrame@uniud.it; bosomarco99@gmail.com; gianni.zorzi@uniud.it; maurizio.polato@uniud.it

E. Scannella and J. Williams (eds.), *Trends, Issues, and Challenges in Banking and Finance*, Palgrave Macmillan Studies in Banking and Financial Institutions,
https://doi.org/10.1007/978-3-031-96066-6_6

statistically significant relation between accounting information relating to financial instruments and firm value. The latter is often replaced by a proxy measure, namely the stock market price (Ball and Brown 1968; Beaver 1968), due to the intrinsic difficulties inherent to the definition of an unambiguous measure of firm value. The existence of a statistically significant relation between accounting information and prices constitutes a useful support to investors in their investment choices, ascribable to an increased trust in accounting figures' capabilities in successfully supporting the interpretation of market measures (Barth et al. 2001).

More in detail, this chapter aims to compare the value relevance of both the IFRS 9 and its predecessor IAS 39 on a sample of 139 European listed banks. The comparison between the two aforementioned accounting standards occurs in the context of the First-Time Adoption (FTA) year of IFRS 9 in the European Union and is performed by exploiting a Ohlson's model framework (Ohlson 1995). The observation of the accounting figures on the occasion of the FTA year holds an essential advantage, as the two standards have been simultaneously employed, in so-called "parallel running," with the processing of accounting data concerning the same financial instruments by exploiting both the "outgoing" international accounting standard, IAS 39, and the "incoming" IFRS 9, thus enhancing the comparability of the two without risking the potential interference of exogenous variables.

The main contribution to the existing literature, however, is represented by an additional analysis aimed at isolating the effects of the transition from one accounting standard to another on a particular item in the balance sheet of banking institutions, namely loans and overdrafts to customers. We consider it useful to study the value relevance of this balance sheet item, as it is one of the most important items in the balance sheet of a banking institution, representing the traditional business of such a kind of firm.

Results highlight how the analysis endorsed the widespread opinion that both accounting standards, IAS 39 and IFRS 9, can be defined as value relevant for investors. However, it is not verifiable, according to the tests conducted, that the new accounting standard IFRS 9 is significantly more relevant to informing the choices of potential investors than its predecessor IAS 39. However, the introduction of IFRS 9 shows an additional ability to explain market stock price compared to IAS 39, but exclusively at the individual loans level and highly significant for equity-strong countries. Inside this framework, the classic net income information is price relevant only within the EU 15 countries, as well as in the so-called "strong-equity countries."

The present work is organized as follows: the next section reports main literature in order to develop the study hypotheses; Sect. 6.3 contains the research design; Sect. 6.4 describes the sample; Sect. 6.5 reports and discusses the results; Sect. 6.6 adds some robustness tests; and finally Sect. 6.7 concludes the work.

6.2 Literature Review and Hypothesis Development

6.2.1 Accounting Standards and Value Relevance

Previous literature has shown that International Accounting Standards and International Financial Reporting Standards (IAS/IFRS) can be qualified as a set of high-quality and globally accepted accounting standards that have the ability to substantially improve the comparability of financial statements of companies in different countries. According to Jacob and Madu (2009), this would provide an impetus for improved investment decisions and a tendency for the investor's allocation of available resources to be improved.

Focusing on accounting standards IAS 39 and IFRS 9 and broadly speaking, it is possible to generally recognize them as value relevant, as they tend to employ a fair value-based approach for the valuation of financial instruments, which is a valuation policy that is generally considered beneficial to investors' decision-making processes. Ahmed and Takeda (1995), analyzing a sample of US-listed banks, reported that the use of the fair-value rule for financial instruments brings a positive effect on the equity market. Barth et al. (1996) also investigated a sample of US-listed banks, reporting that the application of the fair-value measurement method results in a far higher disclosure ratio than the book-value measurement of the same financial instruments. A similar view is given by Eccher et al. (1996) and Nelson (1996), justifying the relationship between the fair-value method and value relevance. The following is our first hypothesis.

H1: Accounting items defined in accordance with IAS 39 and IFRS 9 can be defined as value relevant with respect to the decisions made by investors.

In the next sub-paragraph, we define our second hypothesis, which is represented according to two alternatives: (a) IAS 39 is more value relevant than IFRS9 or (b) otherwise.

6.2.2 *IAS 39 Is More Relevant Than IFRS 9*

The "familiarity" investors have with the accounting standard can constitute a first element capable of affecting the level of value relevance for IAS 39 in respect to IFRS 9. The incremental familiarity of investors with the old accounting standard should have increased the value relevance of financial statement items measured according to it, making the IAS 39 superior to IFRS 9, at least during the first years of adoption of the new standard. This is supported by the studies of Mala and Chand (2015), who consider the "familiarity" that investors establish over time with an accounting standard as a "knowledge-based-variable," which would define, through a constant employment of the same standard, a better confidence with respect to the values shown in the economic–financial disclosure documents, thus defining an improvement in the quality of decision-making by investors.

Sforza and Cimini (2015) dealt specifically with the effects of the growing habit and familiarity among investors with respect to the use of IAS 39 "Financial Instruments." The results of the research come from the analysis of a pool of 55 financial intermediaries listed with 12 EU member states over the period between the years 2010 and 2013. Results confirm that all categories of financial instruments treated according to IAS 39 are value relevant with respect to investment decisions, especially as the investor's ability to better understand the requirements of the accounting standards increases.

Similarly, Liu and Liu (2007) reported that the value relevance of accounting disclosures prepared in accordance with IFRS accounting standards changes as investors become increasingly familiar with such accounting practices. Their analysis focused on the Chinese stock market, with particular reference to three particular categories of shares, called A-Shares (denominated in renminbi only), B-Shares (also denominated in foreign currency, and therefore more attractive to foreign investors), and H-Shares (listed on the Hong Kong stock exchange). The results were also confirmed by Alali and Foote (2012), with reference, in general, to the implementation of IAS/IFRS in the emerging financial markets, with a focus on the Abu Dhabi Stock Exchange (ADX).

Nonetheless, other authors attribute the lower value relevance of IFRS 9 to complexity and higher margins of opportunism of this accounting standard (Gebhardt 2016; Morais 2020; Mechelli and Cimini 2021).

The above arguments lead to our second hypothesis (a):

H2a: accounting items defined according to IAS 39 are more value relevant than those calculated according to IFRS 9.

6.2.3 IFRS 9 Is More Relevant Than IAS 39

The lack of "familiarization" of IFRS 9 is challenged by a usual late adoption of this standard after its first publication (Mechelli and Cimini 2021). This effect is demonstrated, for instance, by Gan et al. (2016), with reference to the Malaysian financial markets. Malaysia has, in fact, introduced mandatory IFRS standards through its standard setters, under, however, different names. For example, the Malaysian standard concerning financial instruments is called FRS139 rather than IFRS 9. Authors of the study were led to define a higher value relevance of the accounting items affected by the new standard in the periods after its introduction, compared to the periods before it. This would, according to the authors, draw sufficient evidence to show that, apart from other factors, the postponement of the introduction of an accounting standard could be the explanation for an increase in the value relevance of the same, when such a postponement has led to an increase in the familiarity of investors and insiders with the aforementioned accounting standard.

Lastly, the replacement of the incurred loss method with the new standard of the expected loss model makes the IFRS 9 more value relevant than the IAS 39. The expected loss model is, in fact, deemed to be more capable of reflecting the economic value of the financial exposure (Novotny-Farkas 2016). Kim and Yoon (2019), analyzing a sample of Korean banks, defined the use of a model based on incurred loss as not being adequately value relevant, adding that IAS 39 was fundamentally incompatible with the expected loss model used to calculate capital adequacy ratios (CARs), in line with Banking Supervision standards. This was even more evident with reference to European financial institutions, which were then subject to IAS 39, as there was never a reconciliation procedure between loan losses recorded according to the application of international accounting standards and those resulting from the application of banking supervisory regulations.

As a value relevance advantage of IFRS 9, it can be argued that the introduction of this standard has defined a lesser influence of discretion in the context of such transactions. This appears to be attributable, according to academics, to the fact that the "management intent" used in IAS 39 for the classification of financial instruments has been replaced by criteria that tend to be considered more objective, such as the joint analysis of the financial intermediary's business model and the intrinsic contractual characteristics of the financial instrument being classified. Consequently, IFRS 9 should prove to be an accounting standard that can be considered more functional in supporting the decision-making process of investors.

The above arguments lead to our second hypothesis (b):

H2b: accounting items defined according to IFRS 9 are more value relevant than those calculated according to IAS 39.

6.3 Research Design

6.3.1 The Standard Model

The basis of the empirical model useful for the analysis is the Ohlson model, adapted in line with our research purpose. More in detail, the model reports the stock price as the dependent variable and the accounting quantities (such as equity and profit) as independent variables.

In order to test the first hypothesis, the following models were used (model 1 and 2, respectively):

$$P_i = \alpha_0 + \alpha_1 \mathrm{BV}_{\mathrm{IAS39}i} + \alpha_2 \mathrm{NI}_i + \varepsilon \tag{6.1}$$

$$P_i = \beta_0 + \beta_1 \mathrm{BV}_{\mathrm{IFRS9i}} + \beta_2 \mathrm{NI}_{\mathrm{i}} + \varepsilon \tag{6.2}$$

where:

P_i is the closing price of a share of bank i at the end of March 2018. The time lag with respect to January 1, 2018 is provided in order for the dependent variable to be able to absorb all information attributable to the equity formation of the sampled banks;

$\mathrm{BV}_{\mathrm{IAS39}i}$ is the book value per share, calculated with reference to bank i as of January 1, 2018, by reference to the regulatory set of IAS 39;

$\mathrm{BV}_{\mathrm{IFRS9}i}$ is the book value per share, calculated with reference to bank i as of January 1, 2018, by reference to the regulatory set of IFRS 9;

NI_i is the profit or loss for the year per share with reference to bank i, computed at the end of the 2017 financial year;

ε is the error term.

Next, in order to test hypothesis 2, we employ a slightly different version of the previous models, which aims to define whether and how much the stock price is affected by the difference between the net worth determined according to IFRS 9 and the same net worth defined according to its predecessor (model 3):

$$P_i = \alpha_0 + \alpha_1 \mathrm{LAC}_{\mathrm{IAS39}i} + \alpha_3 \mathrm{NI}_i + \varepsilon \tag{6.3}$$

where ε is the difference between the book value per share calculated under IFRS 9 in respect of the one calculated under IAS 39.

6.3.2 *The Effect of Loans on Stock Prices*

In this section we try to contribute to the existing literature, proposing an isolation of loans and advances to customers from the other items affected by the introduction of IFRS 9 (model 4 and 5, respectively):

$$P_i = \alpha_0 + \alpha_1 \mathrm{LAC}_{\mathrm{IAS39}i} + \alpha_3 \mathrm{NI}_i + \varepsilon \tag{6.4}$$

$$P_i = \beta_0 + \beta_1 \mathrm{LAC}_{\mathrm{IFRS9}i} + \beta_3 \mathrm{NI}_i + \varepsilon \tag{6.5}$$

where:

LAC_{IAS39i} is presented as the value of loans and advances to customers per share, under IAS 39. The accounting figure is measured as of January 1, 2018;

LAC_{IFRS9i} is presented as the value of loans and advances to customers per share, under IFRS 9. As already reported, this variable stems from the restatement of loans and overdrafts to customers in order to comply with IFRS 9 requirements.

Finally, in line with model 3, a regression is proposed to test the differences between the value of loans under IFRS 9 versus IAS 39 (model 6):

$$P_i = \alpha_0 + \alpha_1 \mathrm{LAC}_{\mathrm{IAS39}i} + \alpha_3 \mathrm{NI}_i + \alpha_4 \Delta \mathrm{LAC}_i + \varepsilon \tag{6.6}$$

where $\Delta \mathrm{LAC}_i$ is the difference between the LAC per share calculated under IFRS 9 in respect of the one calculated under IAS 39.

6.4 Sample

The sample initially comprised 160 listed European banks. However, observations that did not meet the sampling requirements were excluded, resulting in a final sample of 139 banks. The geographical distribution of these banks is presented in Table 6.1.

Similarly to other studies, price data were collected from the Bloomberg platform at the end of March 2018 so that the impact of the adoption of the new accounting standard could be considered as fully absorbed at the financial market level. For the independent variables, it was necessary to manually collect them by referring to individual financial statement files.

Table 6.1 Frequency distribution concerning the state of origin of the sampled banks

EU country	*Number of banks*	*Percentage*
Austria	7	5.04
Belgium	1	0.72
Bulgaria	4	2.87
Cyprus	2	1.43
Croatia	1	0.72
Denmark	22	15.83
Estonia	1	0.72
Finland	4	2.87
France	5	3.61
Germany	10	7.20
Greece	6	4.32
Ireland	3	2.16
Italy	16	11.51
Lithuania	1	0.72
Malta	4	2.87
The Netherlands	7	5.04
Poland	11	7.91
Portugal	1	0.72
Czech Republic	2	1.43
United Kingdom	11	7.91
Romania	2	1.43
Spain	8	5.77
Sweden	7	5.04
Hungary	3	2.16
Total	139	100.00

Source: Author's elaboration

6.5 Results

6.5.1 *Descriptive Statistics*

Table 6.2 provides descriptive statistics on the variables used in the analyses. Please note that the variables (besides price) were related to the number of shares belonging to each sampled bank in order to neutralize the potential distortion owing to the different volumes of sampled banks. Also shown is the variable Total Comprehensive Income (TCI), which will be used instead of the income variable in order to conduct robustness checks.

With reference to the variables set out in the table above, it can be observed that the amount of equity calculated using IFRS 9 is on average lower than that calculated using its predecessor. This is also repeated, predictably, with reference to the variable LAC, which summarizes the level of loans and advances made by banks to customers. This explains why ΔBV presents itself as negative up to its third quartile.

A similar meaning involves the variable ΔLAC, which is also roughly null up to its third quartile. It can be seen that the choice of dividing the observations to the number of shares issued by the banks, as well as the rounding of the values to the second decimal place, rendered a multitude of statistics close to or equal to zero. The analysis of the documents used for the sampling and production of the abovementioned findings may lead to the conclusion, in line with Mechelli and Cimini (2021), that the negative values in the variables ΔBV, as well as ΔLAC, are predominantly

Table 6.2 Descriptive statistics

	Minimum	*First quartile*	*Median*	*Average*	*Third quartile*	*Maximum*
P_i	0.030	2.601	10.136	100.340	35.380	4,011.187
BV_{IAS39}	0.015	2.535	9.802	293.922	29.293	26,334.304
BV_{IFRS9}	0.015	2.294	8.503	290.828	26.536	26,315.797
NI	-788.656	0.163	0.717	19.812	2.947	1,704.89
TCI	-789.481	0.167	0.680	15.63	2.92	1,113.034
LAC_{IAS39}	0.12	9.77	55.06	1,333.58	134.23	33,935.92
LAC_{IFRS9}	0.01	6.91	22.85	595.96	134.72	33,935.92
ΔBV	-118.899	-0.858	-0.186	-3.094	-0.031	4.087
ΔLAC	-128.632	-1.116	-0.124	-4.347	-0.003	22.09

Source: Author's elaboration

Table 6.3 Correlation matrix

	NI	TCI	$BV_{IAS\ 39}$	BV_{IFRS9}	LAC_{IAS39}	LAC_{IFRS9}	P	ΔLAC	ΔBV
ΔBV	-0.17	-0.21	-0.24	-0.24	-0.55	-0.55	0.02	0.51	1
ΔLAC	-0.19	-0.22	-0.34	-0.34	-0.56	-0.56	-0.01	1	0.51
P	-0.04	-0.04	0.01	0.01	-0.02	-0.02	1	-0.01	0.2
LAC_{IFRS9}	0.29	0.32	0.42	0.42	1	1	-0.02	-0.56	-0.55
LAC_{IAS39}	0.29	0.32	0.42	0.42	1	1	-0.02	-0.56	-0.55
BV_{IFRS9}	0.07	0.06	1	1	0.42	0.42	0.01	-0.34	-0.24
$BV_{IAS\ 39}$	0.07	0.07	1	1	0.17	0.17	0.03	-0.07	0.26
TCI	0.97	1	0.06	0.06	0.32	0.32	-0.04	-0.22	-0.21
NI	1	0.97	0.07	0.07	0.29	0.29	-0.04	-0.19	-0.17

Source: Authors' elaboration

attributable to the transition in favor of an impairment model based on the expected loss, as opposed to the previous approach, based on the incurred loss, by virtue of the fact that, in particular, this change would have led banks to record a relatively larger number of loan losses. The changes in IFRS 9 relating to the classification and measurement of financial assets would not, in relative terms, have led to effects of equal magnitude.

The correlation matrix between the different variables is shown for completeness (Table 6.3).

The evident correlation of some variables, such as the book value or the value of loans under the two accounting standards, does not constitute a real multicollinearity problem, as these particular variables are never employed in the same model, rather in different variations of said regression equations.

The variables IAS 39 equity, IFRS 9 equity, IAS 39 LAC, and IFRS 9 LAC are excessively concentrated around zero due to the removal of the scale effect. In order to have a greater variability in the response and thus a fit of the models, a logarithmic transformation of the variables was opted for.

6.5.2 *Regression Results*

Tables 6.4 and 6.5 show the main results of models 1–6. For each of them, two versions are shown: the full version, which displays all variables, and a revisited version, obtained by using a stepwise backward selection based

Table 6.4 Book-value regression models

	Model 1		*Model 2*		*Model 3*	
	All variables	*AIC*	*All variables*	*AIC*	*All variables*	*AIC*
Intercept	1.50336***	1.49732***	1.57367***	1.56719***	1.44557***	1.43681***
	(0.21787)	(0.21815)	(0.21279)	(0.21304)	(0.21812)	(0.21776)
log(BV IAS 39)	0.41450***	0.40764***			0.46924***	0.46819***
	(0.07022)	(0.07009)			(0.07552)	(0.07547)
log(BV IFRS 9)			0.40034***	0.39334***		
			(0.06963)	(0.06949)		
NI	−0.00107		−0.00108		−0.00081	
	(0.00090)		(0.00090)		(0.00090)	
VAR BV					0.02226	0.02391*
					(0.01194)	(0.01179)
Obs.	139	139	139	139	139	139
R^2	0.2063	0.1980	0.1979	0.1895	0.2262	0.2215

Source: Authors' elaboration. ***, **, and * denote statistical significance at the 1%, 5%, and 10% levels, respectively. Standard errors are reported in parentheses

Table 6.5 Loan and anticipation to customers' regression models

	Model 4		*Model 5*		*Model 6*	
	All variables	*AIC*	*All variables*	*AIC*	*All variables*	*AIC*
Intercept	1.03548***	1.03558***	1.06747***	1.06747***	0.96723**	1.03547***
	(0.29342)	(0.29342)	(0.28711)	(0.37480)	(0.30003)	(0.29342)
log(LAC IAS 39)	0.37913***	0.37913***			0.40833***	0.37913***
	(0.06837)	(0.06837)			(0.07351)	(0.06837)
log(LAC IFRS 9)			0.37480***	0.37480***		
			(0.06715)	(0.06715)		
NI	-0.00181		-0.00180		-0.01700	
	(0.00093)		(0.00093)		(0.00094)	
VAR LAC					0.00963	
					(0.00896)	
Obs.	139	139	139	139	139	139
R^2	0.1868	0.1868	0.1888	0.1888	0.1937	0.1868

Source: Authors' elaboration. ***, **, and * denote statistical significance at the 1%, 5%, and 10% levels, respectively. Standard errors are reported in parentheses

on the Akaike Information Criterion (AIC), given in order to use the most significant ones. The aforementioned method is used in this particular case in order to conduct a procedure of iterative skimming of a regression model, progressively removing the less statistically significant variables.

As can be seen from model 1 and model 2, because the logarithms of the assets are always significant, it can be stated that both principles are value relevant, as both the book values as stated in accordance to IAS 39 and in line with IFRS 9 can be deemed as statistically significant. Hence, hypothesis 1 can be confirmed.

Net income, however, conveys little information for the 139 banks involved in the study. In fact, this variable was excluded in the AIC version.

Moving on to model 3, although it may enrich the effectiveness of the model (as suggested by the improvement of R^2 index), it can be stated that this statistical processing does not make it possible to state that the assets quantified through IFRS 9 are more value-relevant information than those quantified through IAS 39, as the difference between the book value measured in accordance with IFRS 9 and IAS 39 is scarcely significant. Moreover, it can be noted that the net income variable is once again discarded by the iterative selection process conducted through the AIC stepwise selection analysis. This suggests that, if both the book value (measured in accordance with either IFRS 9 or IAS 39) and net income are conjunctly considered, the latter variable cannot be considered as statistically significant as the former.

Ultimately, it can be stated that neither version (a) of the analysis (which considers the comparison between model 1 and 2) and version (b) (consisting of model 3) can confirm Hypothesis 2(b), whereas Hypothesis 1 can always be verified.

Relevant are the results of models 4, 5, and 6. Firstly, they highlight the ability to convey value-relevant information to the market considering the measure of loans and advances to customers, for both accounting standards, as both LAC IAS 39 (loans and advances to customers measured complying with IAS 39) and LAC IFRS 9 (as in loans and overdrafts to customers restated in accordance with IFRS 9) can be considered as statistically significant. This leads to confirming Hypothesis 1 also at this level. In addition, although model 5 can be considered approximately as statistically predictive as model 4, it can be argued that IFRS 9 adds relevant information on loans in terms of price. As for Hypothesis 2, it has to be noted that the R^2 index is slightly greater with reference to the IFRS version of the model (model 5), when compared to the IAS version (model 4). Nonetheless, the difference between loans measured in accordance with the two different accounting standards cannot be considered statistically significant in model 6, thus hindering the possibility to fully embrace the confirmation of Hypothesis 2b as a result of this test.

Nevertheless, as already stated, the effect of IFRS 9 on loans and receivables (measured, as always, in terms of price) is far from negligible, especially when models 3 and 4 are, for instance, compared to model 1 and model 2, where book value was considered as a whole. This can be explained in several ways. Firstly, the ability of investors to familiarize with the new standard as it came into force 5 years after its publication (Mechelli and Cimini 2021; Gan et al. 2016). Secondly, particularly relevant at the level of lending is the fact that relying on expected loss versus incurred loss is more relevant in terms of value and brings accounting evidence closer to the market (Novotny-Farkas 2016; Kim and Yoon 2019). Finally, the IFRS 9 criterion therefore seems to be more objective on the valuation of receivables, as stated by Barth et al. (2001).

Table 6.6 Book-value regression models on an EU-15 subsample

	Model 1	*Model 2*	*Model 3*
	AIC	*AIC*	*AIC*
Intercept	1.60663***	1.65575***	1.47971***
	(0.27062)	(0.26690)	(0.27312)
log(BV IAS 39)	0.39910***		0.48674***
	(0.08487)		(0.09327)
log(BV IFRS 9)		0.38967***	
		(0.08496)	
NI			
VAR BV			0.02551*
			(0.01206)
Obs.	108	108	108
R^2	0.1674	0.1605	0.2002

Source: Authors' elaboration. ***, **, and * denote statistical significance at the 1%, 5%, and 10% levels, respectively. Standard errors are reported in parentheses

To conclude, it has to be noted that net income carries on being scarcely statistically significant, even when testing the relevance of loans and advances to customers, in lieu of the book-value figure as a whole.

6.6 Robustness Checks

6.6.1 Analysis of a Subsample of 15 EU Countries

The first robustness check involves carrying out the previously displayed analyses on a subsample, exclusively consisting of banks listed on regulated markets pertaining to countries belonging to the so-called EU-15.[1] The economic–financial reasons underlying the creation of this subsample can be traced back to a number of studies, which revealed that investors, on average, place a lower degree of trust in non-EU-15 banks, resulting in a higher degree of skepticism with respect to their proposed fair values (Fiechter and Novotny-Farkas 2017). In Tables 6.6 and 6.7 we present

[1] EU-15 refers to the EU states that were part of the EU before 2004: Austria, Belgium, Denmark, Finland, France, Germany, Greece, Ireland, Italy, Luxembourg, the Netherlands, Portugal, Spain, Sweden, and United Kingdom.

Table 6.7 Loan and anticipation to customers' regression models on EU-15 subsample

	Model 4	*Model 5*	*Model 6*
	AIC	*AIC*	*AIC*
Intercept	1.17615**	1.19943***	1.17615**
	(0.35901)	(0.35360)	(0.35901)
log(LAC IAS 39)	0.37097***		0.37097***
	(0.08113)		(0.08113)
log(LAC IFRS 9)		0.368621***	
		(0.08035)	
NI	-0.00186*	-0.00185*	-0.00186*
	(0.00093)	(0.00093)	(0.00093)
VAR LAC			
Obs.	108	108	108
R^2	0.1657	0.1666	0.1657

Source: Authors' elaboration. ***, **, and * denote statistical significance at the 1%, 5%, and 10% levels, respectively. Standard errors are reported in parentheses

the results, directly performed on the AIC selected variables, both for the book value and loan and anticipations to customers.

The analysis on the subsample confirms the same results as the analysis on the extended sample. Interestingly, models 4, 5, and 6 show that net income is now also a significant variable. Previously stated results can be said to be in line with the expectations regarding the involvement of a sample composed of banks belonging to 15 EU countries, whose accounting measures are acknowledged by investors as generally more reliable than those of other European banks.

6.6.2 *Analysis of the "Strong-equity" Countries Subsample*

In this paragraph, a second robustness check is provided. Another subsample is used in the analysis, inspired by the subdivision of European countries between "weak equity" countries[2] (whose economic–financial systems are characterized by a certain degree of dirigisme on the part of central

[2] Regarding the countries analyzed in this work, the non-strong-equity countries are Austria, Belgium, Bulgaria, the Czech Republic, Finland, France, Germany, Greece, Hungary, Italy, Poland, Portugal, Romania, Spain, and Sweden.

Table 6.8 Book-value regression models on strong-equity subsample

	Model 1	*Model 2*	*Model 3*
	AIC	*AIC*	*AIC*
Intercept	2.34277***	2.33548***	2.34277***
	(0.47804)	(0.45393)	(0.47804)
log(BV IAS 39)	0.46765**		0.46765**
	(0.16420)		(0.16420)
log(BV IFRS 9)		0.49273**	
		(0.16135)	
NI	-0.01015*	-0.01080*	-0.10156*
	(0.00488)	(0.00485)	(0.00488)
VAR BV			
Obs.	46	46	46
R^2	0.1588	0.1780	0.1588

Source: Authors' elaboration. ***, **, and * denote statistical significance at the 1%, 5%, and 10% levels, respectively. Standard errors are reported in parentheses

administrations and, above all, by a marked incidence of the taxation system) and "strong equity" countries (in which the market is pre-eminently conditioned by commercial logic).[3] This view is in line with Nobes et al. (2008). Therefore, a subsample consisting only of banking institutions from countries considered by the best literature as having "strong equity" will be identified. In Tables 6.8 and 6.9 we present the results, directly performed on the AIC selected variables, both for the book value and loans and anticipations to customers.

The results tend to indicate that the change in accounting standard is perceived as very significant on the stock price in terms of loans, especially in relatively freer economies, where market logics are stronger. This is also confirmed by the higher R^2 values, especially when considering loans and overdrafts granted to customers only. The outcome of the analysis allows to outline a picture in which market-focused economies benefitted more from the additional information delivery granted by IFRS 9. Moreover, a

[3] In the present work, the strong-equity countries are Denmark, United Kingdom, Ireland, Malta, and the Netherlands.

Table 6.9 Loan and anticipation to customers' regression models on strong-equity subsample

	Model 4	*Model 5*	*Model 6*
	AIC	*AIC*	*AIC*
Intercept	1.29345	1.36432*	1.29345
	(0.65594)	(0.63702)	(0.65598)
log(LAC IAS 39)	0.58556***		0.58556***
	(0.16401)		(0.16401)
log(LAC IFRS 9)		0.57587***	
		(0.16093)	
NI	−0.13274*	−0.01314*	−0.01327*
	(0.00493)	(0.00490)	(0.00493)
VAR LAC			
Obs.	46	46	46
R^2	0.2275	0.2283	0.2275

Source: Authors' elaboration. ***, **, and * denote statistical significance at the 1%, 5%, and 10% levels, respectively. Standard errors are reported in parentheses

higher statistical significance of net income can be witnessed, in a similar way to the results regarding the EU-15 subsample.

6.6.3 *Replacing Net Income with Total Comprehensive Income*

The last robustness check, often used in the literature with respect to value relevance research, is related to the possibility of restating the above equations by using total comprehensive income instead of net profit/loss for the year. This is consistent with the assumptions in Ohlson's (1995) price model, which include the so-called clean surplus relation. In Tables 6.10 and 6.11 we present the results, directly performed on the AIC selected variables, both for the book value and loans and anticipations to customers.

This last check confirms the results of the base analysis with reference to the statistical significance of book value and loans and overdrafts to customers, both under IAS 39 and IFRS 9. However, it is possible to notice that, taking models 4–6 into consideration, the total comprehensive income turns out to be statistically significant. This constitutes a major difference with the base analysis, in which the income information was not considered as significant.

Table 6.10 Book-value regression models replacing NI with TCI

	Model 1	*Model 2*	*Model 3*
	All variables	*All variables*	*All variables*
Intercept	1.49732***	1.56719***	1.43681***
	(0.21815)	(0.21304)	(0.21776)
log(BV IAS 39)	0.40764***		0.46819***
	(0.07009)		(0.07547)
log(BV IFRS 9)		0.39334***	
		(0.06949)	
TCI			VAR BV
		0.02391	
		(0.01179)	Obs.
139	139	139	R^2
0.1980	0.1895	0.2215	

Source: Authors' elaboration. ***, **, and * denote statistical significance at the 1%, 5%, and 10% levels, respectively. Standard errors are reported in parentheses

Table 6.11 Loan and anticipation to customers' regression models replacing NI with TCI

	Model 4	*Model 5*	*Model 6*
	AIC	*AIC*	*AIC*
Intercept	1.04781***	1.07912***	1.04781***
	(0.29219)	(0.28596)	(0.29219)
log(LAC IAS 39)	0.37618***		0.37618***
	(0.06786)		(0.06786)
log(LAC IFRS 9)		0.37202***	
		(0.06666)	
TCI	–0.00239*	–0.002383*	–0.00238*
	(0.00183)	(0.00118)	(0.00118)
VAR LAC			
Obs.	139	139	139
R^2	0.1886	0.1906	0.1886

Source: Authors' elaboration. ***, **, and * denote statistical significance at the 1%, 5%, and 10% levels, respectively. Standard errors are reported in parentheses.

6.7 Conclusion

In this chapter, we aim to understand whether the transition between the accounting standard IAS 39 and IFRS 9 constituted relevant share price information for 139 European banks. After confirming that both accounting standards affect the stock price, we tested how changes in equity due to the change in accounting standards had any influence on the price, but without obtaining an affirmative answer. The relevance on price of the change in accounting standards is instead evident at the level of loans and advances to customers, which is the main contribution of this chapter. Secondly, it is evident that the introduction of IFRS 9 compared to IAS 39 is especially relevant for so-called equity-strong countries. However, with regard to the disclosure of net income, it seems that this is somehow included in the effect of equity and is singularly recognized by investors with respect to the effect of loans only where investors pay more attention to value relevance (so-called EU-15, as well as the so-called "equity-strong countries").

This study is, however, subject to at least three limitations, which are set out below.

First, it is conceived that, despite the fact that value relevance is one of the most important aspects of the studies on the interaction between accounting standards and capital markets, the validity of the results of the research pertaining to it is subordinate to the assumptions of the price model declination used from time to time.

Second, it is defined as being difficult to investigate with respect to the value relevance of individual equity items, especially with reference to the impossibility of clearly distinguishing the effects on value relevance attributable to changes in the rules concerning the classification and measurement, impairment, and hedge accounting of financial instruments. Another element of interest is represented by the difficulty of clearly distinguishing the tax implications of the changes, with, even in this case, the possibility of revealing a totally inhomogeneous approach on the part of the sampled banking institutions: only a few of them, from this point of view, did not fail to highlight the tax effects of the transition, while the others, however, did not display this information.

Finally, it is defined that the results in this work refer only to banking institutions with securities listed on regulated markets in EU countries. The conclusions drawn from these results may not be applicable to entities other than those considered in this study, such as banks without EU-listed venture capital securities, or nonfinancial corporations.

References

Ahmed, S., & Takeda, C. (1995). Stock market valuation of gains and losses on commercial banks' investment securities. An empirical analysis. *Journal of Accounting and Economics, 20*, 207–225. doi: https://doi.org/10.1016/0165-4101(95)00396-Z

Alali, F. A., & Foote, P. S. (2012). The value relevance of International Financial Reporting Standards: Empirical evidence in an emerging market. *The International Journal of Accounting*, *47*(1), 85–108, Elsevier. https://doi.org/10.1016/j.intacc.2011.12.005

Ball, R., & Brown, P. (1968). An empirical valuation of accounting income numbers. *Journal of Accounting Research*, *6*(2), 159–178. https://doi.org/10.2307/2490232

Barth, M., Beaver, W., & Landsman, W. (1996). Value relevance of Banks' Fair Value Disclosures under SFAS No. 107. *The Accounting Review*, *71*(4), 513–537. http://www.jstor.org/stable/248569

Barth, M., Beaver, W., & Landsman, W. (2001). The relevance of the value relevance literature for financial accounting standard setting: Another view. *Journal of Accounting and Economics*, *31*, 77–104. https://doi.org/10.1016/S0165-4101(01)00019-2

Beaver, W. H. (1968). The information content of annual earnings announcements. *Journal of Accounting Research*, vol. *6*, 67–92. https://doi.org/10.2307/2490070

Eccher, E., Ramesh, K., & Thiagarajan, S. (1996). Fair value disclosures by bank holding companies. *Journal of Accounting and Economics*, *22*(1–3), 79–117. https://doi.org/10.1016/S0165-4101(96)00438-7

Fiechter, P., & Novotny-Farkas, Z. (2017). The impact of the Institutional Environment on the Value Relevance of Fair Values. *Review of Accounting Studies*, *22*(1), 392–429. https://doi.org/10.1007/s11142-016-9378-7

Gan, C. Y., Chong, L. L., & Ahmad, Z. (2016). Impact of FRS139 adoption on value relevance of financial reporting in Malaysia. *Managerial Finance*, *42*(7), 706–721. https://doi.org/10.1108/MF-06-2015-0167

Gebhardt, G. (2016). Impairments of Greek government bonds under IAS 39 and IFRS 9: A case study. *Accounting in Europe*, 13, 169–196. https://doi.org/10.1080/17449480.2016.1208833

Jacob, R. A. & Madu, C. N. (2009). International financial reporting standards: An indicator of high quality? *International Journal of Quality & Reliability Management*, *29*(7), 712–722. https://doi.org/10.1108/02656710910975778

Kim, H. J., & Yoon, S. Y. (2019). Value-relevance of the regulatory non-GAAP adjustments in the Korean banking industry. *Asia-Pacific Journal of Accounting and Economics*, *26*(1–2), 160–171. https://doi.org/10.1080/16081625.2019.1546974

Liu, J., & Liu, C. (2007). Value relevance of accounting information in different stock market segments: The case of Chinese A-, B-, and H-Shares. *Journal of*

International Accounting Research, *6*(2), 55–81. https://doi.org/10.2308/jiar.2007.6.2.55

Mala, R., & Chand, P. (2015). Judgment and decision-making research in auditing and accounting: Future research implications of person task and environment perspective. *Accounting Perspectives*, *14*(1), 1–50. https://doi.org/10.1111/1911-3838.12040

Mechelli, A., & Cimini, R. (2021). The effect of corporate governance and investor protection environments on the value relevance of new accounting standards: The case of IFRS 9 and IAS 39. *Journal of Management & Governance, Springer; Accademia Italiana di Economia Aziendale (AIDEA)*, *25*(4), 1241–1266. https://doi.org/10.1007/s10997-020-09551-9

Morais, A. I. (2020). Are changes in international accounting standards making them more complex? *Accounting Forum*, *44*(1), 35–63. https://doi.org/10.1080/01559982.2019.1573781

Nelson, K. (1996). Fair value accounting for commercial banks: An empirical analysis of SFAS No. 107. *The Accounting Review*, *71*(2), 161–182. https://www.jstor.org/stable/248444

Nobes, C. (2008). Accounting classification in the IFRS era. *Australian Accounting Review*, *18*(3), 191–198. https://doi.org/10.1111/j.1835-2561.2008.0024.x

Novotny-Farkas, Z. (2016). The interaction of the IFRS 9 expected loss approach with supervisory rules and implications for financial stability. *Accounting in Europe*, *13*(2), 197–227. https://doi.org/10.1080/17449480.2016.1210180

Ohlson, J. (1995). Earnings, book values and dividends in equity valuation. *Contemporary Accounting Research*, *11*(2), 661–687. https://doi.org/10.1111/j.1911-3846.1995.tb00461.x

Sforza, V., & Cimini, R. (2015). The relevance and the reliability of IAS 39 financial instruments categories. Rivista Italiana di Ragioneria e di Economia Aziendale, 10-11-12, 26–39.

CHAPTER 7

The Perks of Market Timing in Mergers and Acquisitions

Gimede Gigante, Beatrice Gobbo, and Andrea Cerri

7.1 Introduction

The merger market has been subject to an increasing trend in Europe since the 1980s.

The mergers and acquisitions (M&A) activity usually happens in clusters, commonly called waves, and in periods where stock markets are highly valued. Moreover, usually, the acquirer company has been priced higher than their target. The reason behind the high intensity in M&A during stock market boom could be explained by the market timing theory of the behavioral hypothesis. This theory assumes that high-valued companies exploit periods of high market value in order to acquire other companies using their stock as a way of payment. This chapter will focus on testing the market-timing behavioral hypothesis for 1985–2019 in the European Union (EU). This research will try to answer if those

G. Gigante (✉) • B. Gobbo • A. Cerri
Department of Finance, Bocconi University, Milan, Italy
e-mail: gimede.gigante@unibocconi.it; beatrice.gobbo@studbocconi.it; andrea.cerri@unibocconi.it

E. Scannella and J. Williams (eds.), *Trends, Issues, and Challenges in Banking and Finance*, Palgrave Macmillan Studies in Banking and Financial Institutions,
https://doi.org/10.1007/978-3-031-96066-6_7

companies that decided to time the market by paying stock are better off than equity-financed acquisitions, which did not time the market. The chapter compares market timers and nonmarket timers' returns to capture the potential benefits. For the sake of completeness, the same analysis can be performed also for cash acquiring companies, in order to provide a long-run comparison.

7.1.1 *Literature Review*

The past literature trying to explain merger waves can be divided generally into two schools: neoclassical and behavioral. The neoclassical hypothesis is based on the economic disturbance theory and efficient reallocation hypothesis. According to Gort (1969) and Mitchell and Mulherin (1996), M&A transactions occur due to shocks in the market, such as new technologies, which increase companies' market value and create discrepancies in valuations. Moreover, restructuring activities tend to improve the allocation of resources. Jovanovic and Rousseau (2002) developed the Q-theory of mergers which proposes that the same forces driving firms' direct investments also drive their decisions about merging with other firms. In this view, M&A is considered as a device for solving an economy-wide problem of capital reallocation. Nevertheless, the neoclassical hypothesis does not take into consideration some significant aspects. It fails to explain why some acquiring companies prefer to pursue stock-based acquisitions while others cash-based ones, and why some bidders have short-term gains after the announcement and others long-term profits. To solve these unexplained trends, behavioral theories were developed to justify the positive correlation between the increase in stock prices and merger waves. The behavioral approach would provide an understanding of M&As from a different point of view. The behavioral hypothesis concerning merger waves is generally based on the incorrect perception of the players in the market. In this context, companies, or better their managers, are able to take advantage of the situation to generate positive returns. According to Shleifer and Vishny (2003), once companies are mispriced in the market, they could be better off performing stock-for-stock mergers by exploiting their overvalued equity. Moreover, for Gugler et al. (2012), the optimism in the market brings growth-seeking managers to engage in transactions that would not have been performed in normal times because considered wealth-destroying.

Following Shleifer and Vishny (2003), the goal of the chapter is to prove that once a firm is conscious about its mispricing and it is able to time the market, they will be well off acquiring a company by using stock as a method of payment instead of cash.

7.1.2 Aims

Essentially, this simple model would like to understand if there are benefits for acquirer companies that time the market and pay with their stock when their stock price is at a pick, in comparison to firms that offered stock as a means of financing but did not time the market. This model will test the assumption mentioned above by Shleifer and Vishny (2003), where market timing companies have a better performance than nonmarket timing companies. Moreover, a further comparison will be made between stock-financed acquisition and cash-financed acquisition.

7.2 Research Methodology

The methodology applied for the Adata evaluation is based on the paper "The benefits of market timing: evidence from merger and acquisition" by Evangelos Vagenas-Nanos. The sample employed in this valuation is based on the EU market. It more specifically involves all the takeovers done in the period between January 1, 1985 and December 30, 2019. For simplicity, this chapter will analyze all the 28 member states, even if many were not part of the EU for the period 1985–2019, dealt with in this chapter. The data have been collected using the Securities Data Company (SDC) Platinum database. The criteria to be met in order to be part of the sample are the following:

- Both target and acquirer are EU listed firms;
- The bidder acquires at least 50% of the shares of the target firm;
- The deal value is at least US $1 million;
- The method of financing the acquisition is either 100% in stock or 100% in cash;
- Those companies falling into the financial and utility firms are discarded (Fuller 2002);
- Deals lacking data for the returns around the announcement date are discarded.

7.2.1 Market Timers and Nonmarket Timers

In order to classify market timer and nonmarket timer companies, Vagenas-Nanos (2012) adopt a sequential procedure. After selecting the sample, daily stock prices for the bidding firms are collected back to 1 year and 2 years before the acquisition announcement date. Then, a comparison is performed between the company's price on the announcement date and the highest and lowest price.

Suppose the difference between the highest price and the price on the announcement date over the difference between the maximum and minimum prices is below a specific alpha percentage. In that case, this deal is classified as market timing.

On the other hand, if the difference between the price on the announcement date and the minimum price over the difference between the maximum price and the minimum price is below a specific alpha percentage, then this deal is classified as nonmarket timing.

This chapter will report results for deals for which prices are 15% away from past pick and minimum prices. The following formulas are adopted to break down market timers and nonmarket timer firms:

$$\text{If } \frac{\text{Max}-P}{\text{Max-Min}} 100 < \%, \text{then the deal is classified as a market timed deal;}$$

$$\text{If } \frac{P\text{-Min}}{\text{Max}-\text{Min}} 100 < \%, \text{then the deal is classified as a non-market timed deal}$$

However, Vagenas-Nanos (2012) argue that it might be necessary to exclude from the sample those firms whose stock price reported very low volatility in the past prices. For this reason, the author constructs a relative range measure that could capture these deals and are excluded from the sample.

$$\text{If } \frac{\text{Max}-\text{Min}}{\text{Average}\left(\text{Max},\text{Min}\right)} < 0.2, \text{then the deal is excluded from the sample}$$

Last but not least, M&A transactions where the difference between the maximum share price of the bidder and the price of the share at the announcement date over the range between the maximum price and the minimum is between 45% and 55% are considered neutral.

The neutral companies are classified by considering the following formula:

$$45\% < \frac{\text{Max} - P}{\text{Max} - \text{Min}} 100 < 55\%, \text{then the deal is neutral}$$

7.2.2 *Event Study Methodology*

The event study methodology is a statistical method to assess the impact of an event on the value of a firm. For example, in this case, the impact of the announcement of a merger among two companies has been considered in order to understand if the investors believe the acquisition will create or destroy value. The simple concept behind this methodology is to assess the abnormal return generated by the event in consideration by adjusting for the return produced by the fluctuations of market prices as a whole (Ball and Brown 1968).

7.2.3 *Short-run Event Study Methodology*

In order to calculate the bidder firms' short-run performance, the following methodology has been used. Firstly, for each firm, abnormal returns (ARs) are estimated both for a 2-day period (0, +1) and for a 4-day period (0, +3) around the M&A announcement date. The AR describes the vast profits or losses generated by a given stock over a specified period. ARs are crucial in assessing a stock performance when compared to the overall market or a benchmark index. The most common type of performance benchmark is a stock market index that tracks the performance of a broad asset class, such as the FTSE100. Comparing the return of a stock in a given market with the return generated by the primary index of the same market is a good proxy for evaluating the ARs of a company.

The equation is as follows:

$$\text{AR}_{i,t} = R_{i,t} - R_{m,t}$$

where $\text{AR}_{i,t}$ is the excess return of the bidder i on day t; $R_{i,t}$ is the return of bidder i on day t measured as "*the theoretical growth in value of a share held over a specified period, assuming that dividends are reinvested to purchase additional units of an equity at the closing price applicable on the ex-dividend date*"; and $R_{m,t}$ is the market return estimated as the percentage change in the corresponding local market index on day t where the companies are listed.

Then to measure the total impact of an event over a particular period of time, the cumulative abnormal returns (CARs) are calculated as the sum of the ARs ($AR_{i,t}$) for the 2 and 4 days around the announcement of the acquisition as per the below-mentioned formula:

$$\mathrm{CAR}_i = \sum_{t=0}^{+t} R_i - R_m$$

To specify whether the CARs are statistically significant, a one-sample t-test will be run. In this case, T-statistics are used to test the null hypothesis that the mean of the CAR is equal to zero for a sample of n firms. The results will be considered statistically significant when the p-value is less than or equal to the level of significance $\alpha = 0.05$; the null hypothesis is rejected. The data favor the alternative hypothesis.

7.2.4 *Long-run Event Study Methodology*

In addition, to examine the long-run ARs for stocks. After Barber and Lyon (1997), the buy-and-hold abnormal return (BHAR) have become the standard method of measuring long-term ARs. BHAR measures the average multiyear return from a strategy of investing in a firm that completed an event and selling at the end of a prespecified holding period. BHAR captures the investor's experience from buying and holding securities for 1–5 years: Vagenas-Nanos (2012) employs the 12-, 36-, and 60-BHAR approach. The BHAR) equation is computed as follows:

$$\mathrm{BHAR}_i = \prod_{1}^{T} (1 + R_{it}) - \prod_{1}^{T} (1 + R_{mt})$$

where R_{it} is the monthly return for the company i measured as "the theoretical growth in value of a share held over a specified period, assuming that dividends are reinvested to purchase additional units of an equity at the closing price applicable on the ex-dividend date"; and R_{mt} is the monthly return of the local market index where the companies are listed.

To specify whether the BHARs are statistically significant, a one-sample t-test will be run. Also in this case, T-statistics are used to test the null hypothesis that the mean of the BHARs is equal to zero for a sample of n firms. The results will be considered statistically significant when the p-value is less than or equal to the level of significance $\alpha = 0.05$; the null hypothesis is rejected. The data favor the alternative hypothesis.

7.3 Empirical Results

7.3.1 *Results of the Event Study in the Short Run*

After collecting the data with the Securities Data Company (SDC) Platinum database, the first skimming to create the sample has been done compliant with the criteria mentioned above. The whole selection accounted for 366 transactions performed during the period January 1, 1985–December 30, 2019.

The extensive sample has been divided into two major categories: acquisitions performed entirely by cash (211) and acquisitions completed fully by stock (155).

For each of the two categories, past stock prices were collected using the Refinitiv database. More precisely, for every bidder involved in such transactions, the stock price at the M&A announcement date, the daily stock prices for the two years preceding the announcement, and the daily stock prices for one year following the announcement were identified.

In the end, the initial sample has been divided into four subsamples: two samples accounting for cash acquirers with 1- and 2-year stock prices and two samples accounting for stock acquirers with 1- and 2-year stock prices.

Then for every company in the sample, the maximum and the minimum price of the stocks at 1 year and 2 years before the M&A announcement have been identified.

Table 7.1 displays the time series distribution of the takeovers by year as well as by stock and cash market and nonmarket timers. The final sample considers a total of 366 transactions between the years 1985 and 2019. The first three columns represent the distribution of the overall sample for 100% stock- and 100% cash-financed acquisitions. The remainder presents the distribution for market and nonmarket timers for stock and cash deals, respectively. Market timers and nonmarket timers are classified according to two different ways. If the share price of the acquiring firm on the date is "close" to its past 2-year or 1-year maximum price (minimum), the deal is classified as a market-timing deal. On the other hand, if the share price of

Table 7.1 Time series distribution for stock and cash acquirers, time span 1985–2019

Year	*All*	*Stock*	*Cash*	*Stock 15%*				*Cash 15%*			
				2 years past prices		*1 year past prices*		*2 years past prices*		*1 year past prices*	
				Market timers	*Nonmarket Timers*	*Market timers*	*Nonmarket Timers*	*Market timers*	*Nonmarket Timers*	*Market timers*	*Nonmarket timers*
1987	1		1					1			
1989	1		1								1
1990	1	1									
1991	2	2		1	1	1	1				
1992	2	2									
1993	1	1		1		1					
1994	5	2	3	1		1			1		1
1996	1		1					1		1	
1997	3	3		2		2					
1998	1		1					1		1	
1999	3	1	2					1		1	
2000	3	2	1								1
2001	4	2	2			1					
2002	19	5	14	1	2	1	2	3	5	1	5
2003	20	13	7	3	6	5	4	1	5	1	5
2004	23	9	14	3		2		4	1	3	1
2005	34	11	23	3	3	3	2	11	1	8	
2006	37	14	23	5	2	5	2	7	2	7	2
2007	28	8	20	2		2	2	10	1	8	

2008	18	5	13		2		2		4		7
2009	29	15	14		6	4	5	1	4	4	2
2010	17	7	10		2		2	3	1	3	1
2011	15	3	12					5	1	4	
2012	14	6	8	1	2		2	2	1	2	1
2013	12	4	8	3		4		3		3	
2014	18	12	6	3	2	2	3		1		1
2015	10	8	2	2	1	2	1	1		1	
2016	7	4	3	1	1	1	2	3		3	
2017	13	5	8	3		2		2	1	4	
2018	13	5	8		1		2	2		1	1
2019	11	5	6	1	1	1	1	1	1	2	1
Tot.	366	155	211	36	32	40	33	63	30	58	30

Source: Securities Data Company (SDC) Platinum database

the acquiring firm on the date is "close" to its past 2-year or 1-year minimum price, the deal is classified as a nonmarket-timing deal.

To define how "close" the price at the announcement date is relative to a past maximum or minimum, Vagenas-Nanos employs the following formulas:

$$\text{If } \frac{\text{Max-}P}{\text{Max-Min}} 100 < \alpha\%, \text{ then the deal is classified as a market timed deal;}$$

$$\text{If } \frac{P\text{-Min}}{\text{Max-Min}} 100 < \alpha\%, \text{ then the deal is classified as a non-market timed deal.}$$

Table 7.1 depicts results for market-timing and nonmarket-timing deals if alpha is 15% or lower.

Once having identified the six different samples, it is now time to understand the returns for the separate M&A transactions in both the short and long run.

For the purpose of identifying the short-run returns both for the stock and cash acquirers, the CARs two and four days after the announcement have been calculated. The CAR will describe the relationship between the expected value of a company's stock by comparing the performance of the market and the stock's current price.

Consequently, the focus will be on the mean distribution of CARs. Specifically, the aim is to assess whether this mean is statistically different from zero. To test this, a one-sample t-test — a parametric test — will be performed. Therefore, before running the t-test, certain assumptions must be met. First, the test variables must be continuous, and the data must be independent.

Moreover, there should be no significant outliers, and the sample should be approximately normally distributed.

The CARs two and four days after the announcement have been identified and tested, first for the general sample distinguishing between market timers and nonmarket timers classified between the past 1 and 2 years. Later on, the analysis has been carried out in more detail, considering both timing and not timing stock and cash acquiring companies. The following tables (Tables 2, 3, and 4) present the results of the CAR analysis described above. This should remove any ambiguity.

All the CARs are statistically significant. The analysis' implications will be provided in the next section.

7.3.2 Results of the Event Study in the Long Run

Once having identified the short-run returns, it is now time to understand the returns for the different M&A transactions in the long run.

To identify the long-run returns both for the stock and cash acquirers, the BHARs 12, 36, and 60 months after the announcement have been calculated. The BHAR can measure the average multiyear return of a stock of a firm that completed the M&A transaction.

Consequently, the focus will be on the mean of the distribution of BHAR and, specifically, one seeks to answer whether the average is different from zero with statistical significance. In order to check whether the mean is statistically significantly different from 0, as for the CAR, a one-sample *t*-test will be performed by previously checking for the parametric conditions.

The BHARs at 12, 36, and 60 months after the announcement have been calculated and tested. The following tables 6 and 7 present the results of this analysis. First, the general sample is examined, distinguishing between market timers and non-market timers, classified based on the 1- and 2-year preannouncement periods. Subsequently, a more detailed analysis is conducted, separating stock and cash acquirers, and again distinguishing between market timers and non-market timers, according to the same time classification.

All BHARs have been statistically tested, and most results are significant. The implications of the analysis will be discussed in the next section.

7.3.3 Discussion of the Findings

This section will present the key results coming from the above-executed analysis of the sample data. Starting from creating the sample and identifying the returns both in the short and long period, it will be possible to identify the main advantages of the market timing in the M&A context.

The creation of the sample highlights the trend of the merger market in Europe between 1987 and 2019. Broadly speaking, the merger market has been able to increase its volume during the last 30 years. It is possible to define the pick of this boom between 2003 and 2008 before the great crisis, but overall, the trend remained positive in the past few years.

As highlighted at the beginning of this chapter, in Europe, an increasing number of takeovers were recorded in the years 1993–2001. The 1990s' merger wave experienced its climax starting from 1997 where the stock market experienced the so-called dot.com bubble, which popped in

2000. In this period, most of the acquisitions occurred where stock acquisition and most companies were able to time the market when pursuing these kinds of transactions. The highest point was reached in 1997 at the beginning of the bubble. However, cash transactions were minimal, and time in the market was not of primary importance.

As highlighted, most of the acquisitions were cash-based acquisitions in the years after the dot.com bubble 2000–2003; stock-based ones represented a minority. It is important to underline here that most of the companies did not time the market during that period, probably due to the poor sentiment in the market conditions.

From the end of 2003 until 2008, before the great crisis, it is possible to distinguish an increase of cash-based acquisitions, which represent the majority, but also stock-based purchases see a surge. Among the cash-based purchases, more than 33% of them were done by considering the market timing. In the same way, also 29% of the stock-based acquisitions were done by considering the market timing.

The 2008 financial crisis marked a dramatic period for the M&A market, especially for stock-based transactions. After the global financial crisis, most deals were completed using cash. That said, it took a few years before stock-based acquisitions made a comeback. What is evident is that, in recent years, most stock-based transactions have been market timed.

On a more general note, respectively, 25% and 29% of the stock-/cash-based transactions during the last 30 years were market timed.

What has been found so far is in line with the past literature concerning the clustering behavior of M&A during the time. Since the seminal contribution by Nelson (1959), pointing out the merger waves of mid-1998, many studies have reported a wave-like pattern in merger activity. In particular, Mueller (1997) and Andrade et al. (2001) have been able to provide further evidence on the merger wave questions with updated facts for the 1990s.

Therefore, data arising from the first sample are consistent with the past literature; M&A tend to cluster in a specific period, notwithstanding the reasons behind this behavior could be multiple. What emerges from Table 7.1 is that the majority of the stock acquirer during a merger wave period tend to time the market. This behavior is consistent with the market timing hypothesis developed firstly by Shleifer and Vishny (2003). This assumption, supported among others by Ang and Cheng (2006), provided a concrete empirical confirmation that equity overvaluation is a valuable driver in M&A transactions. Ang and Cheng determine that stocks' overvaluation raises the chance that firms will perform an M&A transaction and the chance that this transaction will be a stock merger.

After having created a consistent sample to investigate, the analysis' results will proceed to focus on the return of stock and cash acquirers, both considering them as market and nonmarket timers.

Firstly, the short-run returns will be considered, evaluated as CARs, displayed in Table 7.2 Starting from the whole sample, we can say that, for a company pursuing an M&A transaction, in the short run, it is worth to time the market whether it is a cash or stock transaction because, in the end, the resulting gain is coherent both in two days and four days after the announcement.

Going more into detail, the analysis has explicitly focused on stock and cash acquirers to investigate the two M&A transaction groups separately. Table 7.3 shows the result from the CARs of stock acquirers. These data indicate that, whether companies are considered based on their 2-year or 1-year past prices, for stock-based acquisition it is always worth to time the market when considering announcing an acquisition. The average gain, in this case, is around 0.58%. In the same way, the losses resulting from the lack of attention are significant, with an average of about 12%.

Table Table 7.4 shows the result from the CARs of cash acquirers. Also, in this case, the returns for cash acquirers in the short term are higher for

Table 7.2 Short-run abnormal returns CARs (0, +1) and CARs (0, +3) for market timers and nonmarket timers whose share price is 15% away from the past pick-low prices

	CARs (0, +1)			*CARs (0, +3)*		
	All—15%					
	Market timers	*Nonmarket timers*	*Difference (MT-nonMT)*	*Market timers*	*Nonmarket timers*	*Difference (MT-nonMT)*
2 rears past prices						
Mean	1.18%	−6.37%	7.55%	1.9%	−8.12%	9.98%
p	<0.001	<0.001	–	<0.001	<0.001	–
N	99	62	–	99	62	–
1 year past prices						
Mean	1.15%	−7.33%	8.47%	1.8%	−9.02%	10.83%
p	<0.001	<0.001	–	<0.001	<0.001	–
N	98	63	–	98	63	–

Table 7.3 Short-run abnormal returns CARs (0, +1) and CARs (0, +3) for market timers and nonmarket timers whose share price is 15% away from the past pick-low prices, paying in stock

	CARs (0, +1)			*CARs (0, +3)*		
	Stock—15%					
	Market timers	*Nonmarket timers*	*Difference (MT-nonMT)*	*Market timers*	*Nonmarket timers*	*Difference (MT-nonMT)*
2 year past prices						
Mean	0.52%	–9.89%	10.43%	0.67%	–12.16%	12.83%
p	<0.001	<0.001	–	<0.001	<0.001	–
N	36	32	–	36	32	–
1 year past prices						
Mean	0.55%	–11.58%	12.10%	0.68%	–13.47%	14.14%
p	<0.001	<0.001	–	<0.001	<0.001	–
N	40	33	–	40	33	–

Table 7.4 Short-run abnormal returns CARs (0, +1) and CARs (0, +3) for market timers and nonmarket timers whose share price is 15% away from the past pick-low prices, paying in cash

	CARs (0, +1)			*CARs (0, +3)*		
	Cash—15%					
	Market timers	*Nonmarket timers*	*Difference (MT-nonMT)*	*Market timers*	*Nonmarket timers*	*Difference (MT-nonMT)*
2 year past prices						
Mean	1.54%	–2.60%	4.15%	2.53%	–3.70%	6.30%
p	<0.001	<0.001	–	<0.001	<0.001	–
N	63	30	–	63	30	–
1 year past prices						
Mean	1.57%	–2.65%	4.33%	2.59%	–4.14%	6.72%
p	<0.001	<0.001	–	<0.001	<0.001	–
N	58	30	–	58	30	–

those companies that time the market to those companies that decided not to do so. In other words, being a market timer provides some benefits also in this case.

However, as previously mentioned, cash acquiring companies are not included in the market timing theory because the assumption relies on stock acquiring companies. The hypothesis is that firms pursuing a transaction using their stocks as a currency would benefit by paying with their overvalued stocks during market peaks. Therefore, they do not consider transactions with cash currency. Consequently, investor sentiment could explain the high return both for cash and stock acquiring market timing companies. Investor sentiment for high-valued acquiring companies must be considerably high. As Rosen (2006) explained, if investors expect a broad range of mergers to create synergies, they react positively to merger announcements. When investors' expectations are based more on optimistic expectations than on reality, at least there will be a boost in price in the short run.

Moreover, Rosen explains how managerial concerns may operate in addition to investor sentiment. If investors have the above reality expectations about the synergies from a merger, this will reward managers at least in the short-term performance. This literature explains the positive short-term response to merger announcements in hot merger markets. To sum up, when managers announce a takeover at that time, they take advantage of investor optimism and enjoy some short-term benefits whether their method of payment used is either stock or cash.

After having consistently investigated the short-term performance of both cash and stock acquirer, the analysis' results will be focused on the long-run returns of the groups' acquirers, both emerging them as market and nonmarket timers.

While analyzing the long-run performance of both stock and cash acquirers, a price correction is to be expected. In this context, Table 7.5 should show that overvalued market-timing bidders underperform compared to nonmarket-timing companies. In other words, over the long run, the market should be able to assess whether the transaction has truly created value. Therefore, if the initial overvaluation was correctly exploited, no correction would occur.

Firstly, the stock-based acquisition long-run returns will be considered, evaluated as BHAR, which is displayed in Table 7.6. One year after the announcement (BAHR 12), market timers showed slightly positive returns while nonmarket timers suffered significant losses. Three years

Table 7.5 Buy-hold abnormal returns (BHARs) for 12, 36, and 60 months post-acquisition announcement for market and nonmarket timers whose share price is 15% away from past pick-low price

	BHARs12			*BHARs36*			*BHARs60*		
	All—15%								
	MT	*NMT*	*Difference (MT- NMT)*	*MT*	*NMT*	*Difference (MT-NMT)*	*MT*	*NMT*	*Difference (MT-NMT)*
2 years past prices									
Mean	2.22%	−16.91%	19.13%	−19.93%	−35.31%	15.38%	−30.60%	−55.96%	25.36%
p	0.158	<0.001		<0.001	<0.001		<0.001	<0.001	
N	99	62		99	62		99	62	
1 year past prices									
Mean	0.98%	−18.53%	19.51%	−24.38%	−30.21%	5.83%	−37.11%	−59.68%	22.57%
p	<0.001	<0.001	–	<0.001	<0.001	–	<0.001	<0.001	–
N	98	63	–	98	63	–	98	63	–

Table 7.6 Buy-hold abnormal returns (BHARs) for 12, 36, and 60 months post-acquisition announcement for market and nonmarket timers whose share price is 15% away from past pick-low price paying in stock

	BHARs12			*BAHRs36*			*BAHRs60*		
	Stock—15%								
	MT	*NMT*	*Difference (MT- NMT)*	*MT*	*NMT*	*Difference (MT-NMT)*	*MT*	*NMT*	*Difference (MT-NMT)*
2 years past prices									
Mean	2.34%	−33.50%	35.84%	−22.42%	−52.98%	30.56%	−38.00%	−85.57%	47.57%
p	.0.514	<0.001		<0.001	<0.001		<0.001	<0.001	
N	36	32		36	32		36	32	
1 year past prices									
Mean	0.25%	−35.14%	35.39%	−32.76%	−47.31%	14.55%	−52.49%	−97.06%	44.57%
p	<0.001	<0.001	–	<0.001	<0.001	–	<0.001	<0.001	–
N	40	33	–	40	33	–	40	33	–

after the announcement (BAHR 36), market timers statistically significantly outperform nonmarket timers by 14.55%. Even 5 years after the acquisitions (BAHR 60), despite the negative performance of both market and nonmarket timers, bidders who timed the market significantly outperform those that announced a deal when their share price was close to a low. Considering instead stock market timers identified using stock prices from two years prior to the announcement, these acquirers show a higher return–approximately 2.34%–when using one year past prices, measured 12 months after the announcement. However, since this result is not statistically significant, it will not be considered in the final evaluation. In contrast, non-market timers in the same group incurred a substantial loss of –33.50%. Looking further ahead, three years after the announcement (BHAR 36), market timers significantly outperform nonmarket timers by 30.56%. Even five years after the acquisition (BHAR 60), despite negative returns for both groups, bidders who timed the market still significantly outperform those who did not.

The long-term return results are a clear sign that the positive returns of the short run are not the result of investor sentiment. If this was not the case, as Rosen (2006) assumed, one would expect to observe a long-run reversal. However, this is not the case. Stock acquirers who exploit their shares as currency when their price was close to its peak are significantly better off than those nonmarket timing companies, both considering 1, 3, and 5 years after the announcement date.

Therefore, the long-run returns for stock acquiring companies are consistent with the literature proposed by Shleifer and Vishny (2003). This finding directly supports the market timing theory indicating that companies being able to exploit their overvalued equity are better off than those who do not.

Now, the cash-based acquisition long-run returns will be considered, evaluated, also in this case, using the BHAR method (Table 7.7).

One year after the announcement (BAHR 12), market timers showed slightly positive returns while nonmarket timers suffered statistically significant losses. Three years after the announcement (BAHR 36), market timers statistically significantly lost far more than nonmarket timers, around -7.21%. Even 5 years after the acquisitions (BAHR 60), despite the negative performance of both market and nonmarket-timers, bidders who timed the market significantly lost more than those companies announcing a deal when their stocks' price was low. Considering instead stock market timing acquirers identified using stock prices from two years prior

Table 7.7 Buy-hold abnormal returns (BHARs) for 12, 36, and 60 months post-acquisition announcement for market and nonmarket timers whose share price is 15% away from past pick-low price, paying in cash

	BHARs12			*BAHRs36*			*BAHRs60*		
	Cash—15%								
	MT	*NMT*	*Difference (MT- NMT)*	*MT*	*NMT*	*Difference (MT-NMT)*	*MT*	*NMT*	*Difference (MT-NMT)*
2 years past prices									
Mean	2.16%	0.79%	1.37%	–18.5%	–16.46%	–2.04%	–26.37%	–24.37%	2%
p	0.133	0.897	–	<0.001	0.05	–	<0.001	0.018	–
N	63	30	–	63	30	–	63	30	–
1 year past prices									
Mean	1.49%	–0.26%	1.75%	–18.60%	–11.39%	–7.21%	–26.50%	–18.57%	–7.93
p	0.003	<0.001	–	<0.001	<0.001	–	<0.001	<0.001	–
N	58	30	–	58	30	–	58	30	–

to the announcement, they generate a higher return–around 2.16%–based on one-year past prices, measured 12 months after the announcement. However, since the results for both market and non-market timers are not statistically significant, they will not be used for evaluation. Looking further ahead, three years after the announcement (BHAR 36), market timers statistically underperform non-market timers by –2.04%. Even five years after the acquisition (BHAR 60), despite negative performance for both groups, bidders who did not time the market significantly outperform those who did.

The long-run returns for cash-acquiring companies clearly illustrate why cash-based acquisitions are not associated with market timing benefits. Rosen (2006) demonstrated that when short-run abnormal returns are driven by investor sentiment, long-run performance tends to be weaker—a pattern that appears to hold in this case. One year after the announcement, market timers and non-market timers show fairly similar returns. However, a clear reversal emerges three and five years after the announcement, with non-market timers outperforming market timers. This difference grows in favor of non-market timers over time, becoming even more pronounced five years after the acquisition.

In order to wrap up, it is possible to assume that the model has proved the assumption mentioned above by Shleifer and Vishny (2003), where market timing companies have a better performance than nonmarket timing ones. More specifically, the short-run returns for market timers could be justified by investor sentiment for cash acquisition and possibly by market timing benefits and sentiment for stock acquirers. This assumption is then proved in the long run, where the positive returns for cash acquirers are reversed. In contrast, stock market timers enjoy the benefits of having exploited their overvalued equity and keep outperforming their nonmarket timer counterparts. For the sake of completeness, these results are in line with "The benefits of market timing: evidence from merger and acquisition" by Evangelos Vagenas-Nanos. As per the American M&A transactions analyzed in Vagenas-Nanos' paper also, the EU acquisition presents the same market timing behavior. In Europe and the United States, stock acquiring companies try to understand which is the best time for announcing an acquisition by maximizing the value of their stocks. For this reason, as presented by Vagenas-Nanos' results, stock market timers are better off in the long run than cash acquirers. In conclusion, these results provide sufficient evidence for the perks of market timing in M&A.

7.4 Conclusions

The results presented in this empirical chapter can contribute to the market timing theory developed by Shleifer and Vishny in 2003. Firstly, every firm has been identified whether it was adopting a market timer or nonmarket timer behavior. It results in those companies that decided to pursue an acquisition when their stock price was high generate a higher return with respect to those nonmarket timing companies. The results are consistent both in the short and in the long run. Nevertheless, this scenario could be identified only for stock acquirers. The market timing hypothesis does not include cash acquirers. Cash bidders who decided to pursue an acquisition when their stock price was near a pick resulted in a higher return with respect to those who did not market time the announcement date. This fact is just present during the short run because cash acquirers benefit from the positive investor sentiment. In the long run, the opposite happens, indicating consistency with the previously mentioned investor sentiment hypothesis.

This empirical chapter aims to provide additional evidence as to whether it is worth timing the market or not. The investor sentiment assumption proposed by Rosen (2006) could be considered a challenge to Shleifer and Vishny's academic model (2003) presented in the behavioral theory of mergers. In fact, according to Rosen, the stock gains are just temporary and will be subject to a long-run reversal. The results obtained in this chapter discard Rosen's theory by proving the higher return for stock market timers both in the short and in the long run. In conclusion, the data provide sufficient evidence for the perks of market timing in M&A. However, the empirical results reported herein should be considered in the light of some limitations. The primary limitation to the generalization of these results is related to the sample selection. The analysis should provide a focus on the European M&A market, but a clear predominance of the UK market is unavoidable, especially until the beginning of the century. The second limitation instead tackles the sample size. This is mainly due, on the one hand, to the poor activity of the M&A market in Europe and, on the other hand, to the methodology employed during the sample creation. Lastly, the dissertation may raise some concerns, and a deeper analysis is required. Why do some stock acquiring companies decide not to time the market when there is ample proof of this benefit? More generally, why do some companies not use their overvalued equity but rather pay cash? Additional investigation might provide concrete answers to this.

References

Andrade, G., Mitchell, M., & Stafford, E. (2001). New Evidence and Perspectives on Mergers. *Journal of Economic Perspectives, 15*(2), 103–120. https://doi.org/10.1257/jep.15.2.103

Ang, J., & Cheng, Y. (2006). Direct evidence on the market-driven acquisition theory. *Journal of Financial Research, 29*(2), 199–216. https://doi.org/10.1111/j.1475-6803.2006.00174.x

Ball, R., & Brown, P. (1968). An empirical evaluation of accounting income numbers. *Journal of Accounting Research, 6*(2), 159. https://doi.org/10.2307/2490232

Barber, B., & Lyon, J. (1997). Detecting long-run abnormal stock returns: The empirical power and specification of test statistics. *Journal of Financial Economics, 43*(3), 341–372. https://doi.org/10.1016/s0304-405x(96)00890-2.

Datastream. (2012) Thomson Reuters Datastream. Available at: Subscription Service (accessed July 2021).

Fuller, S. (2002). *Social epistemology*. Indiana University Press.

Gort, M. (1969). An economic disturbance theory of mergers. *The Quarterly Journal of Economics, 83*(4), 624. https://doi.org/10.2307/1885453

Gugler, K., Mueller, D., & Weichselbaumer, M. (2012). The determinants of merger waves: An international perspective. *International Journal of Industrial Organization, 30*(1), 1–15. https://doi.org/10.1016/j.ijindorg.2011.04.006

Jovanovic, B., & Rousseau, P. (2002). The Q-Theory of Mergers. *American Economic Review, 92*(2), 198–204. https://doi.org/10.1257/000282802320189249

Mitchell, M., & Mulherin, J. (1996). The impact of industry shocks on takeover and restructuring activity. *Journal of Financial Economics, 41*(2), 193–229. https://doi.org/10.1016/0304-405x(95)00860-h.

Mueller, D. (1997). Merger policy in the United States: A reconsideration. *Review of Industrial Organization, 12*(5/6), 655–685. https://doi.org/10.1023/a:1007797626160

Nelson, R. L., & National Bureau of Economic Research (Etats-Unis). (1959). *Merger movements in American industry, 1895–1956* (No. 66). Princeton University Press. https://doi.org/10.1017/S0007680500045530.

Rosen, R. (2006). Merger momentum and investor sentiment: The stock market reaction to merger announcements. *Journal of Business, 79*(2), 987–1017. https://doi.org/10.1086/499133

SDC Platinum. (2012). *SDC platinum. Thomson Reuters.* [Online]. Available at: Subscription Service (accessed July 2021).

Shleifer, A., & Vishny, R. (2003). Stock market driven acquisitions. *Journal of Financial Economics, 70*(3), 295–311. https://doi.org/10.1016/s0304-405x(03)00211-3

Vagenas-Nanos, E. (2012). *The benefits of market timing: Evidence from mergers and acquisitions. University of Glasgow*. Available at: http://www.efmaefm.org/0EFMAMEETINGS/EFMA%20ANNUAL%20MEETINGS /2012-Barcelona/papers/EFMA2012_0349_fullpaper.pdf

CHAPTER 8

Quid Pro Quotes

Liquidity Provision Opportunity Distribution in the Investment Grade Corporate Bond Market

Karim Henide

8.1 Introduction

Leverage is central to economic cycles and systemic risk; indeed, Geanakoplos (2010) argues that, in times of crisis, "collateral rates (equivalently margins or leverage) are far more important than interest rates," despite the latter's perceived utmost importance by economists dating back to Irving Fisher's writings. Indeed, building on this argument, influential contributions, such as those by Svensson (2018) and Galí (2014), question the use of interest rates altogether in lieu of macroprudential

K. Henide (✉)
Newcastle Business School (NBS), Northumbria University, Newcastle upon Tyne, UK
e-mail: karim.henide@northumbria.ac.uk

E. Scannella and J. Williams (eds.), *Trends, Issues, and Challenges in Banking and Finance*, Palgrave Macmillan Studies in Banking and Financial Institutions,
https://doi.org/10.1007/978-3-031-96066-6_8

tools in response to systematic risks,[1] such as those arising from bubbles, cautioning against utilizing monetary policy to "lean against the wind."[2] The underlying corpus finds meaningful evidence of the negative influence of excess leverage on systemic vulnerability from as early as late modernity; Schularick and Taylor (2012) highlight high leverage and simultaneously low capital/liquidity buffers as significant predictors of financial crises in their study of 14 developed countries over the 1870–2008 period. In a similar vein, Jordà et al. (2015) find in "leveraged bubbles" that the interaction between both asset price bubbles and credit growth poses the greatest risk to financial stability and tends to be significant predictors of financial crises, albeit they find that only housing (not equity bubbles) are significant in their 1870–2013 study spanning 17 countries.[3] Jordà et al. (2015) argue that, as Alan Greenspan had suspected and consistent with the conjectures of Mishkin (2008, 2009b), the role of credit is fundamental to determining the danger of bubbles. While "pure, unleveraged 'irrational exuberance' bubbles may pose a limited threat to financial stability [...] 'Credit boom bubbles', [...] may be a dangerous combination", given the typical development of the positive feedback between "credit growth, asset prices, and increasing leverage" in such bubbles.

Historically, it has been when highly leveraged financial institutions are forced to subsequently deleverage that systemic crises have erupted and economic recessions have followed (Geanakoplos and Pedersen 2012). Adrian and Shin (2010) draw on empirical observations to explain that financial intermediaries have historically tended to proactively adjust their balance sheets in response to changes in prices and measured risks such that leverage becomes procyclical (high during booms and low during busts). Procyclical leverage negatively affects aggregate volatility and particularly the price of risk, as pre-empted to an extent by Gromb and

[1] Inter alia, Grill et al. (2015) and Smith et al. (2017) concur that banks bound by the leverage ratio requirement should see an increase incentive to engage in riskier activity but argue that this is outweighed by the synchronous increase in loss-absorbing capacity due to higher capital.

[2] Mishkin (2009a) offers a robust rebuttal to the view that monetary policy is ineffective during financial crises, arguing that monetary policy is more potent during financial crises because aggressive monetary policy easing can make adverse feedback loops less likely.

[3] Specific to housing bubbles, Khandani et al. (2013) describe the resulting limit to homeowner deleveraging, as a result of the unintentional synchronization of homeowner leverage, as the "refinancing ratchet effect" and find meaningful evidence to suggest that it contributes negatively to systemic risk.

Vayanos (2002). Miller and Stiglitz (2010) similarly add an asset bubble to a canonical model of highly leveraged businesses to illustrate the "vicious downward cycle" that ensues, driving asset price destabilization versus equilibrium, threatening widespread insolvency and a "balance sheet recession" (Koo 2011), following a simulated aggregate financial shock.

8.2 Leverage Ratio Requirement

Given the consensus in the literature, it follows rationally that "monitoring leverage is monitoring systemic risk" (Geanakoplos and Pedersen 2012) and that preventing excess leverage and limiting the effects of weight compression during booms (Adrian and Shin 2010; Altunbasa et al. 2014; Borio and Zhu 2012; Vallascas and Hagendorff 2013) is a prudential necessity. Reflecting the academic rationale in their proposal, the Basel Committee on Banking Supervision (BCBS) was motivated to address the problem of excess bank leverage following the global financial crisis (GFC). The BCBS introduced the Basel III standards in November 2010 (the "Original Basel III Standards"; Basel Committee 2010), then published the "Basel III leverage ratio framework and disclosure requirements" standard in January 2014,[4] the amended full text to the 2013 consultation that prompted criticism (Basel Committee 2013), which recognized the "build-up of excessive on- and off-balance sheet leverage in the banking system" as an underlying cause of the 2008 GFC; the BCBS highlights that in the process of forced deleveraging of bank balance sheets at the height of the crisis "amplified downward pressures on asset prices and exacerbated the feedback loop between losses, falling bank capital and shrinking credit availability" (Basel Committee 2014a). The standard, since consolidated into the Basel Framework, introduces (since Basel II)[5] and outlines the two-pronged intentions of the (non-risk based; Ingves 2014) leverage ratio measure in supplementing risk-based capital requirements. Namely, the ratio is intended to (a) restrict the buildup of leverage

[4] The standard was published with the final stages ("Basel III"; Basel Committee 2017a; Basel Committee 2017b), in December 2017.

[5] Although, per Brei and Gambacorta (2014), the concept is not new, a similar measure has been in force in Canada and the United States since the early 1980s [Crawford et al (2009), D'Hulster (2009)]. The introduction of a leverage ratio requirement for large banking groups has been announced in Switzerland in 2009 [FINMA Swiss Financial Market Supervisory (2009)]. Similar requirements have been proposed more recently in other jurisdictions (Basel Committee, 2014b).

in the banking sector to avoid destabilizing deleveraging processes that can damage the broader financial system and the economy;[6] and (b) reinforce the risk-based requirements with a simple, non-risk-based "backstop" measure. For global systemically important banks (G-SIBs), as identified according to SCO40, the leverage ratio is appended with additional leverage ratio buffer requirements, which must be met with Tier 1 capital, per LEV20.4.[7]

The leverage ratio is defined as a (Tier 1) capital measure divided by a bank's total exposure measure, which consists of on-balance sheet items as well as off-balance sheet items, and is expressed as a percentage. More extensively, based on the leverage ratio common disclosure template (Basel Committee 2014a), the Basel III leverage ratio can be represented as:

$$\frac{\text{Tier 1 capital}}{\begin{array}{c}\text{on-b/s exposure} + \text{derivative exposure} \\ + \text{securities financing exposure} + \text{off-b/s items}\end{array}}$$

Where (per Basel Committee 2014a) on-balance sheet exposures consist of (a) on-balance sheet items (excluding derivatives and securities financing transactions [SFTs], but including collateral); and (b) (asset amounts deducted in determining Basel III Tier 1 capital). Derivative exposures consist of (a) replacement cost associated with all derivative transactions (i.e., net of eligible cash variation margin), (b). add-on amounts for (potential funding exposure (PFE) associated with all derivatives transactions, (c). gross-up for derivatives collateral provided where deducted from the balance sheet assets pursuant to the operative accounting framework, (d) deductions of receivables assets for cash variation margin provided in derivatives transactions, (e) exempted central counterparty (CCP) leg of client-cleared trade exposures, (f) adjusted effective notional amount of written credit derivatives, and (g). adjusted effective notional offsets and add-on deductions for written credit derivatives. Total securities financing transaction exposures consist of (a) gross SFT assets (with no recognition of netting), after adjusting for sale accounting transactions,

[6] As Mishkin (2009b) proposes, post-credit busts, "the resulting deleveraging depresses [...] spending, which weakens economic activity and increases macroeconomic risk in credit markets," which Jordà et al. reasonably argue contribute to explaining the slow resulting recovery from the global financial crisis (Mian and Sufi 2014; Jordà et al. 2013)

[7] LEV40.2 sets out that the leverage ratio buffer will be set at 50% of a G-SIB's higher loss-absorbency risk-based requirements, such that a G-SIB subject to a 2% higher loss-absorbency requirement would be subject to a 1% leverage ratio buffer requirement.

(b) netted amounts of cash payables and cash receivables of gross SFT assets, (c) counterparty credit risk (CCR) exposure for SFT assets, and (d) agent transaction exposures. Off-balance sheet items consist of (a) off-balance sheet exposure at gross notional amount; and (b) adjustments for conversion to credit equivalent amounts.

A minimum leverage ratio of 3%, equating to exposure of a maximum 33.3 % (leverage multiple) vis-à-vis Tier 1 capital, was initially prescribed and settled upon following the finalization of the definition and exposure measure in January 2018. The implementation of the leverage ratio requirements began with bank-level reporting to national supervisors of the leverage ratio and its components from January 2013, and public disclosure started in January 2015. Most recently, various technical amendments were made by the Basel Committee (2023), including expanding the scope of the bank exposure definition to include exposures arising from insurance subsidiaries. Furthermore, a G-SIB buffer became effective from January 2023. The Basel Committee stipulates that the leverage ratio G-SIB buffer should also consist of supervisory Tier 1 capital amounting to 50% of a G-SIB's risk-weighted higher-loss absorbency requirements, behaving akin to the capital buffers in the risk-weighted framework. Capital distribution constraints are imposed on G-SIBs that do not meet the leverage ratio buffer requirement, dependent on Common Equity Tier 1 (CET1) risk-weighted ratio and Tier 1 leverage ratio. A G-SIB that meets (a) its CET1 risk-weighted requirements (defined as a 4.5% minimum requirement, a 2.5% capital conservation buffer and the G-SIB higher loss-absorbency requirement); and (b) its Tier 1 leverage ratio requirement (defined as a 3% leverage ratio minimum requirement and the G-SIB leverage ratio buffer) will not be subject to distribution constraints. Those that do not are subject to the associated minimum capital conservation requirement (the higher of the two associated conservation requirements in the case that both requirements are violated), expressed as a percentage of earnings (Basel Committee 2017a). This is the last of the scheduled Basel III transitional arrangements for the 2017–2028 period.

Academic, practitioner, and policymaker communities identified and expressed key concerns ex-ante surrounding the introduction of a leverage ratio. Given the non-risk weighted nature of the measure, early criticisms pointed to the inherent, reasonably inadvertent, incentivization for certain banks to reduce their risk exposure to low-risk assets and engage in riskier activity (D'Hulster 2009; ESRB 2014; Finansinspektionen 2015; Kiema and Jokivuolle 2014; Lautenschläger 2013; Spinassou 2013; Treanor

2013), thus exacerbating systemic risk, ceteris paribus. Banks may be particularly motivated to engage in riskier activity in pursuit of supplementing their profitability, following the expected impact of debilitated balance sheet capacity (D'Hulster 2009). Furthermore, a clear trade-off emerged between the mitigation of systemic risks and the constraint of market-making activity; introducing a cap on leverage would weaken financial intermediation, giving rise to inefficiencies (limits to arbitrage), reducing credit availability (Spinassou 2013; Treanor 2013) and increasing lending rates (Cosimano and Hakura 2011), which is relevant to the question of real future economic investment and growth. Some researchers also found credence for the prospect of more interconnectedness and risk concentration, particularly as the result of the complicated interplay between bank access to leverage and derivative utilization which "simply cannot be addressed by a reasonable single capital rule" (Blundell-Wignall et al. 2014).

Following the successful finalization and integration of the leverage ratio requirements, academic, practitioner, and policymaking communities, including the BCBS themselves, have sought to assess the intended and unintended implications on systemic risk and agent behavior ex-post, part of a broader initiative to evaluate the impact of prudential regulations introduced after the GFC on markets. In particular, with respect to bond markets, it has been found that bank-affiliated dealers commit less capital (Bessembinder et al. 2018) and that the cost of immediacy has increased (Dick-Nielsen and Rossi 2019); Bao et al. (2018) also find that bonds have become less liquid during times of stress, specifically due to the Volcker Rule.[8] Acosta-Smith et al. (2020) find empirical evidence confirming the anticipated increase in risk-weighted assets by banks bound by the leverage ratio requirement. Securitization activity has also stagnated as a result, consistent with their (2017) proposition(s).

8.3 Corporate Bond Intermediation

Expanding upon the corpus of research that assesses the intended and unintended impact of regulatory changes on the functioning of financial (specifically, corporate bond) markets, and building upon the prior

[8] Bank-affiliated dealers operate in either an agency or principal capacity; the former entails brokering a trade, through counterparty search and matching, without warehousing any risk, whereas the latter which is most relevant to our purposes entails bank-affiliated dealers warehousing the risk on their own balance sheet until they subsequently unload the risk to another counterparty.

work of Anand et al. (2021) and Rapp and Waibel (2023), Giannetti et al. (2023) seek to explore the behavior and performance of unregulated market participants within the context of the constraints on regulated financial institutions and associated spillovers, resulting from Basel III leverage ratio requirements.

Rapp and Waibel (2023), studying the cross-sectional effects of Basel leverage regulations on dealer intermediation, using confidential transaction data from the naturally fragile and fragmented US corporate bond market, demonstrate empirically that bank-affiliated dealers tend to sharply contract their bond inventories, an indication of risk intermediation activity, for approximately 10 days prior to reporting dates which occur at quarter-end. During this period, bank-affiliated dealers are net sellers of positions to nonbank customers, reasonably motivated by an intention to reduce reported leverage ratio. Bank-affiliated dealers' behavior observed around quarter-end in this context is more generally reminiscent of the window dressing behavior engaged in by systematically important banks at year-end with respect to reducing intermediation activity, leading to lower additional capital requirements in the form of G-SIB buffers (Behn et al. 2022). Specifically with respect to the implications of the leverage ratio and banks' incentives to window dress, Bassi et al. (2024) establish a causal link between economically sizeable contractions in repo transactions engineered by banks around regulatory reporting dates, and banks' incentives to engage in window dressing behavior, not only underscoring the importance of leverage ratio in driving such behavior, but also reaffirming the importance of the aforementioned G-SIB framework.

Anand et al. (2021) sought to address the gap in the literature surrounding the linkage between "bond institutions" and fragility risk, finding in their assessments of market structure and mutual fund trading patterns that the marginal mutual bond fund engages in a style of trading that is susceptible to straining dealer positions, although there exists an important subset of mutual funds which "intentionally supply liquidity during episodes of large customer selling (that are associated with significant transitory price effects) and earn a return premium for liquidity services." The latter behavior, exhibited by the subset of liquidity-supplying mutual funds, was found to be consistent during periods of large fund outflows and elevated market stress, contributing positively to alleviating fragility risk in the bond market. This study, as such, offers critical insights into the role of select buy-side firms in persistently supplying liquidity alongside dealers, and that such funds are compensated for their service and, the corollary, for contributing positively to market stability.

Giannetti et al. (2023) leverage data on bonds, mutual funds, and dealers to classify and assess the behavior of market participants, vis-à-vis liquidity demand and supply, around calendar quarter-ends when dealers tend to de-risk their balance sheets and opportunities arise for unregulated market participants to be compensated for supplying liquidity during this time of relative liquidity deficit. The experiments and empirical results are compelling, providing a gamut of original insights surrounding investment grade and high-yield liquidity demand and supply over time. The findings of Giannetti et al. (2023) marry the findings of Rapp and Waibel (2023) and Anand et al. (2021), finding that when and where regulatory concerns hinder bond liquidity provisioning by bank-affiliated dealers, particularly in the case of Basel leverage regulation-induced liquidity hinderances (Rapp and Waibel 2023), liquidity-supplying funds (per Anand et al. 2021) help to bridge the liquidity deficiencies. Giannetti et al. (2023) further find that, with respect to remuneration for liquidity provision, quarter-end purchases of "constrained bonds," where there is inventory overhang,[9] yield higher returns and alpha relative to non-quarter-end months and bonds without inventory overhang. There is also evidence of feedback from fund flows to bond illiquidity, relating poor mutual fund performance and/or outflows to a lower propensity to supply liquidity, and therefore more illiquid bonds at quarter-ends.

8.4 The Selective Distribution of Liquidity Provision Opportunities

In this chapter, we zone-in on the particular insights of Giannetti et al. (2023) with respect to the computations of the excess returns of "constrained" and "unconstrained" bonds prior to and following the introduction of the leverage ratio requirement, as well as regression results

[9] Consistent with the preceding literature (Correa et al., 2020), Gianetti et al. (2023) define European and Japanese bank-affiliated dealers and US bank-affiliated dealers that become subject to the supplementary leverage ratio requirements as "constrained." Furthermore, bonds which are constrained are those subject to an inventory overhang. The degree to which a given bond is constrained in any given month is defined by the share of positive inventory holdings that constrained dealers buildup in bond j during the first twenty days of a month relative to bond j's issue size, where "positive inventory" conveys a dealer's net purchases of a given bond.

pertaining to fund liquidity provisioning by bank-affiliated funds. Constrained bank dealers have been shown to sell their bond holdings primarily to investors and nonbank financial intermediaries in their networks (Rapp and Waibel 2023), which are typically broad and diverse. As Giannetti et al. (2023) highlight that engaging in liquidity provision for investment-grade bonds is profitable and involves limited risk, [so] all mutual fund managers, irrespective of their affiliation with a dealer, should have incentives to compete for these trades, given that we take these agents to be optimizers of respective fund alpha. However, while both bank-affiliated and unaffiliated liquidity-supplying funds equally provide liquidity to constrained banks, it is plausible, although not the only possibility or source of concern, that constrained bank dealers favor their affiliated funds by directing more profitable trades to them. Giannetti et al. (2023) test this preference hypothesis by exploring whether bank-affiliated funds perform better from engaging in liquidity provision following introduction of the leverage ratio (January 2015 onwards). Their results suggest that while all investment-grade bond funds generate alpha from liquidity-supplying strategies after the introduction of the leverage ratio regulations, the alpha of investment-grade liquidity-supplying funds that are bank-affiliated is over three times larger than that of other liquidity-supplying funds (0.034/0.011; the former significant at the 5% level, and the latter significant at the 10% level), suggesting that constrained bank dealers direct their best trades to their affiliated mutual funds. Prior to the introduction of the leverage ratio, the alpha of investment-grade liquidity-supplying funds that are bank-affiliated was materially lower (0.017), though 17× greater than that of other liquidity-supplying funds (0.017/0.001), albeit neither results from the OLS estimates demonstrated statistical significance, which reinforces the narrative around the critical role of the Basel III leverage ratio requirements in altering the pattern of intermediation behavior in the, particularly investment grade, bond trading ecosystem.

The suggestion that constrained bank dealers may be directing their best trades to same-bank-affiliated mutual funds is one of great importance that must be investigated and addressed to mitigate the fairness and sound functioning of markets from being undermined. Furthermore, there are questions to be answered around the potential illegality of such behavior, should it be found that bank-affiliated dealers selectively direct their best liquidity-provision opportunities to same-bank-affiliated mutual funds, as it desecrates the very nature of the principles of the supposed "arm's length relationship" expected between bank-affiliated dealers and same-bank-affiliated mutual funds. This is not, however, the only possibility—and we outline the possibility of aligning with the letter of the law while synchronously posing potential problems for long-term consumer welfare, sound market functioning, and systemic stability, by extension.

In the case of liquidity provision opportunity distribution by purse share

Critically, due to the limitations of the data, namely that Giannetti et al. (2023) do not observe mutual funds' trade but only their monthly position changes, one cannot reasonably establish direct linkages between constrained bank dealers that may be directing their best trades to same-bank-affiliated mutual funds. An alternative plausible theory, which suitably justifies correlation but does not rely on the establishment of causation (contrary to the "same-bank-affiliated mutual fund" theory), is that constrained bank dealers direct their best liquidity-provision opportunities to mutual funds affiliated with bank as a peer group, by virtue of their size and behavioral homogeneity. Future research, with the data used in Giannetti et al. (2023), could explore grouping liquidity-supplying funds by size to validate this theory. Mutual funds affiliated with the world's largest banks constitute among the largest asset managers by AUM as a peer group. It stands to reason that these asset managers exhibit some degree of behavior homogeneity and that, given their size, they are rewarded for their flows in the aggregate through the selective provision of liquidity opportunities. In this paradigm, while no illegality has been alluded to, we highlight the potential adverse impact of the scale economies that could mechanically translate to higher alpha, ceteris paribus, for larger mutual funds. Indeed, the prospect of a positive feedback loop emerges; consider naively the Berk and Green (2004) model which suggests that future fund flows are predicated on prior fund performance, larger mutual funds must benefit disproportionately from future fund flows given their exclusive access to alpha-enhancing liquidity opportunities, intuitively. Such disproportionate absorption of future fund flows should then increase bank-affiliated mutual funds' share of the constrained bank dealers' purse, as a peer group, further entrenching their status and their access to the selective distribution of liquidity-provision opportunities in the future. Independently of computing and comparing prior period returns, assuming otherwise virtually identical characteristics and having knowledge that funds of larger size have selective access to attractive liquidity-provision opportunities, rational wealth-maximizing consumers of mutual funds concerned solely with personal short-term interests must necessarily allocate to larger mutual funds. This behavior can, however, result in suboptimal long-term outcomes, as smaller firms struggle to compete. Reducing competition can be counterproductive for the interests of consumers of mutual funds as a whole in the long term, and it may also negatively influence financial stability; a concentrated industry with virtually behaviorally homogeneous firms suffers from encumbered liquidity, market efficiency, and systemic stability, by extension. We explore this later in the case of the "same-bank-affiliated mutual fund" theory, and draw on the empirical evidence of Massa (2004) to convey our concerns over the loss of a broad and diverse pool of mutual funds.

8.5 Motivation to Collude

The motivation for larger mutual funds to receive attractive, directed, trades is empirically clear vis-à-vis the implications for enhancing fund alpha. Fund alpha, and track record by extension, is important for a manager's personal short-term earnings and career trajectory, given the relevance in determining future fund flows (and therefore higher earnings from management fees, ceteris paribus) as well as performance fees. What, though, could the motivation of the bank-affiliated dealer be? We hypothesize that this could be one or some combination of direct and indirect economic incentives, which synthesize a gap in the literature for further study:

Hypothesis 1 Through fostering strong and transparent relationships with larger mutual funds, bank-affiliated dealers may be pre-emptively fortifying their desks against bouts of counter-cyclicality by establishing a liquidity provider of last resort with a meaningfully large balance sheet and therefore capacity to unload risk, who they reward with attractive trades during periods of systemic stability. This ally, in theory, could protect bank-affiliated dealers from being "cornered" in times of pronounced stress.

Hypothesis 2 Bank-affiliated dealers may benefit from reciprocation, through directing their best trades to larger mutual funds, through selective "second looks" on trades, and therefore opportunities to secure greater trade flows, all within the scope of best execution.[10]

[10] Having established a best price for execution, same-bank-affiliated mutual funds could circle back to their bank-affiliated dealers to inform them of the price to beat, giving them a chance to requote at a lower price. This is a clear informational advantage (competitive disadvantage to the rest of the bank panel competing for the trade) but is conceptually defensible.

Hypothesis 3 In hope of constructing a career safety net, or in pursuit of a more lucrative role with a larger mutual fund, bank-affiliated dealers may seek to build a positive relationship with traders and managers that they face. Such a hypothesis could be supported through investigating bank-affiliated dealers' patterns of employment.

Hypothesis 4 Bank-affiliated dealers may benefit from entertainment at the expense of larger mutual funds, although the potential monetary value of such a benefit would, in theory, be minimal as constrained by the regulator and overseen/enforced by internal compliance teams on both sides—the flow of entertainment also tends to be from the sell-side to the buy-side. There could also be illicit, undocumented, exchanges of products, services, or even cash as, anecdotally, reported publicly in tangential cases of illicit consideration in exchange for insider information.

Notwithstanding the potential concerns of bank-affiliated dealers vis-à-vis the importance of having a close ally in the form of a larger mutual fund to serve as a liquidity provider of last resort to avoid being cornered, selectively directing attractive trades to favored members within a network counteracts the spirit of fairness that regulators seek to maintain in the market and raises some serious questions around competition, long-term consumer welfare, market efficiency, and financial stability, by extension. Having established this and explored possible motivations, we pose the question: how can this behavior be counteracted and how can opportunities to provide liquidity be distributed more symmetrically?

8.5.1 In the Case of Violation of the "Arm's Length Relationship"

Among regulators, there is a clear concern over anti-competitive behavior; antitrust laws, such as the Sherman Antitrust Act and the Clayton Antitrust act, are designed to prevent anti-competitive behavior and protect consumer welfare. Favoritism among banks' dealers and bank-affiliated mutual funds would be an antitrust matter, that could contribute to the systematic stifling of competition in the fund management industry, and the subsequent reduction of consumer choice, and consumer welfare more generally. Inter alia, Coates and Hubbard (2004) speak to the importance of competition as the "best guardian against excessive fees." Furthermore, there are matters of subsequent concern arising from the systematic reduction in competition relating to the functioning of markets.

Specifically, fewer and more concentrated counterparties with less heterogeneous flows in the aggregate do not bode well for market efficiency, or systemic risk more generally. Inter alia, Massa (2004) finds empirical support for the notion that the presence of more and relatively less-informed funds impacts the market, increasing liquidity, albeit the study focused on equity market liquidity—the intuition is reasonably transferable to fixed income markets, though.

Regulators have been clear in their design and communication of best practices and binding rules to set a precedent for ensuring that broker-dealers operating within their purview should ensure fair treatment among their customers. FINMA Rule 5310 establishes rules on best execution, particularly with respect to addressing potential conflicts of interest in principle; FINRA Rule 2122 requires that charges relating to services performed by a broker "shall be reasonable and not unfairly discriminatory among customers," the operative word being "discriminatory." However, against the backdrop of a fragmented market whose business is principally conducted over the counter (OTC) and it is not common, unlike what one may come to expect to observe in some parallel markets, to have tick-by-tick axes on given securities, it is possible for a bank-affiliated dealer to direct their best trades to preselected customers without explicitly discriminating against their other customers on price. Indeed, assuming a bank-affiliated dealer is not prompted to show a price by other customers, would a bank-affiliated dealer solely pitching a constrained bond at an attractive price to a same-bank-affiliated mutual fund be considered discriminatory?

There are, though, also rules that govern selective disclosure more generally.[11] While showing axes selectively to members of a dealer's network may not inherently be a disclosure of material non-publication information, would the declaration by a bank-affiliated dealer to a same-bank-affiliated mutual fund that they were constrained constitute a selective disclosure? In such a scenario, a deal is not necessarily incumbent on such an overt disclosure being made. One can reasonably assume that any one party to

[11] 17 CFR § 243.100(a)(1) stipulates, albeit from the perspective of an issuer (rather than a bank-affiliated dealer), that if an issuer, or any person acting on its behalf, discloses any material nonpublic information regarding that issuer or its securities, the issuer must make public disclosure of that information simultaneously, in the case of an intentional disclosure.

the prices being quoted around the quarter-end bank-deleveraging window would be capable of implying this information from observing the price concession.[12] That is to say that if one takes a bank-affiliated dealer's disclosure, "I am constrained in bond X," to a same-bank-affiliated mutual fund to be [selective] disclosure of material nonpublic information, then directing of attractive trades to favored customers within a network is effectively a covert disclosure of material nonpublic information.

8.6 Addressing the Asymmetric Distribution of Liquidity-Provision Opportunities

We posit a series of propositions which represent possible remedies, motivated by the different agents within the ecosystem, that can redress the balance of liquidity-provision opportunity distribution, or mitigate the need for liquidity provision from unregulated market participants altogether. We assume in our approach that, aside from the aforementioned unintended consequences, the primary endpoint is being met, and the leverage ratio regulation is desirable (should not undergo any modification):

Proposition 1 *The onus is on smaller or unaffiliated mutual funds to proactively seek out liquidity-provision opportunities.*

In theory, mutual funds which are not affiliated with the same bank as a given bank-affiliated dealer can remedy this problem themselves by being more proactive. Assuming their awareness of indicative timelines of bank-affiliated dealers' deleveraging around the quarter-end reporting window, and the resulting opportunities to provide liquidity, such mutual funds could request frequent updates on banks' axes with respect to bonds which they suspect to be constrained, or a broader set of International Securities Identification Numbers (ISIN) from which they can determine the degree of constraint from the implied price concession under fair value. This may be onerous and an unsocial practice, but failure to do this could be perceived as an operational inefficiency in the context, or even a neglect of fiduciary responsibility to seek out optimal opportunities in the case of

[12] Rapp and Waibel (2023), after controlling for some bond characteristics, find economically material and statistically significant price discounts of 2.2 and 3.5 basis points on the average transaction spread for US and European and Japanese bank dealers, respectively, when seeking liquidity supply around quarter-ends.

a fund explicitly mandated to find liquidity-provision opportunities or to maximize alpha capture. In the case that prices of suspected constrained bonds are requested frequently, systematically, any subsequent continuation of outsized alpha generation by larger or same-bank-affiliated mutual funds could be an indication of outright discriminatory pricing, of a scale economies nature and a potentially anti-competitive nature, respectively. Inherent in this study is an assumption that the broader liquidity-supplying mutual fund universe is not proactively seeking prices on suspected constrained bonds around the dealer deleveraging window; if it is the case that the broader mutual universe is proactively seeking frequent pricing of suspected constrained bonds in the aggregate, then Giannetti et al. (2023) does serve as such sufficient indication that discriminatory pricing behavior is inherent in the US corporate investment grade bond market. If, though, the broader liquidity-supplying mutual fund universe is not proactive in identifying such opportunities, beyond the aforementioned speculations, there remains a gap in the literature to understand why this is the case. It is reasonable to suggest that many (smaller) mutual funds simply are not aware of the alpha potential or of the directing of particular trades for larger or same-bank-affiliated mutual funds, hence the inaction, although the work of Giannetti et al. (2023) provides due illumination on the nature of these opportunities, which in itself should encourage more proactive behavior over time, in theory.

Proposition 2 *Securitization as a route for expanding effective security warehousing capacity may supersede the need for liquidity provision from unregulated market participants.*

Bank-affiliated dealers which prefer to maintain or perhaps even opportunistically expand their market presence, rather than to diminish their intermediation capacity, around quarter-end reporting periods can avoid doing so while lowering their reported leverage ratio. This can be achieved through securitization such as, for example, significant risk transfer (SRT) transactions. SRTs provide banks with an opportunity to expand their effective ability to warehouse securities. With their newfound balance sheet access, bank-affiliated dealers can maintain their balance sheet exposure as-is to suit their target reportable leverage ratio, or perhaps even seek to deploy the additional effective capacity to warehouse incremental opportunistic risk—through, for example, allocating to constrained bonds originating from other constrained dealers' balance sheets around quarter-end reporting periods. In addition to introducing additional intermediation capacity, bank-affiliated dealers may be able to decrease their risk-weighted assets (RWA) and therefore mechanically improve their capital adequacy by specifically securitizing and transferring the risk exposure of their riskiest positions and/or by reducing the risk weight density of assets by enhancing the creditworthiness of their asset base, by pivoting the freed-up risk capacity into less risky assets, where "less risky" assets can be defined relatively as those with an RWA value (exposure multiplied by risk weight) below that of the asset they are displacing (whose risk has been transferred via securitization). A marked and sustained growth over time of such aggregate risk transfer tools, which provide an advantage over, for example, AT1 capital (which is relatively costly and does not contribute to CET1 capital), provides investors with targeted exposure to a vetted tranche (or mixed-tranche structure) of obligations as opposed to exposure to the entire bank (as investors would expect from investing in AT1 bonds, for example), and can potentially provide bank-affiliated dealers with an opportunity to hedge but retain their exposure. In the aggregate, it would be expected that such a trend in securitization would contribute to increasing bank-affiliated dealers' ability and willingness to intermediate, reducing the cost of intermediation and increasing the stickiness of constrained bonds, reducing the volume and attractiveness of liquidity-provision opportunities in the aggregate and therefore depriving larger or same-bank-affiliated funds from exclusive alpha capture.

Proposition 3 *Progressive bond market electronification and centralization should level the playing field.*

As bond markets become more liquid, centralized, and less fragmented over time, one would expect transparency and mispricing opportunities to be fewer and more equally visible across the market. Bond markets increasingly trading electronically and showing more frequent axes should increasingly resemble the trading of equities, over time, and should be subject to less human bias. Market structure reforms, influx of capital, and technological development (in particular, the risk of alternative trading platforms) could altogether diminish the need for dealer intermediation completely, with a shift to a more broker-led agency or peer-to-peer trading model. In this scenario, one would expect dealers to be naturally less extended in their intermediation activity and therefore being less constrained and engaging in less aggressive balance sheet deleveraging around quarter-end reporting periods. The implications of this are identical to those of proposition (2).

Proposition 4 *Regulators can dissuade potential anti-competitive behavior, to encourage more equal access to liquidity-provision opportunities.*

Leveraging the methodology of Giannetti et al. (2023), regulators may be able to flag suspect anti-competitive behavior between agents in a network to further investigate for evidence of collusion, in particular where there may be explicit evidence of arguable selective disclosure and/or discriminatory pricing, or perhaps even obfuscation of deal availability. By communicating to the market their awareness of such practices and introducing a sufficiently costly penalty, regulators may be able to generate a credible signal to the market that deters further unfair distribution of liquidity-provision opportunities, promoting simultaneous disclosure of opportunities to provide liquidity to constrained bonds priced with concessions. The work of Giannetti et al. (2023), indirectly, and indeed this chapter, directly, serves as a call to regulators that they should recognize and discuss the potential ethical and legal implications of a suspected selective signal from bank-affiliated dealers to same-bank-affiliated mutual funds to offload risk attractively, with an economically material and statistically significant concession, in constrained securities. This is potentially anticompetitive behavior, and potentially a source of collusive behavior or even a covert sharing of material nonpublic information (where, if a bank-affiliated dealer explicitly communicates that they are constrained and in search of liquidity provision, this could potentially qualify as a source of overt sharing of material nonpublic information). Transplanting the rationale of Henide (2021, 2022) to our context, to penalize offenders, regulators should clarify the rules surrounding such behavior and introduce asymmetric deterrence; a meaningful penalty and clear course of legal recourse should deter anti-competitive behavior. Supplementing the asymmetric deterrence, rules clarifications and asymmetric deterrence should be accompanied by continuous and effective oversight, which may be enabled by following the methodology of Giannetti et al. (2023) to identify suspect collusive behavior among the unmasked identities of funds delivering materially and statistically significant abnormal returns, and their bank trading partners. That the suspected relationship between bank-affiliated dealers and same-bank-affiliated mutual funds does not preclude unethical and potentially illegal behavior of the same spirit existing among other groups, particularly where there is a premise for connectedness; we merely refer to the bank-affiliated group by virtue of study design, and this chapter merely focuses on one angle of connectedness. Recall, also, that the results of Giannetti et al. (2023) may be partially or entirely reflecting the residual economies of scale benefits incumbent among behaviorally homogeneous bank-affiliated mutual funds; the connectedness of bank-affiliated dealers and bank-affiliated mutual funds may be due in part to their relative size. The underlying concern over selectively directing trades impeding competition and, by extension, customer (mutual fund investor) outcomes as well as market functioning, remains regardless of the source(s) of connectedness, although their legal principles are not clearly flouted in this scenario. There remains a gap in the literature to explore whether the described economies of scale benefits are beneficial to long-term consumer welfare, market efficiency, and financial stability, by extension. Extending this gap, there remains a question around how regulators can practically dissolve these economies of scale benefits, beyond effectively increasing bank dealers' risk warehousing capacity.

8.7 Conclusion

Giannetti et al. (2023) expand upon the corpus of research that assesses the intended and unintended impact of regulatory changes on the functioning of financial (specifically, corporate bond) markets, and building upon the prior work of Anand et al. (2021) and Rapp and Waibel (2023). They seek to explore the behavior and performance of unregulated market participants within the context of the constraints on regulated financial institutions and associated spillovers, resulting from Basel III leverage ratio requirements. In this chapter, we zone-in on the particular insights of Giannetti et al. (2023) with respect to the computations of the excess returns of "constrained" and "unconstrained" bonds before and following the introduction of the leverage ratio requirement (post-January 2015), as well as regression results pertaining to fund liquidity provisioning by bank-affiliated funds. Their results, among other meaningful findings, suggest that while all investment-grade bond funds generate alpha from liquidity-supplying strategies after the introduction of the leverage ratio regulations, the alpha of investment-grade liquidity-supplying funds that are bank-affiliated is over three times larger than that of other liquidity-supplying funds (0.034/0.011; the former significant at the 5% level, and the latter significant at the 10% level), suggesting that constrained bank dealers direct their best trades to their affiliated mutual funds.

We postulate that this behavior may undermine the fairness and long-term sound functioning of markets, and how it may be a source of legal concern depending on how this behavior is motivated. This behavior may have negative implications for consumer (mutual fund investor) welfare, market efficiency, and systemic stability, as evidenced in tangential studies. This chapter sets out some hypotheses on the motivation for such behaviors, offering propositions relating to how the adverse effects of preferential trading practices may be mitigated. This may either be facilitated, we envision, through the more equitable distribution of liquidity-provision opportunities among prospective liquidity-supplying mutual funds, or through the opportunities becoming altogether redundant as a result of either subsequent corrections in agent behavior or the reasonable expectations of evolution in technology, market structure and market-making activity. The propositions and their assumptions synthesize new gaps in the literature for further research and academic enquiry, while highlighting the importance of both the findings and the methodology of Giannetti et al. (2023) in motivating the discourse and tools for which to address any adverse behavior, should a consensus be found among regulators to remedy the perceived anti-competitive behavior.

This chapter serves as a call to action for regulators, market participants, and academics alike to confront the inherent complexities and ethical dilemmas posed by selective trading practices within the financial industry, in pursuit of upholding the principles of fairness, transparency, and efficiency that underpin a well-functioning market ecosystem.

References

Acosta-Smith, J., Grill, M., & Lang, J. H. (2020). The leverage ratio, risk-taking and bank stability. *Journal of Financial Stability*, 100833.

Adrian, T., & Shin, H. S. (2010). Liquidity and leverage. *Journal of Financial Intermediation*, *19*(3), 418–437.

Altunbasa, Y., Gambacortab, L., & Marques-Ibanezc, D. (2014). Does monetary policy affect bank risk? *International Journal of Central Banking*.

Anand, A., Jotikasthira, C., & Venkataraman, K. (2014). Procyclical leverage and value-at-risk. *The Review of Financial Studies*, *27*(2), 373–403.

Anand, A., Jotikasthira, C., & Venkataraman, K. (2021). Mutual fund trading style and bond market fragility. *The Review of Financial Studies*, *34*(6), 2993–3044.

Bao, J., O'Hara, M., & Zhou, X. A. (2018). The Volcker Rule and corporate bond market making in times of stress. *Journal of Financial Economics*, *130*(1), 95–113.

Basel Committee. (2009). *Strengthening the resilience of the banking sector*. Bank for International Settlements.

Basel Committee. (2010). *Basel III: A global regulatory framework for more resilient banks and banking systems.* Basel Committee on Banking Supervision.

Basel Committee. (2013). *Revised Basel III leverage ratio framework and disclosure requirements—consultative document.* Bank for International Settlements.

Basel Committee. (2014a). *Basel III leverage ratio framework and disclosure requirements.* Bank for International Settlements.

Basel Committee. (2014b). *Seventh progress report on adoption of the Basel regulatory framework.* Bank for International Settlements.

Basel Committee. (2017a). *High-level summary of Basel III reforms.* Bank for International Settlements.

Basel Committee. (2017b). *Basel III: Finalising post-crisis reforms.* Bank for International Settlements.

Basel Committee. (2023). *Technical amendment—finalisation of various technical amendments.* Bank for International Settlements.

Bassi, C., Behn, M., Grill, M., & Waibel, M. (2024). Window dressing of regulatory metrics: evidence from repo markets. *Journal of Financial Intermediation.*

Behn, M., Mangiante, G., Parisi, L., & Wedowa, M. (2022). Behind the scenes of the beauty contest—window dressing and the G-SIB framework. *International Journal of Central Banking.*

Berk, J. B., & Green, R. C. (2004). Mutual fund flows and performance in rational markets. *Journal of Political Economy, 112*(6), 1269–1295.

Bessembinder, H., Jacobsen, S., Maxwell, W., & Venkataraman, K. (2018). Capital commitment and illiquidity in corporate bonds. *The Journal of Finance, 73*(4), 1615–1661.

Blundell-Wignall, A., Atkinson, P., & Roulet, C. (2014). Bank business models and the Basel system: Complexity and interconnectedness. *OECD Journal: Financial Market Trends, 2013*(2), 43–68.

Borio, C., & Zhu, H. (2012). Capital regulation, risk-taking and monetary policy: A missing link in the transmission mechanism? *Journal of Financial Stability, 8*(4), 236–251.

Brei, M., & Gambacorta, L. (2014). *The leverage ratio over the cycle.* BIS Working Papers No 471.

Coates IV, J. C., & Hubbard, R. G. (2007). Competition in the mutual fund industry: Evidence and implications for policy. *Journal of Corporation Law, 33*, 151.

Correa, R., Du, W., & Liao, G. Y. (2020). *US banks and global liquidity* (No. w27491). National Bureau of Economic Research.

Cosimano, T. F., & Hakura, D. (2011). *Bank behavior in response to Basel III: A cross-country analysis.*

Crawford, A., Graham, C. and Bordeleau, E. 2009. Regulatory constraints on leverage: the Canadian experience. *Financial System Review*, pp.45–50.

D'Hulster, K. (2009). *The leverage ratio.* The World Bank Group, Financial and Private Sector Development Vice Presidency, Note, (11).

Dick-Nielsen, J., & Rossi, M. (2019). The cost of immediacy for corporate bonds. *The Review of Financial Studies, 32*(1), 1–41.

European System of Financial Supervision. (2014). *The ESRB handbook on operationalising macro-prudential policy in the banking sector*. European System of Financial Supervision.

Finansinspektionen. (2015). *The future structure of banks' capital requirements*. Finansinspektionen memorandum: FI Ref. 15–9548.

FINMA Swiss Financial Market Supervisory. (2009). New capital adequacy requirements in Switzerland applicable for large banks: Higher capital ratio targets and leverage ratio.

Galí, J. (2014). Monetary policy and rational asset price bubbles. *American Economic Review, 104*(3), 721–752.

Geanakoplos, J. (2010). The Leverage Cycle. *NBER Macroeconomics Annual*, 24(1), 1–66.

Geanakoplos, J., & Pedersen, L. H. (2012). Monitoring leverage. In *Risk topography: Systemic risk and macro modeling* (pp. 113–127). University of Chicago Press.

Giannetti, M., Jotikasthira, C., Rapp, A. C., & Waibel, M. (2023). *Intermediary Balance Sheet Constraints, Bond Mutual Funds' Strategies, and Bond Returns*. Swedish House of Finance Research Paper, (23–10).

Grill, M., Lang, J. H., & Smith, J. (2015). The impact of the Basel III leverage ratio on risk-taking and bank stability. *Financial Stability Review*, 2.

Gromb, D., & Vayanos, D. (2002). Equilibrium and welfare in markets with financially constrained arbitrageurs. *Journal of financial Economics, 66*(2–3), 361–407.

Henide, K. (2021). Green lemons: Overcoming adverse selection in the green bond market. *Transnational Corporations Journal, 28*(3).

Henide, K. (2022). Voluntary disclosure and adverse selection: Bayesian game theoretical inference for green bond labelling regimes. *International Review of Financial Analysis*, 83.

Ingves, S. (2014). Banking on leverage. *Keynote Address, Bank for International Settlements*, 25.

Jordà, Ò., Schularick, M., & Taylor, A. M. (2013). When credit bites back. *Journal of Money, Credit and Banking, 45*(s2), 3–28.

Jordà, Ò., Schularick, M., & Taylor, A. M. (2015). Leveraged bubbles. *Journal of Monetary Economics, 76*, S1–S20.

Khandani, A. E., Lo, A. W., & Merton, R. C. (2013). Systemic risk and the refinancing ratchet effect. *Journal of Financial Economics, 108*(1), pp. 29–45.

Kiema, I., & Jokivuolle, E. (2014). Does a leverage ratio requirement increase bank stability? *Journal of Banking & Finance, 39*, 240–254.

Koo, R. C. (2011). *The Holy Grail of Macroeconomics: Lessons from Japan's great recession*. Wiley.

Lautenschläger, S. (2013, October 21). *The Leverage Ratio—a simple and comparable measure*. In Speech at the evening reception of the Deutsche Bundesbank/ SAFE Conference "Supervising banks in complex financial systems", Frankfurt am Main.

Massa, M. (2004). *Mutual fund competition and stock market liquidity* (No. 4787). CEPR Discussion Papers.

Mian, A., & Sufi, A. (2014). *House of Debt: How they (and you) caused the Great Recession, and how we can prevent it from happening again*. University of Chicago Press.

Miller, M., & Stiglitz, J. (2010). Leverage and asset bubbles: Averting Armageddon with Chapter 11? *The Economic Journal, 120*(544), 500–518.

Mishkin, F. S. (2008). How should we respond to asset price bubbles. *Financial Stability Review, 12*(1), 65–74.

Mishkin, F. S., (2009a). Is monetary policy effective during financial crises? *American Economic Review, 99*(2), pp. 573–577.

Mishkin, F. S., (2009b). Not all bubbles present a risk to the economy. *Financial Times*.

Rapp, A. C., & Waibel, M. (2023). *Managing regulatory pressure: Bank regulation and its impact on corporate bond intermediation*. Available at SSRN 4500131.

Schularick, M., & Taylor, A. M. (2012). Credit booms gone bust: Monetary policy, leverage cycles, and financial crises, 1870–2008. *American Economic Review, 102*(2), 1029–1061.

Smith, J. A., Grill, M., & Lang, J. H. (2017). *The leverage ratio, risk-taking and bank stability* (No. 2079). ECB Working Paper.

Spinassou, K. (2013). *Basel III Capital Requirements and Regulatory Power: The impact on bank risk-taking and credit supply*. Available at SSRN 2307721.

Svensson, L .E. (2018). Inflation Targeting and "Leaning against the Wind." *35th issue (June 2014) of the International Journal of Central Banking*.

Treanor, J. (2013). Barclays warns on new capital rules. *The Guardian*.

Vallascas, F., & Hagendorff, J. (2013). The risk sensitivity of capital requirements: Evidence from an international sample of large banks. *Review of Finance, 17*(6), 1947–1988.

CHAPTER 9

Regulatory and Performance Differences in US and European Banks in Light of the 2023 Failures

Giusy Chesini

9.1 Introduction—The Background

In March 2023, a few different episodes of bank collapses occurred in the United States and Europe.

Briefly, in the United States, the sudden collapses of Silicon Valley Bank (SVB) and Signature Bank demonstrated that investors had become aware of the precariousness of these banks. Moreover, the same week, the US authorities helped organize an industry bailout of First Republic, which was forced to seek a lifeline, receiving around 30 billion dollars from 11 US banks. First Republic was quickly closed by US regulators and sold to JP Morgan Chase Bank (Shikha and Kapsis 2024); the latter reopened First Republic's offices on May 1, 2023 (Liu et al. 2024).

Differently, SVB, the first to collapse, was abruptly taken over by regulators on March 10, 2023. It was a medium-sized bank whose name recalls

G. Chesini (✉)
Department of Management, University of Verona, Verona, Italy
e-mail: giusy.chesini@univr.it

E. Scannella and J. Williams (eds.), *Trends, Issues, and Challenges in Banking and Finance*, Palgrave Macmillan Studies in Banking and Financial Institutions,
https://doi.org/10.1007/978-3-031-96066-6_9

where the intermediary was based; regardless of size, it was a strategic bank by geographical and operational location, particularly for American technological companies. The difficulties of SVB arose from the loss on fixed-rate bonds, in particular agency mortgage-back securities (i.e., a pool of mortgages underwritten by the government) in its bank portfolio, caused by the increase of the rate of interest decided by the Federal Reserve to counter inflation (Drechsler et al. 2023). In fact, due to liquidity problems, on March 8, 2023, SVB decided to sell the bonds in the market, realizing an after-tax loss of US $1.8 billion and launching external financing with US $15 billion of debt and US $2.25 billion of equity (Liu et al. 2024). Bank depositors, especially those whose deposits were uninsured, partially fueled by social media, thought it was better to withdraw their deposits from the bank. This was a particularly massive problem at SVB, where more than 78% of the deposits exceeded the amounts covered under federal insurance (Jiang et al. 2023). Uninsured deposits played a critical role in the failure of SVB, which experienced 25% of its deposits leaving in a day. A novel aspect of this bank run, not seen during the 2008–2010 downturn, was depositors rapidly withdrawing their funds through online banking. Technological advances increase bank deposit mobility (Krogstrup and Sangill 2024).

To make matters worse, like many other US banks, SVB holds a low percentage of its assets in the form of cash. All this considered, it is understandable why, 2 days after announcing the bond sale, SVB was shut down by regulators, who declared it insolvent. US investors suddenly perceived these collapses, as a possible precursor of similar troubles at other banks and started to run to withdraw their deposits even in financially healthier banks. President Biden's reassuring speech and the financial authorities' prompt intervention were able to halt the rampant confidence crisis.

On March 12, American regulators and the government judged SVB too big to fail and guaranteed all the bank deposits (Ali et al. 2024). If the sale of its assets had not covered the costs of the depositor bailout, a fund financed by all banks should have stepped in, penalizing the whole industry for the problems of a single bank. Furthermore, to avoid other difficulties like the ones by SVB, the Federal Reserve (Fed) announced a program—the Bank Term Funding Program—that offers loans of up to 1 year to banks using the bank's government bonds and certain other assets as collateral. Crucially, the Fed proposed to value the bonds at their original value—not at the lower levels banks stood to receive if they tried to sell them quickly in the markets (Board of Governors of the Federal Reserve System 2023). The Fed's goal was to send a reassuring signal that banks would not have to transform unrealized, potential losses into actual ones. US banks borrowed $153 billion through the Fed's funding program; that was up from less than US $5 billion a week earlier and was the most considerable amount borrowed in a week since the 2008 financial crisis (Glancy et al. 2024).

Finally, nearly together with the SVB crisis, Signature Bank was also mentioned as a collapsed bank. In fact, according to Federal Deposit Insurance Corporation (FDIC) quarterly banking data, the bank was overreliant on uninsured deposits, which accounted for 90% of overall deposits at the end of 2022 (FDIC 2023). The collapse of Signature Bank was mainly due to "poor management"; in particular, they did not fully understand the risks associated with accepting crypto deposits, which comprised more than 20% of its total deposits.

So, another issue related to the March 2023 bank turmoil concerns bank deposit insurance; bank deposits are mainly insured worldwide but in different ways. In the European Union, deposits with a single bank are insured mostly up to €100,000 (Directive 2014/49/EU), while in the United States, up to US $250,000. The amounts are significantly different, and surprisingly, the crisis arose precisely where insurance is higher, and depositors are more protected.

Immediately after the sudden collapse of the mentioned US mid-banks, Credit Suisse (CS), one of the two Swiss investment banking giants with international operations, was bought by Union Bank of Switzerland (UBS), its close competitor, through a quick transaction arranged by Swiss Financial Market Supervisory Authority (FINMA) (the Swiss financial authority). CS was founded in 1856 and was among a group of 30 banks known as systemic banks because a collapse of one of them might devastate the global financial system (Martins 2025). Despite its long history, CS has been plagued by scandals, quick substitutions of top management, and significant losses during the years. CS shares had lost more than 75% of their value over the past twelve months.

So, while the crisis and the collapse of the mentioned US banks were mostly unpredictable, CS's takeover was more predictable because of its long history of damaging episodes primarily attributable to its bad governance. However, the time coincidence shook investors, who began to be concerned about the possible inception of another global financial crisis.

After some weeks, it was clear that the EU and US cases were not comparable episodes and that in the United States a new culprit stressed the financial system: the rapidly rising interest rates.

In general, when central banks tighten monetary policy, there can be negative impacts on the value of the bank's long-term assets (i.e., mortgages and government bonds). Banks may generate losses in this situation due to the maturity transformation that characterizes their business and subsequently fail. This situation can happen in two alternative or consequent steps: first, the liabilities on the balance sheet exceed the value of the assets, and the bank can become insolvent; second, uninsured depositors realize the situation and, fearing potential losses, rush to withdraw their funds, triggering bank default and panic in the financial markets.

The Federal Reserve had undertaken a very aggressive monetary tightening by raising interest rates several times in 2022 to combat high inflation. Banks have faced growing unrealized losses since the Fed began raising interest rates. It must be underlined that interest rates going up is usually a good news story for banks because they can earn more from the net interest rate margin (NIM)—the difference between the interest rate that they charge for loans and the interest rate that they pay on deposits (Farah et al. 2022). Unfortunately, the benefits of interest rate increases do not appear evenly distributed across banks. These depend on factors such as business model and balance sheet structure. So, even if the system-wide effects of rising interest rates should be favorable, idiosyncratic factors may influence outcomes across individual banks (Af Jochnick 2023).

Two distinct but related aspects deserve to be mentioned: banks' regulation and performance in different financial systems. For example, midsize banks like SVB do not have the same regulatory oversight as the US biggest banks, which, among other provisions, are subject to stricter requirements and must hold a certain amount of reserves in moments of crisis. Moreover, in Europe, midsize banks seem more regulated than their US counterparts but less profitable. This induces an investigation of the relationship between regulation and profitability in the two banking systems. Related to these analyses is investigating the effectiveness of the best-known methodologies for predicting bank failures. The remainder of this chapter is structured as follows. The second section presents the relation between profitability and regulation practically and introduces the meaning of the variables used in the quantitative analysis. The third section examines the literature review, while the fourth provides a quantitative data analysis. Finally, the chapter ends up with conclusions.

9.2 The Performance and the Regulatory Issues Together with the Forecast of Bank Failures

Banks play a relevant role in national and international economies; their financial health impacts economic activities and national development. All interested stakeholders constantly assess and measure banks' financial health, using reliable bankruptcy prediction models (King et al. 2005; Casabianca et al. 2019).

To evaluate the vitality of banks it is possible to look at the returns offered to investors by the banking sector in US and EU financial systems. After the financial crisis, US banks soon reached better performance, while EU banks could not perform satisfactorily till 2023 when inflation had a positive impact on a large part of their balance sheets. As it is possible to see in Graph 9.1, the Euro Stoxx Bank Index has never achieved the level of prices shown before the global financial crisis. Conversely, the Dow Jones US Bank Index has continued to grow.

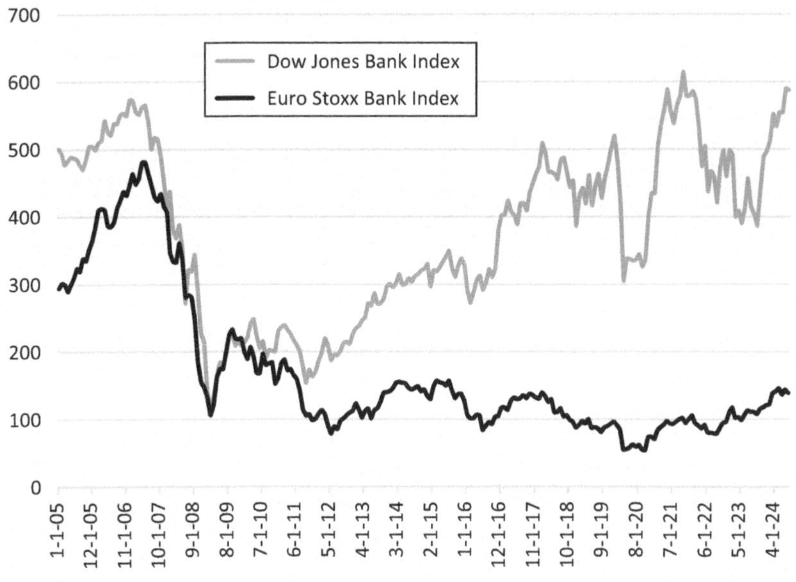

Graph 9.1 Comparison between the Dow Jones Bank Index and the Euro Stoxx Bank Index.

The fact that the performance of US banks since the 2008 crisis has improved much more than that of their European counterparts (Gugler and Peev 2018; Simoens and Vander Vennet 2021) leads us to question whether it is preferable to dispose of well-performing banks even if they are less regulated and more prone to failure. Hence, the first research question arises.

RQ 1: How much profitable is the European banking sector in comparison to the American one?

The interrelationship between profitability and stability in the banking sector is well known in the literature (Xu et al. 2019). Stability is often linked also to the intensity of regulation: European banks appear better regulated (Oliver Wyman 2023) and, therefore, more solvent and stable, but they perform worse in terms of profitability than their US counterparts. This consideration leads us to ask whether the collapse of SVB and other US banks could have been avoided with stricter banking regulation. Hence, the second research question arises.

RQ 2: How regulated is the European banking industry compared to the US banking industry?

Looking at the banks already examined, the SVB's liabilities were represented mainly by deposits, individually large in size, which could run away in minutes (Shikha and Kapsis 2024). At the same time, the assets were primarily held in medium-term fixed-income securities. A balance sheet like this violates the most basic principles of correct banking management in transforming maturities. In these conditions, disseminating news of losses on portfolio securities could cause a rush to withdraw deposits.

Conversely, by considering CS's bankruptcy, the underlying causes are more obscure. In the last few years, several financial scandals and journalistic investigations into illicit trafficking had CS as an actor in money laundering and bad investments, such as those in Greensill Capital and Archeogos. Even in this case, it is possible to recognize several management errors mixed with irregularities.

The issue is whether banking regulation, refined after the global financial crisis, should have prevented the deterioration of banks' economic situations. In fact, both the US and Swiss supervisory authorities failed.

In the American case, softer supervision was favored by the President Trump government's choice (2018) to loosen the supervisory constraints on banks that were not "systematically global." It was asserted that too much regulation would not have helped the economy's growth.

Conversely, in the EU, Basel standards are traditionally implemented more consistently across banks of all sizes (Enria 2023).

It emerges clearly that a crucial safeguard to prevent bank failures from happening again is to have a supervisory authority that acts independently and powerfully, breaking the dangerous entanglement between economic power and political power. The European model, with the European central Bank (ECB), an institution of the EU characterized by strong independence (Chesini and Fauri 2024), appears more reassuring than the US and Swiss ones.

However, even if the latter regulations do not appear strict enough to avoid banking crises, the US and Swiss authorities and governments were quite efficient; in both cases, they activated extraordinary measures, deviating from what was established by consolidated legal institutions.

In particular, in the United States, the Federal Reserve and the Federal Deposit Insurance Corporation (FDIC) interventions have exploited the systemic risk exception, allowing the authorities and government to intervene without limits to avoid financial instability. Precisely the FED and the US Treasury announced on March 12, 2023 the start of a Bank Term Funding Program to improve the liquidity of US banks (Shikha and Kapsis 2024). The actions were accompanied by President Biden's speech, which reassured depositors that they would be fully protected, even beyond the limits set by law, to preserve trust in the banking system, which is essential for financing the economy. In his speech, Biden combined the protection of savers and the need for economic growth, recalling the low unemployment rate in recent years.

The reaction of the Swiss authorities and government was even more surprising. Overnight CS was bought by UBS, the country's other banking giant, in derogating corporate and antitrust rules, thanks to a public guarantee. The concentration took place without the consent of the shareholders' meeting, eliminating the value of a particular class of subordinated bonds called AT1 (Paz Valbuena and Eidenmüller 2023). This decision was an exception to the most elementary rules: shareholders are the residual claimants in the event of bankruptcy, that is, they are paid only if something remains after repaying all creditors. The press release from FINMA (Swiss supervisory authority), which declares the transaction legitimate based on the contractual clauses accompanying the issue of AT1 bonds in Swiss law, could hardly convince the markets (FINMA 2023). It did not convince the homologous authorities; the ECB and the Bank of England hastened in a press release to applaud the initiatives to protect stability but recalled that those choices regarding shareholders and holders of subordinated bonds are inadmissible in the European and English legal systems (ECB 2023).

In Europe, in 2014, a system of rules for managing banking crises aimed at limiting the cost paid by taxpayers was launched.[1] It was a political choice that gave the role of last resort to a public intervention; the principle entails that the price of the crisis must be paid primarily by shareholders and creditors, including depositors, with the sole exception of deposits of up to €100,000, which are reimbursed by deposits insurance schemes. The new rules do not provide flexibility nor a broad "systemic risk exception" like in the United States.

Consequently, if bank bankruptcies—caused by the withdraw of uninsured deposits—should occur in the EU, national governments and authorities would have their "hands tied," unless they adopt the Swiss approach of blatantly violating the rules established ex-ante, with severe damage to the certainty of law, a precious asset for the proper functioning of the markets and the economy.

The regulatory and performance issues mentioned above invoke the opportunity, extensively examined in the literature, to predict bank failures. Several prediction models are often used in different jurisdictions: in the United States, the Texas ratio is frequently used, while in Europe, the Z-score is more commonly used.

This research aims to determine whether it is possible to measure and predict the financial health of banks efficiently and reliably. To this end, different methodologies are compared. In particular, the Texas ratio, the *Z*-score, and the insured deposit coverage ratios are examined.

The Texas ratio was developed to warn of credit problems at particular banks or banks in specific regions. Essentially, the ratio takes the amount of a bank's performing assets plus the value of real assets owned and divides this number by the sum of the bank's tangible common equity and the loan loss reserves (Jesswein 2009). A ratio of more than 100 indicates that nonperforming assets are more significant than the resources the bank may need to cover potential losses on those assets. It was initially applied to banks in Texas in the 1980s and proved helpful in New England banks in the early 1990s. Gerald Cassidy and other analysts at RBC Capital Markets

[1] Bank Recovery and Resolution Directive (BRRD) (Directive 2014/59/EU) and the Single Resolution Mechanism Regulation (SRMR) 806/2014.

developed it (Velliscig et al. 2023). The higher the Texas ratio, the more financial trouble a bank might face. The lower the Texas Ratio, the better.

Texas Ratio = (Nonperforming Assets + Real Estate Owned) / (Tangible Common Equity + Loan Loss Reserves)

Where:

- Nonperforming Assets: Loans that are in default or at risk of default, typically 90 days past due without payment.
- Real Estate Owned: Property owned by a bank, usually acquired through foreclosure after a borrower defaults on a mortgage.
- Tangible Common Equity: A bank's core capital, excluding intangible assets (like goodwill) and preferred equity; a key measure of financial strength.
- Loan Loss Reserves: Funds set aside by banks to cover potential future losses from defaulted loans.

On the other hand, Altman's *Z*-score model is a numerical measurement used to predict the chances of a business going bankrupt in the next 2 years. The model was developed by an American finance professor, Edward Altman, in 1968 to measure companies' financial stability. Altman's *Z*-score model is considered an effective method of predicting the state of financial distress (Ferreira 2023) of any organization by using multiple balance sheet items and corporate income.

***Z*-score** = (Return on Assets + Equity-to-Asset ratio) / σ Return on Assets

Where:

- Return on Assets: A measure of bank profitability relative to its total assets. It indicates how efficiently a bank uses its assets to generate net income.
- Equity-to-Asset ratio: A bank's capital strength by showing the proportion of total assets funded by shareholders' equity; a higher ratio suggests a more solvent institution.
- Return on Assets: The standard deviation of Return on Assets

In the case of SVB, one of the leading causes of the collapse is attributable to the behavior of uninsured depositors. In fact, due to the substantial increase in interest rates, banks registered declines in asset values, which increased their fragility and triggered uninsured depositors runs (Jiang et al. 2023). Therefore, another ratio that might be interesting to estimate is the insured deposit coverage ratio (IDC ratio).

Insured Deposit Coverage = (Mark-to-Market Assets – Uninsured Deposits – Insured Deposits) / Insured Deposits

where:

- Mark-to-Market Assets: The current market value of the bank's total assets, reflecting real-time pricing rather than historical cost.
- Uninsured Deposits: Customer deposits that exceed the government insurance limit and are therefore not protected.
- Insured Deposits: Deposits that fall within the coverage limits of government deposit insurance.

The IDC ratio considers how a bank is financed. In particular, it is relevant to analyze what portion of bank funding is unstable, especially the amount of uninsured deposits. SVB was an extreme case because almost 80% of its assets were financed with uninsured deposits. Uninsured depositors can lose money if the bank fails and the possibility of a bank run makes the bank particularly fragile (Piskorski 2024).

The abovementioned three risk ratios use different balance sheet items, and they can be used to predict bankruptcies in different contexts. Hence, the third research question arises.

RQ3: Which ratio could be most significant in predicting bank insolvency?

In the empirical analysis that follows, an attempt is made to answer these research questions.

9.3 Literature Review

The literature on this topic is extensive and usually focuses on European banks or American banks separately. The works presenting a comparison are few (EBA 2021; Di Vito et al. 2023).

The simplest solution to fragile banking systems often identifies increasing banks' capital requirements and reducing leverage. In this way, the financial system becomes safer, but on the other hand, lending activity decreases, as do banks' profits, and a contraction in economic activity could be generated. Therefore, solutions are usually to strike a balance between profitability and regulation with the goal of preserving stability.

Considering profitability, most euro area banks in a low-interest rate environment until 2022 were unable to earn a return on equity greater than their cost of capital, implying that returns failed to offset risk; this could trigger the conditions for a series of defaults (Soenen and Vander Vennet 2022).

On the other hand, considering the stability, after March 2023, in the United States, some scholars affirmed that many banks had similar but not as extreme characteristics, such as SVB, and therefore the risk of another round of bank runs was not negligible in the short term (Piskorski 2024). This is confirmed also by the International Monetary Fund which demonstrates that vulnerabilities continue to persist in a weak tail of US banks (Adrian et al. 2024). Consequently, the topic remains of great interest for scholars and regulators.

One of the earliest works that analyzed the effects of banking regulation on bank profitability, in particular on banks' return on assets is that of Teixera et al. (2020). This work also investigates the effects of each country's institutional framework on this relationship, considering crisis and noncrisis years.

Recently, several papers have analyzed the causes and repercussions of the SVB bankruptcy since March 2023. Most of them study the possibility of contagion of SVB bankruptcy to other banks and other financial markets.

Bales and Burghof (2024) analyze the default of SVB considering the power of social media. Traditionally, the spread of negative sentiments and information during bank runs relied on conventional media sources like newspapers, television, or radio. However, social media altered the dynamics of information propagation, potentially accelerating the SVB crash due to contagious panic and mass fear. The authors provide evidence that Twitter sentiment and media attention ultimately fueled and accelerated the crash dynamics of SVB. The impact of the social depositor network was also important due to a concentration of deposits among a small group of socially connected venture capitalists.

Several papers have analyzed the recent bankruptcies using the event study methodology. Chen and Nie (2024) investigate the contagion in financial markets following the collapse of SVB using an event study methodology based on nonlinear high-frequency networks. A similar methodology is used by Banerjee et al. (2024) who investigate not only SVB but also Signature Bank and First Republic Bank.

Ali et al. (2024) adopt also an event study methodology and observe that SVB collapse induced negative returns in US and European banks; in particular, SVB's financial distress had a detrimental effect on the share price of banking companies in the United States and in Europe while it had a positive impact on the stocks of technology companies in those countries. Finally, Martins (2025) provide a comprehensive understanding of the impact of SVB and CS collapses on the US equity markets, considering the 100 largest US-listed banks.

Other papers focus on the weak and vulnerable balance sheet and asset–liability profile of SVB. For example, Khoo (2023) stresses the lack of diversification in funding sources and asset pricing risks and the lack of regulatory requirements for stress testing and scenario analysis in SVB. Liu et al. (2024) analyze the corporate history of SVB and the quantitative data of its balance sheets for the years 2020, 2021, and 2022. They find that supervisors did not fully appreciate the extent of the vulnerabilities as SVB grew in size and complexity.

9.4 The Empirical Analysis

The quantitative analysis empirically investigates the factors influencing the performance, regulation, and probability of default of a sample of European and US banks. The sample comprises the banks involved in the March 2023 bankruptcies mentioned above and was basically compiled by Bloomberg considering banks with similar characteristics, defined as comparable.

The dataset comprises 96 banks (75 EU and 21 US banks) and their balance sheet data span from the end of 2005 to June 2024. To compare the financial characteristics of US and European banks, quarterly data on profitability, capitalization, liquidity, asset quality, and efficiency are collected. In addition, the Texas ratio, the *Z*-score, and the IDC ratio are computed. Only for American banks it is possible to dispose of data on insured deposits and so the IDC ratio is calculated only for American banks. The data of uninsured deposits are offered to Bloomberg by the FDIC. Conversely, in Europe, the European Deposit Insurance Scheme (EDIS), which constitutes the third pillar of the European Banking Union (EBU), is not in force yet, so it is not possible to dispose of data like the US sample.

Tables 9.1 and 9.2 show the descriptive statistics of the main variables examined in the econometric models.

After some preliminary tests, such as the Variance Inflation Factor (VIF) and the Hausman tests, we eliminated some variables due to collinearity and we run a series of panel regressions with random effects.

First of all, the analysis aims to examine if there is a different trade-off between profitability (ROA) and regulatory capital (Tier 1 ratio) in the datasets of European and American banks.

Table 9.1 Descriptive statistics for European banks

Variable	*Obs*	*Mean*	*Std. Dev.*	*Min*	*Max*
Z-SCORE	1,244	17.89	13.30	-5.41	82.04
TEXAS_RATIO	1,047	39.40	49.85	0	1,014.30
EFF_RATIO	1,265	71.44	70.71	-117.55	2,027.54
NUM_OF_EMPLOYEES	1,230	46,208.96	51,364.12	633	315,520
GROWTH_IN_TOT_LOA	1,205	5.09	38.02	-91.28	1,136.51
GROWTH_IN_TOT_DPST	1,247	5.93	19.36	-93.40	225.94
RETURN_ON_ASSET	1,248	0.23	0.98	-12.37	4.43
TOT_LOAN_TO_TOT_DPST	1,232	142.77	96.20	0	1,495.92
NON_PERF_ASSET_TO_TOT_ASSET	1,183	3.12	5.092	0.0009	35.68
TIER1_CAPITAL_RATIO	1,309	12.67	5.60	-6	40.5
COM_EQY_TO_TOTAL_ASSETS	1,266	5.22	2.35	-5.72	30.65

Table 9.2 Descriptive statistics for American banks

Variable	*Obs*	*Mean*	*Std. Dev.*	*Min*	*Max*
Z SCORE	367	23.14	12.79	0.75	52.75
TEXAS_RATIO	364	9.51	10.73	0.07	64.88
EFF_RATIO	370	58.56	14.59	24.07	165.21
NUM_OF_EMPLOYEES	358	26,905.03	53,995.39	416	281,000
GROWTH_IN_TOT_LOAN	367	11.88	19.47	-23.63	148.948
GROWTH_IN_TOT_DPST	367	12.61	19.51	16.53	133.22
RETURN_ON_ASSET	367	0.98	0.83	-5.84	2.85
TOT_LOAN_TO_TOT_DPST	369	90.63	19.41	28.82	154.82
NON_PERF_ASSET_TO_TOT_ASSET	368	1.95	21.87	0.00	419.922
TIER1_CAPITAL_RATIO	378	11.32	2.77	0	19.55
COM_EQY_TO_TOTAL_ASSETS	369	9.89	2.11	4.97	18.99

Secondarily we try to understand the different usages of the three ratios (Texas ratio, Z-score, and IDC ratio) in Europe and in the United States considering their statistical significance.

The model proposed is the following:

$$\textbf{Risk ratio}_{b,i,t} = \beta_0 + \beta_1 \text{ Growth in total loans}_{b,i,t} + \beta_2 \text{ Growth in total deposits}_{b,i,t} + \beta_3 \text{ Total loans to total deposits}_{b,i,t} + \beta_4 \text{ Nonperforming assets to total assets}_{b,i,t} + \beta_5 \text{ Efficiency ratio}_{b,i,t} + \beta_6 \text{ Return on assets}_{b,i,t\,+} + \beta_7 \text{ Tier 1 capital ratio}_{b,i,t} + \delta i + \phi t + \epsilon b,i,t$$

The independent variables in the models are the following: Growth in total loans, Growth in total deposits, Tier 1 capital ratio, Total loans to total deposits, Nonperforming assets to total assets, Efficiency ratio, and Return on assets (ROA).

We run different regressions using the complete dataset or alternatively the dataset of European banks and American banks separately.

A dummy variable, called Eubanks_dummy, is created to evaluate how the performance and the regulation of European banks differ from the American ones in the time period 2005–2024.

Table 9.3 shows the result of a panel regression with random effects run to evaluate the performance of European banks in respect to their American counterparts. It emerges that American banks performed better than the European banks in the time period considered, in particular the ROA of American banks is around 43% better than the one of the American banks. Other variables are significant (***) in the regression: the Z score, the Texas ratio, the Growth in total deposits, and the Common equity to total asset ratio (the leverage).

Differently, Table 9.4 shows the results of a panel regression with random effects run to evaluate the level of regulation of European banks concerning their capitalization, that is, the level of stability, in respect to their American counterparts. In this case, a basic ratio is used as dependent variable: the Tier 1 ratio. It emerges that European banks have higher levels of Tier 1 ratios than the American banks in the time period considered, in particular 5,6 higher. Other variables are significant in the regression: the Growth in total loans (**), the Growth in total deposits (**), the Total loan to total deposits (a measure of liquidity), and the Common equity to total assets (leverage) (***). Finally, Tables 9.5 and 9.6 aim to identify which ratio is more significant in evaluating bank bankruptcy separately for the European and American datasets. Precisely, Table 9.5 shows

Table 9.3 Panel regression results (dependent variable: return on assets)

Banks	*Obs*	*1,394*
	Group	*95*
Return on assets (ROA)	*Coef.*	*P > z*
• Z score	.0134672	0.000***
• Texas ratio	-.0054502	0.000***
• Growth in total loans	.0008562	0.197
• Growth in total deposits	.0098237	0.000***
• Total loans to total deposits	.0050347	0.396
• Nonperforming assets to total assets	-.0001778	0.563
• Efficiency ratio	-.0021465	0.251
• Common equity to total assets	-.0031043	0.000***
• Eubanks_dummy	-.4355159	0.000***
• cons	.7392427	0.000***
R^2:		
Within	0.1587	
Between	0.7380	
Overall	0.3166	

Table 9.4 Panel regression results (dependent variable: Tier 1 capital)

Banks	*Obs*	*1,519*
	Group	*95*
Tier 1 capital ratio	*Coef.*	*P > z*
• Growth in total loans	-.0090914	0.001**
• Growth in total deposits	-.0151054	0.002**
• Total loans to total deposits (liquidity)	-.0124863	0.000***
• Nonperforming assets to total assets	-.0065766	0.390
• Efficiency ratio	.0006129	0.665
• Common equity to total assets (leverage)	.7226024	0.000***
• Eubanks_dummy	5.652562	0.000***
. cons	5.923363	0.000***
R^2:		
Within	0.2512	
Between	0.0000	
Overall	0.0999	

Table 9.5 Panel regression results (dependent variable: *Z*-score)

Z-SCORE	*European banks*		*American banks*	
	Obs	*1,147*	*Obs*	*366*
	Group	*74*	*Group*	*21*
	Coef.	*P > z*	*Coef.*	*P>z*
• Growth in total loans	0.033307	0.323	.0001357	0.994
• Growth in total deposits	-0.0098599	0.164	−.0166824	0.314
• Tier 1 capital ratio	0.5632535	0.000 ***	.4251559	0.001 **
• Total loans to total deposits	-0047537	0.017*	.0662183	0.000***
• Nonperforming assets to total assets	-0093735	0.789	.0103994	0.211
• Return on assets (ROA)	0.9853286	0.012*	2.395867	0.000 ***
• Efficiency ratio	-0045275	0.000***	.0541448	0.009 ***
• cons	11,13924	0.000	6.627789	0.002
R^2:				
Within	0.3113		0.2004	
Between	0.1832		0.1390	
Overall	0.1440		0.0895	

the results of two distinct regressions where the *Z*-score is the dependent variable; the R^2 is lower than in the following regressions (Texas ratio) for both European and American banks. So, the model works worse for the examination of the *Z*-score than for that of the Texas ratio. Consequently, also the significance of the regressors is lower than in the following regression. The ROA is significant (***), and the coefficient is positive because the higher the ROA, the higher the *Z*-score; this means that the higher the distance of the bank from insolvency, the lower the probability of default. Regarding the Tier1 capital ratio, it is significant (*** for European and ** for American banks) for both groups of banks, and the coefficients have positive signs. This means that the higher the capitalization of banks, the higher the *Z*-score is, and the lower the probability of insolvency.

Table 9.6 shows the results of the panel regression where the Texas ratio is the dependent variable; the R^2 is higher than in the previous regressions for both European and American banks. So, the proposed model works better for the examination of the Texas ratio, where also the significance of the regressors is higher. The ROA) is significant (***), and the coefficient is negative because the higher the ROA, the lower the Texas ratio and the lower the probability of default of the bank. Regarding the Tier 1 capital

Table 9.6 Panel regression results (dependent variable: Texas ratio)

TEXAS RATIO	*European banks*		*American banks*	
	Obs	*1,035*	*Obs*	*363*
	Group	*74*	*Group*	*21*
	Coef.	*P > z*	*Coef.*	*P>z*
• Growth in total loans	-.0313831	0.311	–.1606803	0.000***
• Growth in total deposits	.2871086	0.000***	.1270188	0.001**
• Tier 1 capital ratio	–.9144295	0.002**	1.456259	0.002**
• Total loans to total deposits	.0630963	0.000***	.1674435	0.000 ***
• Nonperforming assets to total assets	4.434682	0.000***	.0112563	0.564
• Return on assets (ROA)	–7.664929	0.000***	-5.986218	0.000***
• Efficiency ratio	–.007505	0.673	.0152855	0.752
• cons	2.984.111	0.000	-1.742.141	0.013
R^2:				
Within	0.2003		0.4250	
Between	0.6695		0.0375	
Overall	0.4009		0.3327	

ratio, it is significant (**) for both samples of banks, but the coefficients have different signs. For European banks, the higher values of the capital ratio contribute to reducing the Texas ratio and have a positive influence on the solvability of the banks; on the contrary, for American banks, it has a negative influence, probably because the high capitalization reduces the amount of money available for profitable investments and this negatively influences the Texas ratio.

9.5 Conclusions

The paper takes its cue from the recent failures of several US mid-banks. Immediately, the finding that crises have again hit some US banks suggested that the cause could be attributed to poor regulation of their operations. In addition, the further finding that US banks are, on average, more profitable than European banks suggests that they have fewer regulatory constraints and can operate with lower capitalization, allocating more funds to profitable activities. In fact, although rising inflation and restrictive policy by monetary authorities have had a similar impact on the balance sheets of European and US banks, only the latter have experienced a number of failures.

After summarizing the causes of bank failures and the subsequent actions implemented by the authorities in the respective countries, the research highlights the profitability and regulatory characteristics of two comparable samples of banks, one European and the other American.

Over the 2005–2024 period, the higher average profitability of US banks (+43%) and the lower average level of capitalization imposed by regulation, particularly the Tier 1 ratio (–5,6), was noted.

After that a comparison between the statistical significance of the *Z*-score and of the Texas ratio is performed through a set of panel regression analyses with random effects, separately run for the evaluation of European and American banks. The regressions where the *Z*-score is the dependent variable show a lower R^2 than the following regressions (Texas ratio) for both European and American banks. The R^2 is higher for the European banks and this would explain why in the literature the *Z*-score is more used in European samples. Concerning the independent variables, the ROA is significant (***), and the coefficient is positive because the higher the ROA, the higher the *Z*-score; this means that the higher the distance of the bank from insolvency, the lower the probability of default. Regarding the Tier1 capital ratio, it is significant for European (***) and for American banks (**), and the coefficients have positive signs. This means that the higher the capitalization of banks, the higher the *Z*-score is, and the lower the probability of insolvency.

Finally, two-panel regressions where the Texas ratio is the dependent variable show that the R^2 is higher than in the previous regressions for European and American banks. So, the proposed model works better for the examination of the Texas ratio, where also the significance of the regressors is higher. The ROA is significant (***), and the coefficient is negative because the higher the ROA, the lower the Texas ratio and the lower the probability of default of the bank. Regarding the Tier 1 capital ratio, it is significant (**) for both samples of banks, but the coefficients have different signs. For European banks, higher capital ratios help lower the Texas ratio and positively impact their solvency. Conversely, for American banks, higher capital ratios have a negative effect, likely because increased capitalization reduces funds available for profitable investments, adversely affecting the Texas ratio.

The quantitative analysis, even using two relatively small datasets, confirms the different relationships that characterize the profitability, regulation, and stability of European and American banks. In addition, the comparison between the *Z*-score and the Texas ratio offers an explanation as to why the former is more used in the analysis of the stability of European banks while the latter is more used in the analysis of American banks.

References

Adrian, T., Abbas, N., Ramirez, S. L., & Dionis, G. F. (2024, March). *The US Banking Sector since the March 2023 Turmoil: Navigating the Aftermath.* IMF Global Financial Stability Note.

Af Jochnick, K. (2023, January). Boosting bank resilience to adverse external shocks. *Inforbanca, No. 127,* 2–12.

Ali, S., Naveed, M., Gubareva, M., & Vo, X.V. (2024). Reputational contagion from the Silicon Valley Bank debacle. *Research in International Business and Finance, 69,* 102275.

Bales, S., & Burghof, H. (2024). Public attention, sentiment and default of Silicon Valley Bank. *North American Journal of Economics and Finance, 69,* 102026.

Banerjee, A. K., Pradhan, H. K., Sensoy, A., & Goodell J. W. (2024). Assessing the US financial sector post three bank collapses: Signals from Fintech and financial sector ETFs. *International Review of Financial Analysis, 91,* 102995.

Board of Governors of the Federal Reserve System. (2023, March 12). Federal Reserve Board announces it will make available additional funding to eligible depository institutions to help assure banks have the ability to meet the needs of all their depositors. *Press release.*

Casabianca, E. J., Catalano, M., Forni, L., Giarda, E., & Passeri, S. (2019, August 2019). *An early warning system for banking crises: From regression-based analysis to machine learning techniques.* Marco Fanno Working Papers, August 2019.

Chen, J., & Nie, C. (2024). Impact of the collapse of silicon valley bank on the banking sector: An analysis based on non-linear high frequency networks. *Finance Research Letters, 62* 105187.

Chesini, G., & Fauri, F. (2024). *From one crisis to another: The European Central Bank's Role from the Great Recession to the Ukraine War.* Constitutional Political Economy.

Di Vito, L., Fuentes, N. M., & Leite, J. M. (2023). *Understanding the profitability gap between euro area and US global systemically important banks.* ECB Occasional Paper Series No. 327.

Drechsler, I., Savov, A., & Schnabl, P. (2023, March 13). Why do banks invest in MBS? https://pages.stern.nyu.edu/~pschnabl/research/DSS_SVB.pdf.

EBA. (2021). *Differences in provisioning practices in the United States and European Union.* Thematic Note EBA/REP/2021/13.

ECB. (2023, March 20). ECB Banking Supervision, SRB and EBA statement on the announcement on 19 March 2024 by Swiss Authorities. *ECB Press Release.*

Enria, A. (2023, March 28). *A new stage for European banking supervision*. Keynote speech by the Chair of the Supervisory Board of the ECB, 22nd Handelsblatt Annual Conference on Banking Supervision, Frankfurt am Main.
Farah, E., Austen, M., & Carchen, E. (2022). *The good, the bad and the ugly. The impact of inflation on European banking and what to do about it*. Oliver Wyman.
FDIC. (2023, April 28). *FDIC's Supervision of Signature Bank*. FDIC Internal Review Report.
Ferrarin, A., Polato, M., & Velliscig, G. (2020). Disentangling the Texas ratio: The case of the Italian banking sector. *International Journal of Managerial and Financial Accounting, 12*(3/4). 217–241
Ferreira, C. (2023). Competition and Stability in the European Union Banking Sector. *International Advances in Economic Research, 29*, 207–224.
FINMA. (2023, March 19). *FINMA approves merger of UBS and Credit Suisse*. Press Release.
Glancy, D., Ionescu, F., Klee, E., Kotidis, A., Siemer, M., & Zlate, A. (2024). *The 2023 Banking Turmoil and the Bank Term Funding Program. Finance and Economics Discussion Series 2024–045*. Board of the Governors of the Federal Reserve System, https://doi.org/10.17016/FEDS.2024.045.
Gugler, K., & Peev, E. (2018). The persistence of profits in banking: an international comparison. *Applied Economics, 50*, 55, 5996–6009.
Jesswein, K. R. (2009). An examination of the "Texas ratio" as a bank failure model. *Academy of Banking Academy of Banking Studies Journal, 8*(1–2) 63–73.
Jiang, E., Matvos, G., Piskorski, T., & Seru, A. (2023, March 13). *Monetary Tightening and US Bank Fragility in 2023: Mark-to-market losses and uninsured depositor runs?* Available at: https://ssrn.com/abstract=4387676
King, T. B., Nuxoll, D .A., & Yeager, T. J. (2005). *Are the causes of bank distress changing? Can researchers keep up?* FDIC Center for Financial Research Working Paper, N° 3.
Khoo, G. (2023). Commentary: Lessons from SVB's collapse on sustainability and sustainable finance: Ensuring resilience from "unsustainability". *The Journal of Risk Finance, 24*(3), 386–389.
Krogstrup, S., & Sangill, T. (2024). New technologies and the Future Governance of Bank Run Risk. *Journal of Financial Regulation, 10*, 135–141.
Liu, X., Megginson, W., Tran, N., & Wei, S. (2024). Who loses most when big banks suddenly fail? Evidence from Silicon Valley Bank Collapse. *Finance Research Letters, 59*, 104806.
Martins, A. M. (2025). The collapse of Silicon Valley Bank and Credit Suisse and their impact on other U.S. Banks. *Applied Economics Letters, 32*(8), 1126–1130.
Paz Valbuena, X., & Eidenmüller, H. (2023). Bailout Blues: The Write-Down of the AT1 Bonds in the Credit Suisse Bailout. *European Business Organization Law Review, 24*, 409–419.

Piskorski, T. (2024). Could Silicon Valley Bank happen again? "The short answers, yes" says professor who sees $2 trillion of losses on the books. *Fortune Future of Finance Conference*. https://fortune.com/2024/05/16/silicon-valley-bank-aftermath-2-trillion-exposure-underwater/

Shikha, N., & Kapsis, I. (2024). Bank crisis management and resolution after SVB and Credit Suisse: Perspectives from India and the European Union. *International Insolvencies Review, 33*(1), 55–88.

Simoens, M., & Vander Vennet, R. (2021). Bank performance in Europe and the US: A divergence in market-to-book-ratios. *Finance Research Letters*, 40, 101672.

Soenen, N., & Vander Vennet, R. (2022). Determinants of European banks' default risk. *Finance Research Letters*, 47, 102557.

Teixeira, J. C. A., Silva, F. J. F., Costa, F. A. T., Martins, D. M. C., & da Graça Batista, M. (2020). Banks' profitability, institutions, and regulation in the context of the financial crisis. *International Journal of Financial Economics*, 25, 297–320.

Velliscig, G., Floreani, J., & Polato, M. (2023). Capital and asset quality implications for bank resilience and performance in the light of NPLs' regulation: A focus on the Texas ratio. *Journal of Banking Regulation, 24*, 66–88.

Wyman, O. (2023). The EU banking regulatory framework and its impact on banks and the economy. Reference study. January.

Xu, T., Hu, K., & Das, U.S. (2019). Bank profitability and Financial Stability. IMF Working Paper, WP/19/5.

CHAPTER 10

The Impact of Nonperforming Loan Restructuring Programs in the European Union Following the Global Financial Crisis

Ewa Miklaszewska, Krzysztof Kil, and Radosław Ciukaj

10.1 Introduction

Since the 1990s, there was a significant trend to decline the share of bank credit to nonfinancial firms, relative to the real estate or consumer loans. This tendency was further reinforced after the 2008 global financial crisis (GFC) and the COVID-19 outbreak (ECB 2019; ESRB 2023). A sharp decline in bank loans to nonfinancial corporations (NFCs) in many European Union (EU) countries after the GFC raised a concern over sustainable economic growth and posed a serious policy concern (Gambacorta et al. 2014).

For long-term economic growth, efficient lending, especially corporate credit, is essential (Beck and Keil 2020). Financial literature suggests that

E. Miklaszewska (✉) • K. Kil • R. Ciukaj
Department of Banking and Global Financial System, Institute of Finance, Cracow University of Economics (Uniwersytet Ekonomiczny w Krakowie), Kraków, Poland
e-mail: miklasze@uek.krakow.pl; kilk@uek.krakow.pl; ciukajr@uek.krakow.pl

E. Scannella and J. Williams (eds.), *Trends, Issues, and Challenges in Banking and Finance*, Palgrave Macmillan Studies in Banking and Financial Institutions,
https://doi.org/10.1007/978-3-031-96066-6_10

in many cases an efficient and well-performing banking system may not be sufficient to influence the volume and structure of a loan (Miklaszewska and Kil 2016). Banks tend to respond to regulatory incentives (Elliot and Willesson 2018) and by implementing specific public policies, governments aim to stimulate corporate lending, faciliate access to finance for business and promote economic growth. Credit policies, instruments, and institutions that could affect the negative lending trend are of utmost importance (Bezemer et al. 2023). There are a number of possible policy tools to influence bank lending, such as the following:

- central banks can use monetary policy tools (interest rate adjustments, open market operations), to influence the overall cost and availability of credit in the economy;
- governments can apply credit guarantee schemes to reduce the risk associated with corporate lending, particularly for small- and medium-sized enterprises that may have limited collateral or credit history. Governments may also offer subsidized loan programs, where the government provides financial support to reduce the interest rates or fees charged on corporate loans;
- governments may also implement regulatory reforms to invigorate lending processes and enhance the efficiency of credit markets.

After the experience of the GFC, many banks and governments in the EU countries have established systems and measures to manage the nonperforming loan (NPL) portfolios and to the deal with the accumulation of nonperforming exposures (Karkowska 2024). Thus, this chapter aims to analyze whether the post-2008 crisis regulatory reforms and restructuring programs, particularly aiming to reduce the NPL portfolios, have been effective in incentivizing banks to extend loans in general, and loans to businesses in particular. The main objective of the research was to assess whether the selected methods of restructuring of low-quality loans and the intensity of their application have affected the changes in the value of the NPL ratio. The main hypothesis verified in the article is whether the methods of restructuring the NPL portfolio in the European Union countries after the GFC period, applied at the level of countries and banks, were effective in improving credit availability and in affecting credit structure.

As the research methodology, first the author's index of the intensity and diversity of application of restructuring actions and tools was constructed, then linear regression of panel data was used (based on dynamic models SYS-GMM) to assess the statistical significance of factors affecting the allocation of bank credit. The econometric analysis covers the period 2014–2022. The positive verification of the main hypothesis allowed us to form the conclusion that public policies toward areas of banking fragility have positively impacted credit availability and structure.

10.2 Credit Allocation and Its Importance in the Financial System

The key responsibility of banking sector is to provide credit to consumers, corporations, and small firms. In case of the nonfinancial corporations (NFCs), bank credit is an essential part of financing investment activities, particularly within the European financial model. In 2023, the volume of outstanding loans to households and NFCs in the EU reached 13 trillion euros, which was approximately 77% of the EU's GDP and 86% of loans originated from euro area countries, particularly from the four economies—Germany, France, Italy, and Spain. In 2023, total lending to NFCs amounted to 5.3 trillion euros, accounting for 41% of total loans and equivalent to 31% of the EU's GDP. Between 2012 and 2023, the EU credit market was relatively volatile—it experienced three consecutive years of contraction (from 2012 to 2014), followed by 8 years of expansion (2015 to 2022). Loans to NFCs in the EU have expanded only since 2016, with a growth rate ranging between 0.1% and 6.4% in most years, and recorded a slight decrease of 0.65% in 2023 (Andersson and Trevisan 2024). As pointed out by ESRB (2023), the COVID-19 pandemic was an interesting experiment in the response of bank lending to an exogenous relaxation of prudential requirements and to support measures impacting credit demand, like loan guarantees and moratoria. Following the widespread public support measures, EU banks significantly expanded their corporate loan books between 2020 and 2021. However, the amounts borrowed by NFCs were largely retained as cash reserves. Households use debt primarily to finance consumer spending and mortgages, but for firms an external source of finance is essential for their investments, which in the long run is fundamental to the GDP growth. Hence, it is particularly important to understand what factors influence credit structure and composition and what lessons can be learned from post-GFC lending support measures.

Among the determinants of banks' lending policies, an important role is played by indicators related to the credit market, including the quality of their loan portfolio. The analysis of the quality of banks' loan portfolios is also important from the point of view of the economy as a whole, as the materialization of credit risk in banks often reduces the scale of their lending and thus has negative repercussions on economic activity (Berger and De Young 1997; Falagiarda et al. 2020). Another important issue is the question of stability of lending policies and countercyclical credit dimension (Beck at al. 2008). One of the causes of the GFC was the inadequate management of credit risk in the housing loan market in the United States, which manifested itself in expansive lending policies, banks' involvement in trading in risky financial instruments, and significant involvement in real estate markets, in particular, holding a large number of so-called subprime loans. The decline in asset prices in the US real estate market has led to a deterioration in their financial condition. The extensive interconnectedness of US banks with other financial institutions resulted in the materialization of systemic risk. The deterioration of the macroeconomic situation in many European economies after the GFC led to difficulties in settling the financial obligations of many borrowers, and thus significantly worsened the quality of banks' loan portfolios. The high levels of NPLs were holding down credit growth and economic activity. NPLs influence bank lending through three interrelated key channels: profitability, capital, and funding. Bank profitability suffers because banks have to raise provisions; NPLs may also tie up substantial amounts of capital due to higher risk weights on impaired assets. Also, a deteriorating balance sheet raises bank's funding costs because of lower expected revenue streams and, hence, heightened risk perceptions on the part of investors. Together, these factors result in some combination of higher lending rates, reduced lending volumes, and increased risk aversion (IMF 2016).

The GFC led also to a rapid accumulation of government debt in most countries of the euro area. After the 2020 economic crisis, the increase in public debt was mainly the result of an expansionary fiscal policy in a number of countries. The COVID-19 pandemic created a number of vulnerabilities for the banking sector, such as pushing out bank loans by public grants and subsidies and endangering the portfolio of corporate loans. The governments were reacting to external shock by employing fiscal stabilization measures at a massive scale, which were successful in reduction of shocks and stimulation of the recovery, but at the same time resulting in largely expanding budget deficits (Miklaszewska and Kil 2024). The crisis itself exacerbated fiscal challenges faced by countries and, in many cases, fiscal burden constrained lending growth (Fed. 2023).

An important contribution to understanding the role of banks in the economy and in emphasizing the importance of systemic stability for effective lending was made by the 2022 winners of the Bank of Sweden's Alfred Nobel Prize in Economics: Ben Bernanke, Douglas Diamond, and Philip Dybvig (KVA 2022). They stressed that the main goal of stabilizing banks and preventing banking crises is precisely to sustain effective lending. Moreover, the economic literature frequently treated banking crises as consequences of economic problems and the Nobel laureates' contribution was to point out that the opposite is most often true—it is the disruption of credit that causes economic problems, recessions, or crises. Diamond and Dybvig (1986) showed that a bank undertakes costly monitoring of loan contracts, having a cost advantage over other forms of capital allocation, while the alternative is either duplication of effort or a free-rider problem, resulting in a stampede of the loan market. Bernanke emphasized the role of credit for economic development, easing the business cycle and recovering from economic recessions (Bernanke 1993), pointing to new elements of analysis, such as the functioning of the economy in an environment of information asymmetry. He also emphasized, as have many other empirical works, the role of relationship lending for small businesses, which has a significant macroeconomic effect. Analyzing the role of bank credit in the post-2008 crisis period, he concluded that changes in the credit market deserve more attention from economists when analyzing the economic effects of financial crises, but also when studying business cycles (Bernanke 2018). An efficient credit market plays a fundamental role in economic development, which is also shown by empirical data. In the global market, bank credit to GDP increased from 56% to 147% in the period 1960–2020 and there are some dramatic differences in access to credit between low-income and high-income countries—private sector credit to GDP for the former was 13% and for the latter 140% in 2018 (The World Bank 2022).

Credit availability can impact the economy in a number of ways and is based on a number of linkages. The first link is based on the lending availability standards (non-price loan terms). Another link is based on the feedback between the balance sheets of banks, firms, and households. Many studies showed that banking sector stability also appears to be an important driver of GDP growth, while financial deepening plays an important role for banks transferring funds to the real sector (Danielsson et al. 2022). In financial crises, credit activities of banks decline, and this has an impact on the availability of resources for financing the economy, although there appears to be no clear evidence of a systemic retrenchment from bank core activity of providing credit (Buch and Dages 2018, Casanova et al. 2021).

10.3 Methods of Restructuring the NPL Portfolio in the EU Countries in the Post-2008 Crisis Period

When assessing the quality of banks' loan portfolio, the typical approach is to identify the percentage of NPLs in the total loan portfolio. The most common characteristics of nonperforming receivables are the length of time they are past due (delays in repayment of more than 90 days) and signals of possible difficulties of the borrower in timely payment of his/her loan obligation (BCBS 2017). High levels of NPLs can reduce bank capital and liquidity, making it more difficult for banks to provide funding to the real economy (EC 2023). In Eurozone countries alone, the level of NPLs tripled in the 5 years since the beginning of the GFC. As traditional mechanisms for dealing with NPLs, such as their restructuring or write-off, proved insufficient, many European banking sectors decided to implement so-called market-based methods for reducing high levels of NPLs (OECD 2021). Many governments and supervisory authorities have recognized the need for a comprehensive approach, implementing a series of structural reforms, particularly in the 2014–2020 period (Wyman 2018, Asian Development Bank 2021). The analysis of NPL reduction methods revealed a diverse approach to the issue among analyzed countries in terms of both the methods chosen and the timing of their implementation. Government–backed schemes have helped to start NPL securitization transactions, as in a case of government–backed schemes in Italy (Garanzia Cartolarizzazione Sofferenze, GACS) and Greece (Hellenic Asset Protection Scheme, HAPS) (Linaritis 2020). The most popular methods include the creation of asset management companies and transferring nonperforming credit exposures to them and securitizing them or selling them directly to investors (Cerruti and Neyens 2016; Fell et al. 2017). Other methods supporting the restructuring of the NPL portfolio included strengthening prudential supervision, carrying out reforms to strengthen debt enforcement systems, insolvency frameworks and tax systems, or measures and reforms aimed at developing markets for NPLs by improving market infrastructure and eliminating information asymmetries (EBA 2019 and 2022).

To capture the intensity of measures taken by individual countries to reduce its NPL portfolio, a comprehensive index was used: ***NPL Reduction Intensity Index (NPL_RII)*** (Ciukaj 2025). In the index, "intensity" was defined as the scale and scope of diversification of NPL reduction methods implemented in a given country to reduce the high value of NPLs.

The NPL_RII index was calculated as the sum of the values of the following variables:

- Value of NPL sales ratio, calculated as the relationship between the value of the NPL portfolio sold in individual country in a given year and the sum of NPL portfolios sold in all analyzed countries in the same year;
- Value of NPL securitization ratio, calculated as the relationship between the value of the securitized NPL portfolio in individual countries in a given year and the sum of securitized NPL portfolios in all analyzed countries in the same year;
- Level of development of the NPL market, measured as the relationship between the value of *Getting Credit index* in a given year in a given country and the value of the *Getting Credit index* in the country that recorded its highest value in a given year. Getting Credit index is a variable published in World Bank's Doing Business Reports, which measures the quality of borrowers' and lenders' information in loan agreement and the level of available credit information in a given country and represents limits on information asymmetry;
- Level of quality of bankruptcy and judicial processes in a given country, measured as the relationship between value of *Resolving Insolvency index (RII)* value in a given country in a given year and the value of RII in the country that recorded the highest its value in a given year, where RII is a World Bank variable published in Doing Business reports. It measures the quality of bankruptcy and litigation processes in a country in a given year;
- Binary variables for asset protection scheme (AMC), supervisory actions, and tax reforms, where the value of 1 means that a given NPL reduction method was applied in the given year and in a given country and the value of 0 means that a given NPL reduction method was not applied in the given year and in a given country.

Table 10.1 presents values of NPL_RII index for the EU countries where such measures were used, between 2010 and 2020.

Based on the data presented in Table 10.1 we can observe a variety of approaches to the intensity of NPL reduction measures, introduced by selected EU countries. The country that was most intensively engaged in reducing the NLPs' level was Italy in 2016 (index value of 6.48), followed by Ireland (3.88 in 2015), Portugal (3.60 in 2016), and Cyprus (3.58 in 2020). Looking at the average values of the index for the whole period, the

Table 10.1 Values of NPL_RII index for the EU countries between 2010 and 2020

Country	*2010*	*2011*	*2012*	*2013*	*2014*	*2015*	*2016*	*2017*	*2018*	*2019*	*2020*	*Avg.*
Austria	2,61	2,61	2,61	2,51	2,63	2,77	2,63	2,59	2,57	2,57	2,56	2,61
Bulgaria	1,62	1,47	1,48	1,5	1,47	1,51	2,49	1,44	1,45	1,47	1,45	1,58
Cyprus	1,21	1,33	1,34	2,32	2,23	2,44	1,54	1,66	2,64	3,57	3,58	2,17
Spain	2,63	2,63	2,67	3,07	3,50	3,45	3,05	3,37	3,26	2,97	2,87	3,04
Greece	2,2	2,18	2,18	2,21	2,21	2,24	2,22	2,25	2,35	3,13	2,44	2,33
Croatia	1,39	1,43	1,44	1,22	1,31	1,35	1,35	2,36	1,35	1,38	1,29	1,44
Hungary	1,43	1,41	1,36	1,34	2,31	2,58	2,54	2,54	2,55	2,56	2,53	2,10
Ireland	2,89	3,86	2,89	3,87	3,83	3,88	3,18	2,91	2,95	2,99	2,79	3,28
Italy	1,36	1,35	1,38	1,37	1,67	4,27	6,48	4,44	4,45	5,45	4,45	3,33
Lithuania	2,36	1,34	1,34	1,33	1,48	1,47	1,42	1,38	1,38	1,38	1,38	1,48
Latvia	1,51	2,52	1,75	1,74	1,7	1,73	1,7	1,76	1,71	1,71	1,71	1,78
Portugal	1,53	1,53	1,53	1,53	1,57	1,63	3,60	2,59	2,59	1,6	1,51	1,93
Romania	1,61	1,58	1,6	2,59	2,58	2,75	2,74	2,65	1,67	1,66	1,64	2,10
Slovenia	1	1,02	1,16	3,2	2,19	3,24	2,45	2,42	2,54	2,53	2,41	2,20
Avg.	**1,81**	**1,88**	**1,77**	**2,13**	**2,19**	**2,52**	**2,67**	**2,45**	**2,39**	**2,50**	**2,33**	**2,24**

Source: Ciukaj (2025).

highest value was reached by Italy and Ireland, and the lowest by Lithuania and Latvia. Moreover, the majority of analyzed EU countries showed a maximum value of NPL_RII index in 2015 (five countries) and 2016 (three countries), while only two countries (Greece and Cyprus) started to intensify the NPL restructuring effort late (in the 2018–2020 period).

10.4 Research Design and Results

10.4.1 Factors Influencing Availability of Credit

Lending policies and credit availability to the nonfinancial sector (NFS) are key determinants of bank efficiency and performance. To analyze credit availability in the EU countries, the following key indicators were used:

- the share of loans to NFS in total assets (L/A),
- the rate of change in the value of loans to NFS (including corporate loans, consumer loans, and housing loans),
- the structure of the loan portfolio (share of consumer, corporate, and housing loans in total credit to NFS).

To assess the statistical significance of factors affecting the allocation of bank credit, linear regression of panel data was used. The following three groups of data were used:

- microeconomic data, characterizing individual banks (based on BankFocus database);
- macroeconomic and sectoral data, characterizing economic environment in each country (based on the data from Eurostat and ECB databases);
- experimental variables, characterizing the methods to restructure low-quality loan portfolios used in the EU countries. In order to consider the long-term effects of the applied restructuring instruments, 2-year lags of the variables were introduced. The data for experimental variables were extracted for each country from a number of reports of national supervisory authorities and other official publications.

Based on completeness of available data, the base model used statistical information for 1,457 banks from 27 EU countries with business continuity in 2014–2022. The variables used in the construction of the model were identified based on the literature review and expert assessment and are presented in Table 10.2. Due to the presence of correlations between variables, some variables were excluded from the model. The analysis of correlation coefficients is presented graphically in Fig. 10.1.

Considering the characteristics of the variables, dynamic models were used (Generalized Method of Moment version of SYS-GMM, based on Blundell and Bond 1998), commonly used in banking studies with panel data. The GMM estimators allow for a departure from the standard assumption of strict exogeneity of regressors and the inclusion of lagged values of the dependent variable. The SYS-GMM estimator can also give more reliable and accurate results in similar cases (Baltagi 2005). Statistical inference regarding the significance of the model parameters was performed based on the one-step estimator. For diagnostic purposes, the Sargan test for the two-step method (Hansen's test) was used, as well as the Arellano-Bond AR(1) and AR(2) autocorrelation tests.

The final shape of the estimated dynamic regression models is determined by Eq. 10.1:

$$CR.ALOC_{it} = const + a1*CR.ALOC_{i,t-1} + a2*MICRO.VAR_{i,t} + a3*MACRO.VAR_{i,t} + a4*CR.REST_{i,t-2} + V_{it} \quad (10.1)$$

Table 10.2 Characteristics of the set of variables employed in the base model

Variable	*Definition*	*Area of analysis*
• **Explanatory variables—credit allocation**		
NFSL_TA	Loans to the NFS / total assets	Credit policy
CORPL_TL	Corporate loans / total loans for the NFS	Credit policy
CONSL_TL	Consumer loans / total loans for the NFS	Credit policy
MORTL_TL	Mortgage loans / total loans for the NFS	Credit policy
• **Explanatory variables—microeconomic characteristics**		
LOG_TA	Natural logarithm of total assets	Bank size
ROE	Net profit / average shareholders' equity	Bank profitability
NPL	Share of impaired loans in total loans	Assets quality
NIM	Net interest margin - net interest income/ total assets	Bank profitability
ZSC	Z-score = ROA+CAR/standard deviation of ROA	Bank stability
TCR	Total equity / RWA	Bank stability
II_TI	Net interest income/ total income	Diversification of incomes
C_I	Cost/Income	Cost efficiency
DEP_TA	Total deposits/total assets	Financing strategy
DD_TD	Current deposits/total deposits	Stability of financing
SEC_TA	Treasury securities/total assets	Dependence on public sector risk
DEP_IB_TA	Deposits from the interbank market/total assets	Dependence on wholesale financing
SPEC	Bank specialization—binary variable. 0-universal or commercial bank; 1-specialized bank (including cooperative and savings banks)	Business model
• **Explanatory variables—macroeconomic and sectoral characteristics**		
GDP	Change in GDP of the country of bank's operation	Economic growth
HICP	A harmonized measure of inflation in the EU	Inflation
PU_DEBT	Public sector debt/GDP	Public debt
LT_IR	Long-term interest rate (according to the Maastricht convergence criteria)	Interest rate
HHI	Herfindahl–Hirschman concentration measure	Concentration

Source: Own presentation.

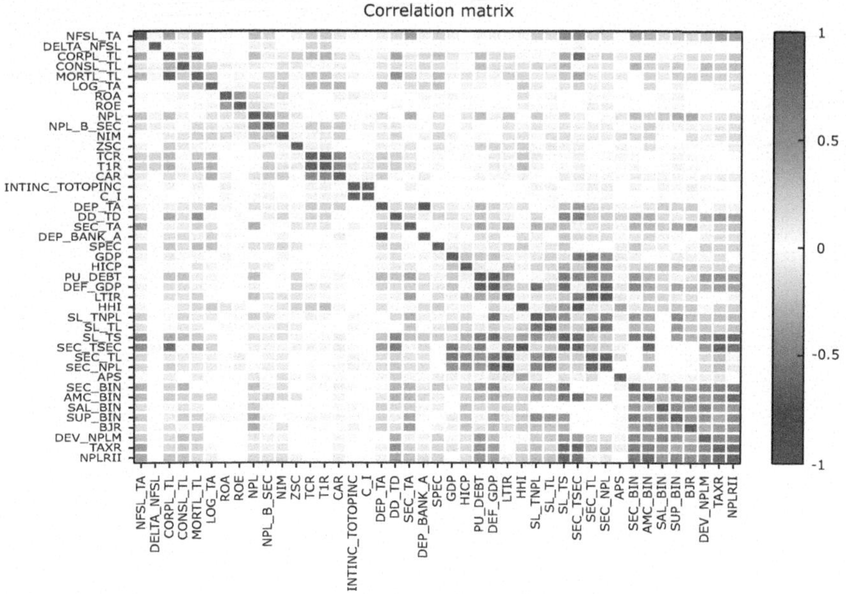

Fig. 10.1 Correlation matrix for the underlying set of variables. Source: Own presentation.

where:

CR.ALOC represents characteristics of the bank's credit allocation;
MICRO.VAR is a vector of microeconomic control variables;
MACRO.VAR is a vector of macroeconomic and sectoral control variables;
CR.REST denotes experimental variables—characteristics of the NPLs' restructuring tools used in a given country, added in the extended model (2).

First, parameter estimation was carried out for the base model (1). The results for all explanatory variables are presented in Table 10.3.

Table 10.3 Results of parameter estimation in the base model (1) for the variables: NFSL_TA, CONSL_TL, MORTL_TL, CORPL_TL

Variable	*NFSL_TA*	*CONSL_TL*	*MORTL_TL*	*CORPL_TL*
DEP.VAR(-1)	0.657*** (0.041)	0.764*** (0.091)	0.580*** (0.053)	0.813*** (0.147)
CONST	17.181*** (3.128)	7.899 (7.78)	14.722** (6.176)	10.692 (8.664)
LOG_TA	−0.247 (0.157)	0.246 (0.194)	−0.132 (0.271)	−0.416 (0.412)
ROE	−0.009 (0.029)	-0.029 (0.057)	−0.040* (0.022)	−0.003 (0.031)
NPL	−0.227*** (0.033)	0.001 (0.045)	−0.336*** (0.061)	0.062 (0.131)
NIM	0.204 (0.23)	0.447 (0.317)	-0.765 (0.668)	−0.455 (0.295)
ZSC	0.000* (0)	0.012* (0.007)	0.000 (0.003)	−0.015 (0.026)
TCR	−0.165*** (0.040)	−0.057 (0.053)	−0.086** (0.041)	0.002 (0.034)
II_TI	0.083*** (0.023)	−0.005 (0.026)	0.082** (0.032)	0.039 (0.045)
C_I	−0.012 (0.007)	−0.002 (0.01)	−0.028** (0.011)	−0.024 (0.016)
DEP_TA	0.006 (0.025)	−0.014 (0.041)	−0.039 (0.047)	0.018 (0.065)
DD_TD	0.038*** (0.01)	−0.027 (0.018)	0.07*** (0.026)	−0.013 (0.027)
SEC_TA	−0.297*** (0.03)	0.099*** (0.029)	0.247*** (0.029)	0.009 (0.041)
DEP_IB_TA	−0.026 (0.03)	−0.043 (0.047)	−0.165*** (0.05)	0.014 (0.074)
SPEC	1.302** (0.607)	−1.244 (0.86)	3.447*** (1.291)	-3.554 (3.632)
GDP	0.043** (0.02)	0.064 (0.047)	−0.022 (0.039)	−0.052 (0.06)
HICP	−0.328*** (0.059)	0.267** (0.117)	0.49*** (0.149)	−0.024 (0.186)
PU_DEBT	0.064*** (0.008)	−0.024 (0.016)	0.005 (0.018)	−0.044 (0.035)
LTIR	2.315*** (0.173)	−0.969*** (0.336)	−2.708*** (0.517)	0.707*** (0.272)
HHI	−11.213** (5.073)	22.445** (9.499)	0.111 (20.102)	24.092* (13.289)
No. of observations	4821	2706	2433	823
No. of instruments	55	55	55	55
Test AR 1	−11.2449 (0.0000)]	−4.32394 (0.0000)	-9.33951 (0.0000)	−3.03833 (0.0024)
Test AR 2	−1.47647 (0.1398)	0.57773 (0.5634)	−0.395975 (0.6921)	0.212609 (0.8316)

Notes: AR (1) – first-order autocorrelation test. AR (2) – second-order autocorrelation test. Robust standard errors in parentheses and p-values in brackets. Time effects are included but not reported. System GMM (1 lag used as instrument). Source: Own calculations.

Table 10.4 Factors influencing bank credit for major types of loans

Loan structure	*Positive influence*	*Negative influence*
Consumer loans/ TL	• bank stability (Z-Score index) • bank exposure to the Treasury debt securities market (SEC_TA) • inflation rate, • banking market concentration.	• the level of long-term interest rates.
Housing loans/TL	• the share of net interest income in profits, • the share of current deposits in assets, • exposure to the treasury securities (SEC_TA), • bank specialization, • the inflation rate.	• bank profitability (ROE), • the quality of loan portfolio (NPL), • bank capital adequacy (TCR), • C/I ratio, • share of deposits from the interbank market in total assets, • the level of long-term interest rates.
Corporate loans/ TL	• the level of long-term interest rates, • market concentration.	

Source: Table 10.3.

The results of the baseline model (Table 10.4) demonstrate that total credit exposure of banks (NFSL) is significantly affected:

a. **positively**:
   - bank stability as measured by the *Z*-Score index,
   - traditional business model—share of net interest income in banking profit and share of current deposits in total deposits,
   - bank specialization (the use of a cooperative or savings bank model),
   - macroeconomic factors: high GDP growth and level of long-term interest rates.
   - public finance sector balance and country's public debt in relation to GDP.

b. **negatively**:
   - the quality of loan portfolio (NPL ratio),
   - the value of the TCR ratio,
   - bank's exposure to the Treasury debt securities market (SEC_TA ratio),
   - the level of current inflation and the level of market concentration.

Consequently, it could be concluded that the increase in bank lending to the economy (NFS) is supported by bank stability, traditional business model with a high level of interest incomes and large portfolio of current deposits as a source of financing, and the high quality of the existing loan portfolio. Among the macroeconomic factors supporting banks' credit exposure are the high rate of economic growth, an increase in the level of interest rates, and a reduction in the inflation rate. When analyzing parameters related to public finance, a positive relationship between public debt and the share of loans to NFS in total assets has been demonstrated. However, the tightening of bank capital regulations after the GFC might have contributed to the reduction of bank credit (negative influence), as illustrated also by other sources (ESRB 2023).

The determinants influencing bank *credit* for a different type of loans are summarized in Table 10.4.

Analyzing the determinants of access to credit for different types of loans, in all cases there is a strong tendency of continuation of the trends. It should also be noted the different impact of interest rates - lowering rates favors a reduction in corporate loans to total loans and an increase of consumer and housing loans in the total exposure. For consumer and housing loans, the higher share of treasury securities in bank assets is also a positive factor. The higher share of housing loans is supported by the better quality of total exposures. Higher banking market concentration has a positive impact on the share of corporate and consumer loans.

10.4.2 The Impact of the NPLs' Restructuring Strategies on the Availability of Credit

In the next step of the analysis, the econometric model was extended by adding experimental variables, which represented the NPLs' restructuring methods applied in a given country, which are shown in Table 10.5.

The aim was to assess the long-term effects of the NPLs' restructuring programs on the overall credit availability. The experimental variables were applied with a 2-year lag. Because of a significant correlation between the experimental variables, they were included in the model separately. After inclusion of the experimental variables, all models retained a high level of stability of results. Tables 10.6 and 10.7 present the estimation results for the total loan exposure and for corporate loans, which can be summarized as follows (for statistically significant influence):

For the aggregated loan portfolio (NFSL_TA):

- positive effect of the variables:
  - the comprehensive NPLs' restructuring intensity index (NPL_RII),
  - variables related to the sale of NPLs (SL_TL, SL_TS, SAL_BIN) and their securitization (SEC_BIN),

Table 10.5 Extended model (2): characteristics of experimental variables, representing types of NPL restructuring policies at the country level

SL_TNPL	% Sale / Total NPL
SL_TL	% Sale / Loans
SL_TS	% Sale / Total sale
SEC_TSEC	% Securitization /Total securitization
SEC_TL	% Securitization /Loans
SEC_NPL	% Securitization / NPL
APS	Asset Protection Program—binary variable; 0- did not occur in a given year in a given country; 1- actions taken in a given year in a given country
SEC_BIN	Securitization—binary variable; 0- did not occur in a given year in a given country; 1- activities undertaken in a given year in a given country
AMC_BIN	AMC—binary variable; 0- did not occur in a given year in a given country; 1- activities undertaken in a given year in a given country
SAL_BIN	Direct sales—binary variable; 0- did not occur in a given year in a given country; 1- activities undertaken in a given year in a given country
SUP_BIN	Supervisory activities—binary variable; 0- did not occur in a given year in a given country; 1- actions taken in a given year in a given country
BJR	Bankruptcy and judicial reforms—binary variable; 0- did not occur in a given year in a given country; 1- actions taken in a given year in a given country
DEV_NPLM	Development of NPL markets—binary variable; 0- did not occur in a given year in a given country; 1- actions taken in a given year in a given country
TAXR	Tax reforms—binary variable; 0- did not occur in a given year in a given country; 1- actions taken in a given year in a given country
NPL_RII	An index computed by the authors, measuring intensity of NPL reduction methods in a given country in a given year, lagged by 2 years

Source: Own presentation.

  - the existence of asset management company (AMC_BIN),
  - supervisory action (SUP_BIN),
  - bankruptcy code reform (BJR) and tax reform (TAXR),
  - development of NPL market (DEV_NPLM).
- negative effect of Asset Protection Program (APS).

It can be concluded that a number of tools used in each country to restructure the portfolio of low-quality loans, including in particular the sale of impaired loans, securitization, the development of NPL markets, and the establishment of AMCs, as well as the supervisory actions and

Table 10.6 Model 2 with experimental variables for NFSL_TA

	Experimental variables											
Variable	*NPL_RII*	*SL_TNPL*	*SL_TL*	*SL_TS*	*APS*	*SEC_BIN*	*AMC_BIN*	*SAL_BIN*	*SUP_BIN*	*BJR*	*DEV_NPLM*	*TAXR*
NFSL_TA(-	0.565***	0.459***	0.462***	0.383***	0.488***	0.399***	0.498***	0.499***	0.41***	0.5***	0.494***	0.483***
1)	(0.041)	(0.043)	(0.042)	(0.042)	(0.042)	(0.039)	(0.041)	(0.041)	(0.039)	(0.041)	(0.041)	(0.04)
const	27.293***	25.394***	25.707***	35.437***	23.62***	36.337***	28.051***	28.246***	31.522***	27.211***	28.486***	30.922***
	(3.919)	(5.61)	(5.599)	(5.99)	(4.518)	(5.067)	(4.52)	(4.525)	(4.867)	(4.487)	(4.641)	(4.521)
LOG_TA	-0.506***	-0.377	-0.375	-0.241	-0.398*	-0.379	-0.517**	-0.538**	-0.475*	-0.503**	-0.526**	-0.462**
	(0.196)	(0.234)	(0.232)	(0.252)	(0.231)	(0.25)	(0.222)	(0.226)	(0.25)	(0.222)	(0.229)	(0.226)
ROE	-0.046	-0.087*	-0.087*	-0.093*	-0.064*	-0.067*	-0.06*	-0.059*	-0.071**	-0.059*	-0.061*	-0.061*
	(0.033)	(0.049)	(0.049)	(0.049)	(0.035)	(0.035)	(0.035)	(0.035)	(0.035)	(0.035)	(0.035)	(0.035)
NPL	-0.129***	-0.256***	-0.25***	-0.131**	-0.205***	-0.086**	-0.19***	-0.209***	-0.087**	-0.193***	-0.212***	-0.188***
	(0.039)	(0.048)	(0.047)	(0.054)	(0.038)	(0.044)	(0.04)	(0.038)	(0.044)	(0.04)	(0.038)	(0.039)
NIM	0.445*	0.454**	0.45**	0.511*	0.456*	0.629*	0.527**	0.447*	0.583	0.562**	0.452*	0.504*
	(0.26)	(0.201)	(0.201)	(0.275)	(0.264)	(0.341)	(0.264)	(0.256)	(0.357)	(0.262)	(0.26)	(0.268)
ZSC	-0.003	-0.007	-0.007	-0.004	-0.006	0.002	-0.004	-0.004	-0.001	-0.004	-0.004	-0.003
	(0.006)	(0.006)	(0.006)	(0.007)	(0.006)	(0.007)	(0.006)	(0.007)	(0.007)	(0.006)	(0.007)	(0.007)
TCR	-0.161***	-0.162***	-0.162***	-0.196***	-0.172***	-0.22***	-0.178***	-0.179***	-0.207***	-0.177***	-0.179***	-0.185***
	(0.042)	(0.047)	(0.047)	(0.051)	(0.047)	(0.051)	(0.046)	(0.047)	(0.05)	(0.046)	(0.048)	(0.047)
INTINC_	0.097***	0.167***	0.167***	0.178***	0.118***	0.123***	0.113***	0.113***	0.126***	0.112***	0.115***	0.115***
TOTOPINC	(0.031)	(0.029)	(0.029)	(0.029)	(0.036)	(0.037)	(0.035)	(0.035)	(0.037)	(0.035)	(0.035)	(0.035)
C_I	-0.024***	-0.04***	-0.04***	-0.043***	-0.029***	-0.033***	-0.028***	-0.028***	-0.034***	-0.028***	-0.029***	-0.029***
	(0.009)	(0.013)	(0.013)	(0.014)	(0.01)	(0.01)	(0.01)	(0.01)	(0.01)	(0.01)	(0.01)	(0.01)
DEP_TA	-0.012	0.064	0.062	0.041	0.054*	0.018	0.027	0.035	0.031	0.03	0.041	0.023
	(0.032)	(0.04)	(0.04)	(0.044)	(0.033)	(0.038)	(0.034)	(0.034)	(0.036)	(0.034)	(0.034)	(0.035)
DD_TD	0.057***	0.065***	0.065***	0.054***	0.069***	0.063***	0.077***	0.072***	0.07***	0.078***	0.076***	0.064***
	(0.014)	(0.017)	(0.017)	(0.019)	(0.015)	(0.017)	(0.015)	(0.015)	(0.016)	(0.015)	(0.015)	(0.016)
SEC_TA	-0.338***	-0.454***	-0.45***	-0.401***	-0.432***	-0.369***	-0.407***	-0.428***	-0.391***	-0.412***	-0.43***	-0.411***
	(0.033)	(0.034)	(0.034)	(0.034)	(0.032)	(0.033)	(0.033)	(0.032)	(0.032)	(0.033)	(0.032)	(0.032)
DEP_	-0.089**	-0.015	-0.02	-0.068	-0.026	-0.076	-0.052	-0.035	-0.054	-0.045	-0.035	-0.052
BANK_A	(0.039)	(0.057)	(0.057)	(0.06)	(0.043)	(0.048)	(0.043)	(0.042)	(0.047)	(0.042)	(0.043)	(0.043)

Variable	*Experimental variables*											
	NPL_RII	*SL_TNPL*	*SL_TL*	*SL_TS*	*APS*	*SEC_BIN*	*AMC_BIN*	*SAL_BIN*	*SUP_BIN*	*BJR*	*DEV_NPLM*	*TAXR*
SPEC	2.109**	2.571*	2.543*	2.790*	2.468**	2.408*	2.413**	2.430**	2.280*	2.452**	2.340**	2.468**
	(1.04)	(1.34)	(1.332)	(1.431)	(1.167)	(1.289)	(1.159)	(1.155)	(1.283)	(1.159)	(1.170)	(1.170)
GDP	0.058**	0.119***	0.123***	0.084**	0.041	0.037	0.048*	0.047*	0.043*	0.046*	0.033	0.048*
	(0.026)	(0.036)	(0.037)	(0.034)	(0.026)	(0.026)	(0.027)	(0.027)	(0.026)	(0.026)	(0.026)	(0.027)
HICP	-0.154**	-0.661***	-0.569***	-0.875***	-0.335***	-0.263***	-0.384***	-0.371***	-0.234***	-0.346***	-0.324***	-0.366***
	(0.078)	(0.133)	(0.136)	(0.128)	(0.085)	(0.088)	(0.087)	(0.087)	(0.086)	(0.086)	(0.085)	(0.086)
PU_DEBT	0.012**	0.053***	0.052***	0.014**	0.066***	0.005**	0.034**	0.039***	0.042***	0.042***	0.038***	0.029**
	(0.009)	(0.017)	(0.017)	(0.006)	(0.014)	(0.004)	(0.014)	(0.013)	(0.013)	(0.014)	(0.014)	(0.013)
DEF_GDP	0.326***	0.293***	0.279***	0.275***	0.374***	0.209***	0.276***	0.281***	0.31***	0.306***	0.313***	0.262***
	(0.065)	(0.085)	(0.081)	(0.076)	(0.069)	(0.076)	(0.073)	(0.075)	(0.073)	(0.072)	(0.072)	(0.073)
LTIR	1.392***	2.898***	2.732***	1.89***	2.156***	1.449***	2.044***	2.093***	1.398***	1.904***	1.939***	1.884***
	(0.242)	(0.419)	(0.419)	(0.384)	(0.275)	(0.284)	(0.285)	(0.279)	(0.278)	(0.287)	(0.276)	(0.273)
HHI	-23.378***	-39.63***	-43.587***	-37.067***	-13.217	-30.324***	-24.412***	-31.887***	-39.399***	-32.209***	-27.678***	-30.171***
	(8.029)	(11.258)	(11.59)	(9.679)	(10.672)	(9.894)	(9.165)	(9.051)	(9.532)	(9.343)	(9.296)	(8.98)
EXP.VAR.	1.473***	0.017	0.259**	0.217***	-11.522***	6.806***	2.146***	1.689***	5.79***	2.034***	1.218***	2.921***
	(0.152)	(0.013)	(0.105)	(0.031)	(3.059)	(0.762)	(0.491)	(0.473)	(0.673)	(0.477)	(0.419)	(0.500)
AR 1 TEST	-9.17464	-6.97258	-6.99992	-6.6623	-8.0128	-7.06251	-8.6852	-8.13249	-7.10801	-8.63057	-8.09631	-8.68888
	(0.0000)	(0.0000)	(0.0000)	(0.0000)	(0.0000)	(0.0000)	(0.0000)	(0.0000)	(0.0000)	(0.0000)	(0.0000)	(0.0000)
AR 2 TEST	-0.441785	-0.855988	-0.861236	-0.718059	-1.09212	-1.32498	-0.24446	-2.48428	-1.35908	-0.349492	-2.15448	0.00970379
	(0.6586)	(0.3920)	(0.3891)	(0.4727)	(0.2748)	(0.1852)	(0.8069)	(0.1132)	(0.1741)	(0.7267)	(0.0312)	(0.9923)
NB. OBS.	2558	2033	2033	2033	2558	2558	2558	2558	2558	2558	2558	2558
NB. INSTR.	56	56	56	56	56	56	56	56	56	56	56	56

Notes: AR(1) – first order autocorrelation test. AR(2) – second-order autocorrelation test. Robust standard errors in parentheses and p-values in brackets. Time effects are included but not reported. System GMM (1 lag used as instrument).

Table 10.7 Model 2 with experimental variables for CORPL_TL

	Experimental variables											
Variable	*NPLRII*	*SL_TNPL*	*SL_TL*	*SL_TS*	*APS*	*SEC_BIN*	*AMC_BIN*	*SAL_BIN*	*SUP_BIN*	*BJR*	*DEV_NPLM*	*TAXR*
CORPL_	0.836***	0.963***	0.961***	1.017***	0.797***	0.841***	0.841***	0.834***	0.834***	0.832***	0.836***	0.826***
TL(-1)	(0.09)	(0.077)	(0.078)	(0.11)	(0.096)	(0.09)	(0.089)	(0.091)	(0.091)	(0.085)	(0.093)	(0.093)
const	6.165	2.825	2.871	−2.387	17.218	5.366	5.28	6.017	6.017	6.252	5.739	7.19
	(8.979)	(9.966)	(9.969)	(12.684)	(11.33)	(9.123)	(9.075)	(9.099)	(9.099)	(8.815)	(9.094)	(8.736)
LOG_TA	−0.219	0.054	0.048	0.231	−0.663	−0.237	−0.239	−0.281	−0.281	−0.268	−0.236	−0.367
	(0.362)	(0.38)	(0.383)	(0.458)	(0.449)	(0.367)	(0.361)	(0.376)	(0.376)	(0.346)	(0.36)	(0.361)
ROE	0.006	0.009	0.009	0.013	0.005	0.006	0.005	0.005	0.005	0.010	0.007	0.007
	(0.025)	(0.024)	(0.024)	(0.029)	(0.025)	(0.025)	(0.025)	(0.025)	(0.025)	(0.026)	(0.026)	(0.025)
NPL	0.024	0.022	0.025	0.004	0.040	0.030	0.035	0.042	0.042	0.011	0.032	0.036
	(0.107)	(0.066)	(0.066)	(0.058)	(0.094)	(0.109)	(0.103)	(0.105)	(0.105)	(0.106)	(0.103)	(0.102)
NIM	−0.561	−0.151	−0.153	0.026	−0.713	−0.548	−0.545	−0.575	−0.575	−0.653*	−0.561	−0.610
	(0.37)	(0.284)	(0.282)	(0.352)	(0.380)	(0.367)	(0.362)	(0.368)	(0.368)	(0.376)	(0.372)	(0.376)
ZSC	−0.045	−0.01	−0.009	−0.008	−0.045	−0.046	−0.045	−0.044	−0.044	−0.046	−0.047	−0.051
	(0.045)	(0.011)	(0.011)	(0.013)	(0.045)	(0.047)	(0.045)	(0.045)	(0.045)	(0.044)	(0.047)	(0.046)
TCR	0.006	−0.003	−0.004	−0.009	−0.001	0.006	0.005	0.005	0.005	0.002	0.005	0.007
	(0.025)	(0.017)	(0.017)	(0.022)	(0.023)	(0.025)	(0.025)	(0.024)	(0.024)	(0.024)	(0.024)	(0.025)
INTINC_	0.047	−0.011	−0.011	−0.018	0.043	0.047	0.048	0.047	0.047	0.055	0.049	0.050
TOTOPINC	(0.038)	(0.027)	(0.027)	(0.03)	(0.036)	(0.038)	(0.039)	(0.038)	(0.038)	(0.04)	(0.039)	(0.038)
C_I	−0.019	0.012	0.012	0.024	−0.030	−0.022	−0.022	−0.026	−0.026	−0.017	−0.02	−0.021
	(0.022)	(0.028)	(0.028)	(0.031)	(0.023)	(0.023)	(0.022)	(0.023)	(0.023)	(0.022)	(0.023)	(0.022)
DEP_TA	0.021	−0.054	−0.056	−0.060	−0.003	0.018	0.016	0.015	0.015	0.020	0.014	0.018
	(0.071)	(0.039)	(0.039)	(0.038)	(0.066)	(0.069)	(0.068)	(0.067)	(0.067)	(0.070)	(0.067)	(0.068)
DD_TD	−0.008	−0.011	−0.011	0.001	−0.005	−0.006	−0.006	−0.008	−0.008	−0.009	−0.008	−0.001
	(0.020)	(0.017)	(0.017)	(0.027)	(0.020)	(0.020)	(0.020)	(0.020)	(0.020)	(0.02)	(0.021)	(0.020)
SEC_TA	0.028	0.029	0.03	0.049	0.031	0.036	0.042	0.039	0.039	0.038	0.041	0.026
	(0.043)	(0.034)	(0.034)	(0.074)	(0.045)	(0.044)	(0.048)	(0.045)	(0.045)	(0.044)	(0.045)	(0.042)
DEP_	0.046	0.011	0.012	−0.010	0.055	0.040	0.037	0.044	0.044	0.026	0.038	0.038
BANK_A	(0.06)	(0.045)	(0.046)	(0.062)	(0.066)	(0.057)	(0.058)	(0.059)	(0.059)	(0.054)	(0.058)	(0.058)

Variable	*Experimental variables*											
	NPLRII	*SL_TNPL*	*SL_TL*	*SL_TS*	*APS*	*SEC_BIN*	*AMC_BIN*	*SAL_BIN*	*SUP_BIN*	*BJR*	*DEV_NPLM*	*TAXR*
SPEC	−1.297	1.543	1.488	2.466	−2.519	−1.341	−1.425	−1.621	−1.621	−1.726	−1.306	−1.580
	(2.304)	(1.951)	(1.968)	(2.151)	(2.475)	(2.401)	(2.306)	(2.379)	(2.379)	(2.218)	(2.302)	(2.303)
GDP	0.033	0.019	0.015	0.023	0.003	0.022	0.020	0.021	0.021	0.029	0.025	0.015
	(0.037)	(0.043)	(0.044)	(0.054)	(0.032)	(0.035)	(0.034)	(0.036)	(0.036)	(0.035)	(0.036)	(0.034)
HICP	−0.186	0.045	0.036	0.007	−0.181	−0.178	−0.184	−0.207	−0.207	−0.183	−0.184	−0.142
	(0.259)	(0.144)	(0.140)	(0.312)	(0.254)	(0.253)	(0.261)	(0.262)	(0.262)	(0.256)	(0.259)	(0.240)
PU_DEBT	−0.036	−0.031	−0.030	−0.021	−0.077**	−0.038	−0.041	−0.043	−0.043	−0.036	−0.04	−0.037
	(0.029)	(0.026)	(0.026)	(0.019)	(0.036)	(0.031)	(0.03)	(0.029)	(0.029)	(0.027)	(0.028)	(0.028)
DEF_GDP	−0.032	−0.213**	−0.193**	−0.189**	−0.105	−0.039	−0.038	−0.050	−0.050	−0.050	−0.048	−0.040
	(0.162)	(0.091)	(0.077)	(0.077)	(0.155)	(0.156)	(0.158)	(0.16)	(0.16)	(0.152)	(0.149)	(0.156)
LTIR	0.708**	0.433	0.446	0.442	0.573*	0.700**	0.716**	0.771**	0.771**	0.780**	0.748**	0.613**
	(0.325)	(0.304)	(0.299)	(0.295)	(0.324)	(0.320)	(0.320)	(0.349)	(0.349)	(0.345)	(0.344)	(0.311)
HHI	33.007*	27.358	28.296	21.047	26.909**	34.527*	35.567*	36.006**	36.006**	39.196**	35.763**	36.091*
	(18.137)	(17.840)	(18.139)	(14.505)	(13.718)	(18.638)	(18.332)	(18.259)	(18.259)	(17.922)	(17.868)	(18.556)
EXP.VAR.	−0.363	**−0.009**	−0.04	0.023	9.547*	−0.398	0.143	0.687	0.687	−1.801	−0.511	1.841*
	(0.309)	**(0.017)**	(0.105)	(0.101)	(4.911)	(1.012)	(1.078)	(0.746)	(0.746)	(1.213)	(1.106)	(1.11)
AR 1 TEST	−2.69109	−1.84148	−1.84771	−1.84771	−2.69753	−2.68558	−2.68916	−2.72469	−2.72469	−2.63303	−2.65912	−2.65836
	(0.0071)	(0.0456)	(0.0446)	(0.0446)	(0.0070)	(0.0072)	(0.0072)	(0.0064)	(0.0064)	(0.0085)	(0.0078)	(0.0079)
AR 2 TEST	1.86477	−0.536451	−0.57861	−0.57861	1.97148	1.92064	1.9077	1.95749	1.95749	1.81494	1.86162	1.77598
	(0.0622)	(0.5916)	(0.5629)	(0.5629)	(0.0487)	(0.0548)	(0.0564)	(0.0503)	(0.0503)	(0.0695)	(0.0627)	(0.0757)
NB. OBS.	516	341	341	341	516	516	516	516	516	516	516	516
NB. INSTR.	56	56	56	56	56	56	56	56	56	56	56	56

Notes: AR(1) – first order autocorrelation test. AR(2) – second-order autocorrelation test. Robust standard errors in parentheses and *p*-values in brackets. Time effects are included but not reported. System GMM (1 lag used as instrument). Source: Own calculations.

Source: Own calculations.

bankruptcy and judicial reforms and tax reforms, all had a positive impact on extending credit to the economy. An aggregate approach, based on a comprehensive index of intensity and diversity of restructuring tools (NPL_RII index), allows also to confirm a positive impact of public and market-based restructuring tools on banks' ability to expand lending. The only restructuring tool that shows an adverse effect on banks' lending was the implementation of the asset protection program (APS).

- For corporate loans (CORPL_TL): positive effect of asset protection program (APS) and tax reform (TAXR).

10.5 Conclusions

GFC has influenced many processes and actions, resulting not only in a public finance crisis in many EU countries, but also in creating many economic and social challenges. One of those challenges was the NPL crisis, particularly in the euro area countries. In the aftermath of the GFC, NPLs have been a major concern for supervisors, policymakers, and market participants. Many countries used a variety of restructuring tools, including the creation of impaired loans secondary markets with an extensive servicing network, structured credit solutions, and creation of bad banks or AMCs. As the empirical study in this chapter has shown, those actions were successful not only in reducing the NPL ratios in the EU, but also in creating incentives to extend bank credit to the economy.

Based on the econometric analysis, the chapter demonstrated that the methods of restructuring the low-quality loan portfolio and the intensity of measures used were an important determinant not only for the change in the quality of the loan portfolio, but also in extending bank lending to the economy, particularly the corporate loans. An increase in bank lending to the economy was supported not only by bank-based factors (bank stability, traditional business model with a high level of interest incomes, the large portfolio of current deposits as a source of financing, and the high quality of the existing loan portfolio), by the macroeconomic factors (the high rate of economic growth, an increase in interest rates, and a reduction of the inflation rate), but also by intensity and diversity of methods used to restructure the NPL portfolios, as measured by synthetic index NPL_RII. Thus, the empirical research confirmed a positive role of public involvement in reducing bank fragility and in resolving obstacles to efficient allocation of credit.

References

Andersson, F., & Trevisan, L. (2024, December). *Lending to European households and non-financial corporations: Growth and trends. Key findings from the ECRI Statistical Package*. European Credit Research Institute. https://ecri.eu/sites/default/files/key_findings_ecri_sp_2024.pdf.

Baltagi, B.H. (2005). *Econometric analysis of panel data*. Wiley & Sons, Chichester.

BCBS. (2017). *Guidelines: Prudential treatment of problem assets—definitions of non-performing exposures and forbearance*. Bank for International Settlements.

Beck, T., Büyükkarabacak, B., Rioja, F., & Valev, N. (2008). Who gets the credit? And does it matter? Household vs. firm lending across countries. The World Bank Working Paper, No. 4661.

Beck, T., & Keil, J. (2020). Are *b*anks *c*atching *c*orona? Effects of COVID on *l*ending in the U.S. https://ssrn.com/abstract=3766831.

Bezemer, D., Ryan-Collins, J., Van Lerven, F., & Zhang, L. (2023). Credit policy and the "debt shift" in advanced economies. *Socio-Economic Review*, 21(1). https://doi.org/10.1093/ser/mwab041.

Blundell, R. W., & Bond, R. W. (1998). Initial conditions and moment restrictions in dynamic panel model data models. *Journal of Econometrics*, *87*(1), 115–143.

Casanova, C., Hardy, B., & Onen, M. (2021). *COVID-19 policy measures to support bank lending, BIS Quarterly Review*. Bank for International Settlements.

Ciukaj, R. (2025). *Methods of restructuring portfolios of low-quality loans in the European Union in the post-crisis period*. Cracow University of Economics (in print).

EBA. (2019). Final Report on Guidelines on management of non-performing and forborne exposures. https://www.eba.europa.eu/activities/single-rulebook/regulatory-activities/credit-risk/guidelines-management-non-performing.

EBA. (2022). Report on NPLs – progress made and challenges ahead. https://www.eba.europa.eu/risk-analysis-and-data/npls.

EC. (2023). European financial stability and integration review. https://europa.eu/!hywqdP

ECB. (2019), Burlon L., Dimou M., Drahonsky A.C., Köhler-Ulbrich P., *What does the bank lending survey tell us about credit conditions for euro area firms?* ECB Economic Bulletin, Issue 8.

Elliot, V., & Willesson, M. (2018). Does bank regulation spill over to firm financing? In M. Garcia-Olalla & J. Clifton (eds), *Contemporary issues in banking: Regulation, governance and performance*. Palgrave MacMillan Studies in Banking and Financial Institutions.

ESRB. (2023, June). Beck T., Peltonen T., Perotti E., Serrano A.S., Suarez J., *Corporate credit and leverage in the EU: recent evolution, main drivers and financial stability implications*, Reports of the Advisory Scientific Committee No 14.

Falagiarda, M., & Köhler-Ulbrich, P., Maqui E. (2020*), Drivers of firms' loan in the euro area - what has changed during the COVID-19 pandemic? ECB Economic*

Bulletin, issue 5. https://www.ecb.europa.eu/press/economic-bulletin/focus/2020/html/ecb.ebbox202005_08~ce5f790f76.en.html

Fed. (2023). Aizenman J., Jinjarak Y., Spiegel M., *Fiscal Capacity and Commercial Bank Lending Under COVID-19, FED San Francisco Working Paper 2022–04*, https://doi.org/10.24148/wp2022-04.

Fell, J., Grodzicki, M., Krušec, D., Martin, R., & O'Brien E. (2017), Overcoming non-performing loan market failures with transaction platforms. *Financial Stability Review*. European Central Bank. November. pp. 130–144.

Gambacorta, L., Yang, J., & Tsatsaronis, K. (2014, March). Financial structure and growth. *BIS Quarterly Review*. https://www.bis.org/publ/qtrpdf/r_qt1403e.htm

IMF. (2016). Staff Discussionn Note, A Strategy for Resolving Europe's Problem Loans. https://www.imf.org/en/Publications/Staff-Discussion-Notes/Issues/2016/12/31/A-Strategy-for-Resolving-Europe-s-Problem-Loans-43286

Karkowska, R. (2024). The influence of the COVID-19 pandemic on bank lending: Evidence form European countries. In P. Wachtel & E. Miklaszewska (eds), *COVID-19 and European banking performance: Resilience, recovery and sustainability*. Routledge.

Miklaszewska, E., & Kil, K. (2016). Bank-specific, macroeconomic or structural variables: Which explains bank enterprise lending? The evidence from transition countries. In S. Carbó Valverde, P. J. Cuadros Solas, & F. Rodríguez Fernández (eds.), *Bank funding, financial instruments and decision-making in the banking industry*, Palgrave Macmillan Studies in Banking and Financial Institutions.

Miklaszewska, E., & Kil, K. (2024). The impact of the COVID-19 pandemic on bank stability and performance in the CRR region In P. Wachtel & E. Miklaszewska (eds.), *COVID-19 and European banking performance: Resilience, recovery and sustainability*. Routledge.

Asian Development Bank (2021). *Nonperforming loans in Asia and Europe—causes, impacts, and resolution strategies.* https://www.adb.org/publications/nonperforming-loans-asia-europe-causes-impacts

OECD. (2021). *Resolution strategies for NPLs in the post-COVID-19 landscape.*,

World Bank. (2022). Public asset management companies: International experience—policy brief. https://thedocs.worldbank.org/en/doc/614221527523160699-0130022018/original/ PublicAMCsinternationalexperiences.pdf

Wyman, O. (2018). The non-performing loans jigsaw: Pieces starting to fit? https://www.oliverwyman.com/content/dam/oliver-wyman/v2/publications/2018/march/the-non-performing-loans-jigsaw.pdf

Index

E. Scannella and J. Williams (eds.), *Trends, Issues, and Challenges in Banking and Finance*, Palgrave Macmillan Studies in Banking and Financial Institutions,
https://doi.org/10.1007/978-3-031-96066-6

The manufacturer's authorised representative in the EU is Springer Nature Customer Service Centre GmbH, Europaplatz 3, 69115 Heidelberg, Germany. If you have any concerns regarding our products, please contact ProductSafety@springernature.com

Printed and bound by CPI Group (UK) Ltd, Croydon, CR0 4YY

01/10/2026

02225953-0009